The Cuillin in rare winter raiment. Left to right: Sgurr Mhic Choinnich, Sgurr Alasdair and Sgurr Sgumain, from Glen Brittle

INTRODUCTION

Size, as they say, is not everything. In comparison to the greater ranges, Scotland's mountains might look diminutive, but they punch above their weight. Although they tend to be short by international standards, Scottish scrambles, traditional rock climbs and winter routes are as good as any of their type. What Scottish peaks lack in altitude they make up for in attitude: long walk-ins, rough terrain and mercurial weather are the norm. It is often claimed that those who learn to handle Scotland's mountain mood swings can adapt their climbing to pretty much anywhere in the world – and it's more or less true, give or take hypoxia and crevasses. But why climb elsewhere at all, when what we have here in Scotland is so good? While we're spouting old clichés it just remains to say that in the trade-off between quantity and quality, the Highlands hold their own. The Scottish hills contain an almost limitless supply of superb objectives – challenging trips in beautiful settings. Metre for metre, there can be no finer mountains.

It is amazing just how much is packed into such a small country. One of Scotland's great strengths is the diversity of its distinctive landscapes. From the Cuillin's seaside saw-teeth to the magnificent buttressed face of Ben Nevis, from the sub-arctic desolation of the Cairngorm plateau to the sandstone monsters sprouting out of the waterlogged Assynt moors, variety abounds. The landforms are underpinned by a complex geology, a gift to climbers. In this book alone there are routes on granite, gabbro, basalt, rhyolite, andesite, gneiss, schist, quartzite and sandstone – sometimes even a combination of these in one day. Each is a different climbing medium, a different experience.

The pointiest peaks, specifically those of Skye, demand compulsory scrambling. But other than these few notable exceptions, relatively non-technical hillwalker's trails can be followed up almost every mountain in the country. Those who are keen to tick off arbitrary shortlists of summits might see this as good news, though they are in danger of missing out. Some Highland hillwalks may be fantastic, but a summit-focused mentality can blind Munro-baggers to the obvious merits of smaller hills and more interesting routes. In contrast, people for whom the quality of the ascent experience is at least as important as the peak itself can find more challenging and more aesthetic climbs by the score, only the easiest of which receive much attention from hillwalkers. Where the going gets tough, the fun really starts. Delve into Scotland's rich horde of classic ridges and you'll discover mountain climbs as satisfying as any, anywhere.

The market is already saturated with mountain books. If we read them all we'd never have time to climb. So is this particular book sufficiently different to deserve your attention? I'd like to think so. The answers to the following questions go some way to explaining why.

Why a ridges theme?
Surely every mountaineer loves a good ridge? Threading a bristling gendarmed spine; inching around an extravagantly fluted cornice; balancing gracefully along a stone tightrope in the clouds – these are some of the finest things a climber can get up to. We all live on a metaphorical knife-edge; sometimes it's instructive to be reminded of that fact by pitting ourselves against the real thing. Ridges are airy and elegant, among the most attractive features of any mountain. There is a compelling narrative quality to ridge climbs, a linear development from beginning to eventual resolution via the twists and turns of plot along the way. A ridge is a story in stone. There may be technically harder climbs on any roadside crag, but few have the charisma of Scotland's classic ridges. These are some of the grandest mountaineering lines in the country, each a memorable and unique adventure.

Why a 'best-of' selection?
Quite simply because there are too many potential inclusions to cover in one book (perhaps there's scope for a volume II?). The selection leans

INTRODUCTION

towards the classics, alongside which are a few that are more obscure, and yet equally worthwhile. Though seasoned Highlands aficionados might already know many of these routes, it seems a fair bet that only a tiny handful of climbers will have done them all. There may be no information here that you couldn't glean from days spent poring over a small library of area-specific climbing, scrambling and hillwalking guides, but bringing these routes together in a single volume gives the ridge enthusiast a compact source of reference, one that also aims to serve as a celebration of Scottish ridges. It is a personal selection, and not everyone will necessarily agree with all of my choices. Have I included a dud, or overlooked a gem? If this gets one or two people talking about something other than football, even for a minute, then the book will have served a useful purpose.

What are the criteria for including or omitting routes?

Enduring favourites such as Suilven or the Dubhs Ridge could hardly be left out, but there are many other excellent climbs worthy of inclusion. There's something special about every featured route, be it beautiful line, quality climbing or stunning location. Of course, the best days out are a combination of all three. One prerequisite at least is self-evident – that any included route must resemble a ridge, more or less. That is, it must be longer than it is wide, with steep sides and a defined crest. Obvious really. The chosen routes

Small is beautiful: Arran's Cir Mhor (Routes 3 and 4) is less than 800m high but with lines like these, who cares? To the right is A'Chir (Route 1)

Life on the edge...or is it? The Imposter of Clach Glas (Route 47)

also need to be exciting. Wonderful ridge walks abound in Scotland, but only those that involve a modest degree of technicality and exposure – danger, if you like – make the shortlist. This is a mountaineer's guide, and scrambles are the bottom line. There is no intrinsic upper grade limit, though the hardest climbs described weigh in at only VS or winter III. Sticking to relatively moderate winter grades was a conscious choice; though far harder (and just as good) under snow, celebrated ridge climbs such as those of Ben Nevis remain classics even in summer, at which time they can be enjoyed by a wider range of people. The selection aims to reflect the diversity of the Scottish mountaineering experience, which is a rich mix of roped and unroped scrambles, roped summer climbs and winter routes.

Who is the book aimed at?

Experienced mountain walkers will doubtless have done plenty of scrambling in their time, and should feel pretty confident on the easier routes described here. But many scramblers will have set their sights a little higher still, aspiring to the classic low-grade rock and winter climbs. This is where the ground gets really interesting, while still remaining technically feasible for a majority of able-bodied people. Unhelpfully, it is exactly at this point that scrambling and hillwalking guidebooks tend to fizzle out. In contrast, climbing guidebooks often make only fleeting reference to some very attractive easier routes, and ignore others altogether.

It would be a strange sort of climber who did not find A'Mhaighdean's North West Ridge

Introduction

deeply satisfying, though it could hardly be classed as a technical trip, and receives only a passing mention in the SMC area climbing guide. But just as the blinkered Munro-bagger ignores the best bits of a hill in pursuit of their summit tick, so some accomplished climbers scoff at the low-grade adventures, preferring instead the pursuit of ever-higher numbers. Both groups are in danger of missing out. Though they have their uses, grades and figures are merely abstractions, and shouldn't blind us to the merits of any route. Quantifiable goals like the next E5 or that final Munro are all very well, so long as people remember to enjoy themselves along the way. To paraphrase American alpinist Alex Lowe, 'the greatest climber is the one having the most fun'. If this is true then the most enjoyable climbs must also be the best. And it's hard to imagine routes more entertaining than the ones detailed in this book. The selection plugs something of a gap in the literature by ranging widely across the grades, on the basis that accomplished hill users, from stately hillwalkers to honed rock jocks, can find their middle ground on classic Scottish ridges, and all go home enriched.

Getting there

Mainline bus and rail links to Highland towns such as Fort William, Kyle of Lochalsh and Aviemore are fairly good, in the main, though beyond Scotland's Central Belt public transport can be frustratingly slow. At a local level public transport coverage in the mountains is at best patchy. Although Glencoe, Lochaber, the Cuillin and the Northern Cairngorms are all more or less accessible by a combination of rail, bus and leg power, some areas are rather harder to reach. Public buses in Wester Ross, for example, can

Pedal power: cycling to Ben Alder (Route 23) saves hours of foot slogging

be woefully infrequent. Visitors who find this arrangement inconvenient should spare a thought for the local inhabitants, who have to live with it permanently.

Bikes can be used to good effect. Where decent tracks stretch far into the hills cycling can get you much closer to the climbs than a car, sparing a lot of walking. But if you are relying on pedal power as sole means of road transport over the huge distances of the Highlands, time obviously has to be on your side. The sad fact is that the majority of the routes described are most easily and quickly accessed by those with a car. Environmental concerns aside, the fastest and perhaps the most convenient way for long-distance visitors to reach the Highlands is to catch a train to Inverness or Glasgow, and continue by hire car. Flights from the south of England to, for example, Inverness are also a realistic way to access many of the routes.

Accommodation

In major tourist centres such as Fort William and Aviemore the choice of lodging ranges from spartan campsites through to swanky hotels. Elsewhere accommodation options are more widely scattered, though you're usually likely to find something that suits the budget within a short drive of your chosen route, be it a Youth Hostel, bunkhouse, campsite or B&B. Each chapter includes a brief list of some of the more conveniently placed local accommodation providers. This is a selection that errs towards low-cost offerings, in recognition of the habits and finances of the average climber. Hiring self-catering accommodation is an option for groups or families intending to base themselves in one area for several days, while climbing clubs can make similar use of club-owned huts.

Sleeping out

Although most of the routes described in this book fit comfortably into a single day out, a minority involve such long distances on the ground, in such remote areas, that they are best treated as only part of a longer stay in the hills. Overnighting in the wilds is one of the most satisfying of mountain experiences, stretching out a day trip into an extended mission. There's nothing better than dumping your monstrous rucksack with relief beside a mirror-flat lochan, pitching the tent and brewing up in time to enjoy sunset and moonrise, without another soul for miles around. No fee to pay, no neighbours to disturb the peace; just you and nature.

Nature, of course, offers a variety of experiences from the uplifting to the downright maddening. At the annoying end of the scale, rain and midges are two obvious cases in point, about which the less said the better. Downsides apart, idyllic wild camp sites can be found in their thousands throughout the Highlands and Islands. Freedom, self-sufficiency and profound solitude – who needs hotels when tents offer so much for so little? If carried out responsibly, discreet low-impact wild camping is perfectly appropriate almost anywhere in the Highlands. The usual caveats about taking only pictures and leaving only footprints apply; but then only a thoughtless idiot would crap near a stream or leave tin cans under a rock.

The other popular night-time option is the bothy, a Scottish mountain institution. There are dozens of these old huts tucked into quiet corners of the Highlands, serving as free shelter to all comers – a wonderfully egalitarian concept in keeping with the generous spirit of the hills. Some are exceptionally spartan, while the better-equipped examples could just about make a comfortable permanent home. Bothies have several major advantages over camping: they don't have to be carried in on your back; they mitigate the worst vagaries of the midges; and they can provide instant friends. If your new hut-mates insist on staying up all night with several bottles of malt – well, who could blame them? Would you really leave them to it, when it's so much better to join in? The locations of the better-known bothies are widely publicised in magazines and books such as this, and in busy periods they can be packed to the rafters. Others seem to exist more on the level of rumour than concrete bricks and mortar.

Well-placed bothies and possible wild camps and bivvys are mentioned in each route chapter.

Introduction

There's nothing better than a wild camp such as this one beneath Suilven (Route 42)

Maps
At 1:50,000 the OS Landranger series is sufficiently detailed in almost every case, and the relevant sheet is indicated in the information section at the start of each route. One notable exception is the Skye Cuillin, where the terrain is so complex and the contours so close-packed that the 1:25,000 scale Explorer map (sheet number 411) proves marginally easier to follow. The Harvey's Superwalker 1:25,000 (and 1:12,500 enlargement) of the Cuillin is perhaps the clearest of all.

Route descriptions
At the start of each route, distance and ascent stats are given for the day as a whole – that is, a total for the approach, the climb and the descent. Where there is a choice of approach, descent and/or continuation, these stats refer to the option given precedence in the text. Timings are fairly liberal, being based on the estimated fitness and abilities of average mountaineers in reasonable conditions; poor weather, nightfall or thick snow might double or more the time it takes to do anything. Route grades refer only to the climb itself. Where possible, the overall length of each technical climb is listed. Individual pitch lengths and blow-by-blow pitch descriptions are given only where it seems most logical to do so. If the ground offers a variety of possible lines and places to belay, the route description will be broader, and may explicitly mention only the most salient features – the rest is left to your judgement on the day, which is as it should be. Compass directions are abbreviated (W, NW, etc), and are approximate. 'Left' and 'right' are relative to the direction of travel.

Grades and difficulty
The majority of these routes involve long days out in tough terrain. Climbing ability aside, you'll enjoy yourself a lot more if you have a healthy level of strength and fitness. No attempt has been made to grade the walking sections, as the nature of the walk-in should be obvious from the accompanying map and route description. Mountaineers must take rough and remote ground

Home from home: Culra bothy and Ben Alder's Leachas ridges (Route 23)

in their stride – it's all part of the fun. Technical sections are classified using the conventional scrambling grades 1–3, rock climbing grades from Moderate upwards (see grade table) and Scottish winter grades.

British grading systems seem to respect a distinction between scrambling and climbing, as if they were two essentially different classes of activity on the ground. This has led to all sorts of semantic entanglements, with people trying, for instance, to define exactly where a 'scramble' becomes a 'climb'. Is it the point at which a rope is deemed necessary? Given the vast spread of abilities within the outdoor community, if this were so then some people would be 'climbing' on a summer traverse of An Teallach, while others might happily 'scramble' the crux pitches of the Rosa Pinnacle's South Ridge. It is more helpful to view the apparent divide as a defect of our methods of classification, and not as something set in stone. As soon as you begin using your hands on the rock, and start trying not to fall off, you are climbing – with a small 'c' – an activity that stretches as an unbroken continuum from the simplest scramble to the most superhuman Extreme. This book abides by conventional grades, but only because they are well understood.

Summer routes are described and graded for ideal summer conditions – that is, dry and snow free – but each could also be tackled as a winter climb, and where possible winter grades are listed in the text. Those that are much more worthwhile if climbed in the winter are described accordingly.

Grade table

The climbing community likes nothing better than a good old-fashioned grade debate. While it is tricky to accurately collate international grading systems to everyone's satisfaction, this table should give overseas visitors or those new to real (that is, outdoor trad) climbing a rough field translation between different schemes.

INTRODUCTION

UK Adjectival	UK Technical	UIAA	France (sport)	USA
1 scramble				5.1
2 scramble		I	1	
3 scramble				5.2
Moderate				
Difficult		II	2	5.3
Very Difficult		III	3	
				5.4
Severe		IV		5.5
			4	
	4a	V-		5.6
Hard Severe				
	4b		5	
		V		
Very Severe				5.7
	4c			
		V+		
				5.8
			5+	
Hard Very Severe	5a	V1-		
				5.9
		V1	6a	
Extremely Severe 1	5b			5.10a
		V1+	6a+	5.10b
Etc…				

CLIMBING GRADES

Winter grades

Thanks to the ever-changing nature of winter ground, these grades can only sensibly be treated as a rough indication of a route's overall difficulty, in average conditions. There are no guarantees. Often on winter routes, and certainly for climbs at the harder end of the spectrum, an Arabic numeral denoting the technical grade of the hardest move appears alongside the Roman numeral describing the route's overall difficulty and seriousness, a system similar to that used for British rock. In this book I have provided such a detailed breakdown in a couple of cases where the technicality of a short passage of climbing could be said to differ from the overall grade – a move or two of 3 on a grade II route, for instance. In the table below, approximate Alpine grades are listed in brackets beside their Scottish equivalent.

Gear and skills

Enthusiastic climbers and hillwalkers are already likely to own most of the necessary clothing and general accessories. Let's face it, this lowly branch of mountaineering is hardly the most image-driven side of the sport. You don't need to splash out on the latest trendy soft shell just to climb a Moderate ridge, when a shabby old fleece and waterproof jacket will do the job. A pair of walking boots should see you right on ground graded up to around Diff, or even on short occasional pitches of VDiff (as appear on the Cuillin Traverse, for instance). Beyond this point most people are usually happier stowing boots in the rucksack and slipping on a pair of rock shoes. That said, the latest walking/scrambling/climbing hybrid boots might take all but the hardest of these routes in their stride, though they often fall down on waterproofing – a major failing in soggy Scotland. The ideal Scottish summer mountaineering boot is an optimum compromise between apparently contradictory qualities, combining lightness and dexterity with support, water resistance and sufficient durability to withstand the rigours of rough terrain. The sole unit should be sturdy and grip well on a variety of surfaces including wet rock and vegetation.

Winter Climbing Grades

I (F – PD)	Just a notch up from the more engaging end of the winter hillwalking spectrum; simple snow gullies up to around 45° and snowed-up low-grade summer ridge scrambles. Reasonable conditions underfoot often permit competent climbers to solo at this grade.
II (PD – AD)	Slightly steeper, with short ice pitches or basic technical climbing on mixed ground. Ropes are usually appreciated, and should always be carried. Classic summer ridge traverses such as Liathach and Aonach Eagach are benchmark winter IIs (though subject to conditions they may prove hard, or easy, or anything in between). In comparison to typically straightforward grade II gullies, ridge routes can often feel challenging, with high exposure and long, complex passages on corniced gendarmed crests.
III (AD – D-)	Appreciable technical pitches demanding confidence and competence. Imperfect conditions can make an epic out of a grade III; Tower Ridge is an infamous example.
IV (D – D+)	Steeper ice or more difficult mixed pitches; more serious and sustained than III, requiring considerable strength, skill and climbing experience. VDiff summer ridges such as North East Buttress and Observatory typically become winter IVs, though there is no hard and fast correlation.
V (TD)	Steep, sustained and serious ice routes, or very technical mixed routes demanding a high degree of all-round climbing ability.
VI (ED1)	As for V, only more so in every respect…

Moving together is a good option on exposed low-grade ground such as Pygmy Ridge (Route 26). In this picture the leader has reached a belay stance, and is bringing the rest of the party up.

Mountains tend to shed loose rock, and **helmets** are always a wise idea; you'll look less silly wearing one than you will with a hole in your head, as they say. Few scramblers seem to bother with them, myself included, though perhaps they ought; falling rocks respect no grade boundaries.

The appropriate level of protection on any route is a matter for personal judgement on the ground, though it's clearly better to be safe than sorry. The vertiginously challenged would probably appreciate a **rope** and associated hardware on all but the easiest of these ridges, while for the majority of mountaineers the urge to tie in tends to start making itself felt on exposed Mod/Diff routes, or thereabouts. Many Scottish ridge climbs involve significant sections of low-grade rock or snow, the sort of ground that competent climbers might solo, but on which ropes are often sensibly employed.

Some people will opt to move roped together with running belays on large stretches of all but the hardest routes herein. Speed is of the essence on long, remote climbs, and moving together is the best way to travel fast in reasonable security. The steepest and most technical ridges, however, tend to be climbed in pitches throughout.

In planning what safety kit to bring these general rules may prove helpful: **Easy scrambles** require nothing; on **grade 3 scrambles**, Mods and Diffs carry one rope and a stripped-down rack (some nuts of varying size, a couple of bigger chocks/cams, three/four quickdraws, several slings and screwgates at most). Unless your party opts to move together it will probably stay in the rucksack on all but the hardest pitches, but at least it's ready to resort to if needed; ice, rain or wind can turn even a scramble into a mini epic.

GEAR AND SKILLS

Ridges can be better in winter conditions: Aonach Eagach (Route 13) is a case in point

Climbs graded VDiff and upwards require a full rack, often best complemented with two half-ropes rather than a single one. Sixty metre ropes seem to be becoming the vogue in some circles, and even on the traditional mountaineering routes detailed here the extra length can be welcome on occasion. I have tried to highlight where this is particularly so.

Even in early summer **crampons** and an **axe** can be invaluable. A walking axe and 10-point crampons will do for grade I winter ridges – welcome news for those who are already equipped for winter hillwalking and who have only modest winter ridge-climbing ambitions. If Beinn Alligin or the Carn Mor Dearg (CMD) Arete under snow are your goals, you need not remortgage the house to buy shiny new climbing kit. Traditionalists of the long wooden-handled axe and step-cutting era may mutter darkly through their beards about it not being like that in their day, but the general consensus seems to be that winter climbs of more than grade I are best tackled using standard modern technical climbing gear – two short axes and 12-point crampons.

'Four season' boots are another winter necessity. Those designed for steep terrain rather than hillwalking are *de rigeur* on all but the easiest winter climbs.

The safe negotiation of any mountain route owes as much to route-finding nous, hill skills and smooth efficiency as it does to technical climbing ability of the sort on display at indoor and roadside venues. The easier routes described in this book are ideal places in which to build the

The Horns and Beinn Dearg from Sgurr Mor (Route 35)

necessary competence and confidence. However this is not an instruction manual. Before they go off half-cocked and end up bumbling into a nightmare, readers lacking the appropriate proficiency should, consult *The Hillwalker's Guide to Mountaineering* by Terry Adby and Stuart Johnston (Cicerone). If unsure of your abilities, then consider taking a course at an instruction centre such as Glenmore Lodge – some of the best climbers started out this way. Or perhaps a more experienced friend would be willing to show you the ropes?

Seasonal notes

Winter brings wild weather and short daylight hours. Deep snow sometimes blankets the terrain, threatening mountaineers with the dangers of cornices and avalanche. In such conditions the walk-in can be extremely arduous, and yet snow cover is rarely consistent enough to justify the use of skis or snowshoes. Encased in a glistening crust or swamped in powder, even lowly scrambles can become challenging mixed climbs, while summer rock routes take on a whole new character. At this time of year you've got to start earlier, move faster, carry heavier loads and be prepared to tackle technical ground using axes and crampons. Starting and, frequently, finishing your day in the dark is commonplace. The increased workloads, tougher conditions and higher risks associated with winter mountaineering demand greater fitness and stamina, and a broad range of skills. If you can't assess the snow for avalanche risk, navigate accurately in a whiteout or cope with longer runouts between poorer runners, then be sensible and either downgrade your winter ambitions or look into the possibility of taking an appropriate course.

Doom and gloom aside, it has to be said that full-on winter conditions transform the character of any mountain, arguably improving it. Few things in life can be better than a traverse of Liathach or the Cuillin in perfect winter nick. Sadly, perfection is a rare and fleeting thing in Scotland's changeable maritime climate, as in life generally. The state of snow and ice might vary by the hour, and no two ascents of the same route are ever certain to be identical. This means that winter grades are more fluid than summer ones, and route descriptions less concrete. Take both with a pinch of salt. However, ridges can be found in some kind of climbable state more often than other types of winter route. Should global climate change wreak its predicted worst, this will be even truer in future years. When gullies and faces are thin and marginal, or when they're overloaded and avalanche prone, the day's climbing might be salvaged by heading to the nearest ridge.

Avalanches

Early pioneers of Scottish mountaineering tended to ignore the risks, some even pooh-poohing the very existence of avalanches in Scotland. On forays to the Alps and beyond they would, of course, have been awed by the devastating force of monster avalanches that can swallow entire villages. As the Highlands do not suffer such whoppers, perhaps it was natural that they were somewhat complacent about the relative tiddlers on their home turf. Yet even a tiddler can bite. Thanks to the lessons of harsh experience, collective wisdom has since accrued. It is now common knowledge that avalanches occur throughout the Scottish winter season. As the number of winter climbers has grown, so too have avalanche-related incidents. Injuries and fatalities are all too regular, and even the wiliest climbers are sometimes caught out.

Major avalanches are rare, and yet they do happen. Famously, the entire Great Slab of Cairngorm's Coire an Lochain can slide to the full depth of the snowpack; that must be quite a sight, though best viewed from a distance. History, too, provides an example – the infamous Loss of Gaick (1800), when four men were buried and killed in a hut as they slept. Events this dramatic might be uncommon, but even a minor snow slide can damage a climber, particularly if it dislodges them. Indeed, damage can just as readily be caused through falling as burying.

Convex slopes are more likely to slide than concave ones, while the prime ground for big slabs in particular is a slope between 30° and 45°. Do not get hung up on these generalisations, however, as no snow slope is ever entirely above suspicion. The massive airborne avalanches sometimes seen overseas are not thought to be a feature in Scotland. Here there are several broad types of common avalanche, each more likely to occur in a different set of conditions.

Powder, spindrift or loose-snow avalanches take place when slopes are overloaded with unconsolidated snow, either during and after heavy snowfall or as a result of wind action. Such slides may be fairly minor, and yet sufficient to knock people off the mountain.

Wet-snow avalanches usually strike during a thaw, when layers in the snowpack become saturated. Bonds between layers, or even those between the snow and the ground beneath, are subsequently weakened. A slide can then occur, either with a trigger such as the footsteps of a passing climber, or simply at 'random' due to the increased weight and instability of wet snow. These avalanches move relatively slowly, but they can be big. The debris is dense and has minimal air content, rapidly setting hard to entomb any unfortunate victims. It is imperative that victims are dug out as quickly as possible, bearing in mind the risk to rescuers from further slides.

Windslab is formed by an accumulation of wind-borne snow crystals on lee slopes, and in sheltered hollows such as the head of gullies. The intricate structure of each crystal is damaged as it blows along, so that when billions drift together they mesh into a single bonded layer. The bond between the slab and the underlying snow pack tends to be weak, so that it is delicately poised and needs little excuse to slide. **Windslab avalanches** are a common danger in Scotland, thanks in part both to the stormy weather and to the rolling topography over which snow can be blown for great distances. Because they are formed simply by wind action, the risks posed by windslabs can persist long after any snowfall. To roughly predict the slope aspects on which they are most likely to occur you need to have closely scrutinised the weather for several days prior to your climb with particular attention to wind direction, though remember that mountain landforms can redirect the prevailing wind in unpredictable ways. Windslab has a characteristic dull or

Introduction

'chalky' appearance, and makes a weird squeaky noise under your boots. Misleadingly, it may vary in texture from quite soft to very hard.

Cornice collapse can be a variation of either a windslab or a wet-snow avalanche. The effect of preceding wind conditions on cornice stability can be hard to judge until you're actually up there getting avalanched, but at least it's easy to spot a thaw in advance, and thus avoid a wet collapsing cornice.

Avalanche prediction is a complex – though still inexact – science. Sensible climbers make good prior use of the detailed forecasts provided by the Scottish Avalanche Information Service (see Appendix 3: Useful contacts), backing these up with their own in-the-field assessments of the snowpack throughout the day. Not to do so is the mountaineering equivalent of playing Russian roulette.

Access

Scotland long had an unwritten tradition of free access to open hill country. The problem with such arrangements, of course, is that they're not worth the paper they're not written on; and in some cases traditional freedoms were threatened, as landowners sought to challenge the informal understanding. Thankfully the Scottish Executive has now replaced this ad-hoc arrangement with the long overdue Land Reform (Scotland) Act of 2003, a new statutory enshrinement of responsible access that came into force early in 2005. This has put Scotland at the vanguard of progressive land legislation.

In pursuit of outdoor recreation people are now officially free to wander at will, provided that they follow guidelines laid down in the Scottish Outdoor Access Code. This code encourages recreational activists to respect the needs of other countryside users, in particular landowners and managers. In accordance with current discourse, these *rights* could be said to be tempered by attendant *responsibilities*. Countryside users cannot interfere with agriculture; they must keep a 'sensible distance' from houses, use tracks where possible and, inevitably, abide by access restrictions brought about by stalking activity. That the overwhelming majority of hill users are still obliged

Wild land is a unique and dimishing resource: in the wonderful Letterewe Forest, approaching the wilderness peaks of Beinn Lair (Route 38) and A'Mhaighdean (Route 39)

to make allowances for the habits of a tiny minority, the blood sports enthusiasts, seems a little out of kilter with the democratic ideal. Quibbles aside, we must be thankful that the law is now generally on the hill user's side. For a copy of the code visit: www.outdooraccess-scotland.com. For details of the legislation visit: www.scotland.gov.uk.

Land ownership and management

Climbers cannot venture into the mountains without occasionally thinking about their ownership and management. We do not operate in a vacuum. Despite recent moves to redress the balance, Scotland's land distribution is among the most unequal in the developed world. Since the Clearances and before, the Highlands have been subdivided into vast estates owned by a handful of aristocrats and plutocrats. In deciding how this land is used, the influence of the non-landowning majority is less decisive than it might be.

Traditional estate activities give rise to an apparent conflict of interest, namely stalking versus habitat regeneration. Landowners see themselves as protective custodians of the land. They argue that shooting deer is the only way to keep numbers down and mitigate grazing damage. Perhaps so; yet the case is far from closed. Many believe that commercial stalking actually helps perpetuate an unbalanced ecology. Because estate finances rely overwhelmingly upon visitors paying vast sums to hunt, it is in their interests to maintain an unnaturally high deer population. Deer numbers are estimated to have trebled over the last 40 years. As a result overgrazing herds munch the mountainsides into barren sterility, denuding native woodlands and the biodiversity that goes with them. In society at large support is growing for the idea of restoring the 'original' Highland ecology, recreating a great richness in place of a degraded environment devoted to deer hunting. Whether or not these two ends will prove mutually exclusive, perhaps the time has come for estates to diversify.

Conservation of wild land

Do guidebooks undermine the very things they describe? Is it hypocritical or counter-productive to write in praise of wild land if it helps to swell a growing tide of visitors? Personally I'd say no. Guidebooks help propagate the notion of mountains as a resource for all – valuable in and of themselves – and not just as a hitherto untapped commercial opportunity. A voice *for* the wilderness can sometimes sound like a voice *in* the wilderness; if more people were inspired to visit the Highlands then perhaps their protection would move further up the nation's agenda. It is an issue of increasing urgency.

Wild land is a unique kind of resource, in short and diminishing supply globally. Scotland is blessed with some of the least developed and most scenic areas left in Europe, with an inestimable conservation and recreational value that attracts visitors from around the world. Tourism is the single most profitable local industry, and one that relies heavily upon the popular perception of the Highlands as 'unspoilt'. Yet this is a landscape shaped by centuries of human intervention, from deforestation to dam building. The modern world has already blazed its mark across swathes of irreplaceable countryside. How best to use what remains?

The current storm of windfarm proposals represents arguably the biggest threat to wild land in generations, with dozens of planned developments, some of truly monstrous size. Laudable as they can be, renewable power technologies insensitively applied have destructive capacities as profound as any other means of generating electricity. Poorly planned windfarms and their associated road and power-line infrastructure threaten to tarnish Scotland's exceptional beauty to no clear benefit.

The impulse to wreak great damage to special places in the very name of protecting our environment springs from an ironic sort of doublethink. Yet with a little clear thought we could both substantially cut CO_2 emissions and preserve vast patches of internationally important landscape. Unwillingness to do so reflects the low regard in which wild land is held in some influential quarters.

So why should we leave wild land lying unsullied and (ostensibly) commercially underproductive? In today's political climate, influenced as it

Introduction

Where better to contemplate the infinite than up mountains? Wintry Liathach (routes 36 and 37) looks divine.

is by changes in the actual climate, talk of visual pollution may not be fashionable. Yet it affects the quality of our lives as profoundly as air pollution. Aesthetics are as legitimate a benchmark as any other by which to judge the health of an environment and a society. Visible for miles around, a mountaintop covered in wind turbines in an area hitherto dominated by natural landforms is an intrusion. Love them or loathe them, it is impossible to deny that windfarms adulterate wild places.

But many of us need unspoilt areas. Simply being out there fulfils an urge of the same order, perhaps, as that which leads some towards religion. A mountainscape is like a vast roofless church in which we can experience something significant above and beyond ourselves. Mountains feed the soul (for want of a less ambiguous word).

Appropriate respect for our environment springs in part from recognising that civilisation is but a fractional and fleeting part of a far grander universe. Despite the human impulse to master everything we touch the elements still rage freely, and time and space remain unfathomable. During the daily grind these truisms are easily ignored, yet when we escape into the hills, with their weather and geology, they strike us forcefully. Where better to contemplate the infinite than up mountains? Such experiences are, of course, degraded in proportion to the level of visible industrial development. Were I to gaze from the summit of An Teallach or Braeriach to see the mess of a windfarm or power line in the distance, a small but important part of me would shrivel – and for once I wouldn't be able to blame the cold.

'The greatest climber is the one having the most fun': high spirits on the NE Ridge of Angel's Peak (Route 28), above a frozen Lochan Uaine

ARRAN AND THE SOUTHERN HIGHLANDS

Barely 60km from the middle of Glasgow, the tight-grouped granite peaks of Arran are like no others in Scotland, basking in the balmy climate of the Costa del Clyde. The elevations may be modest, yet these hills rise straight out of the sea, sweeping to rugged crests and spearhead summits that make a mockery of many a Munro. This is a wonderfully accessible mountain sanctuary.

The Southern Highlands are listed here for convenience. It is a large area, with many fine mountains and plenty of rock and winter climbing. Ridge routes however are in short supply, with the best of them on the Cobbler and Ben Lui as described.

Cir Mhor (Routes 3 and 4) from the A'Chir Ridge (Route 1).
The huge prominent buttress is the Rosa Pinnacle.

Route 1 – A'Chir Traverse

Grade	1.5km Moderate
Distance	15km
Ascent	950m
Time	7 hours
Start/finish	Glen Rosa Campsite (NS000377) – limited car parking beside the track
Maps	OS Landranger (1:50,000) 69
Accommodation	Lochranza Youth Hostel (0870 004 1140) is about 30 minutes' drive from Glen Rosa. Glenrosa campsite (01770 302 380) in the mouth of the glen is basic, but well positioned. Beware the mighty midge. Aldersyde Bunkhouse, Lamlash (01770 600 959), is an alternative.
Sleeping out	Glen Rosa provides some wild camping opportunities.
Public transport	If basing your trip at Glen Rosa, a car is unnecessary. Regular Caledonia Macbrayne ferries run from Ardrossan on the mainland to Brodick. The mouth of Glen Rosa is a 3.5km walk (or even a taxi ride) from the ferry terminal.
Seasonal notes	Being small, southerly and surrounded by water, Arran's mountains often escape the iciest grip of winter; but when it takes hold the climbing is superb. Because of its many tricky sections on slabby rock A'Chir is no soft touch, with pitches of III,3.

A'Chir is a fabulous little mountain, proving beyond question the truism about size not being everything. Standing at the heart of Arran's dramatic granite massif, it is a ridge not to be missed. Despite its diminutive stature the traverse of this knobbly crest rates as one of the most entertaining routes of its kind anywhere, with plenty of sustained top-end scrambling enlivened by several harder bits. Route finding is continuously challenging, and in all but perfectly dry conditions a rope might be a welcome reassurance, particularly as it allows you to abseil the infamous Mauvais Pas (Bad Step). The rock might be sound and rough, but it's also rounded and blocky, demanding a strenuous approach. The effort is generously rewarded.

The southern half of the A'Chir crest, rising to the summit

ARRAN AND THE SOUTHERN HIGHLANDS

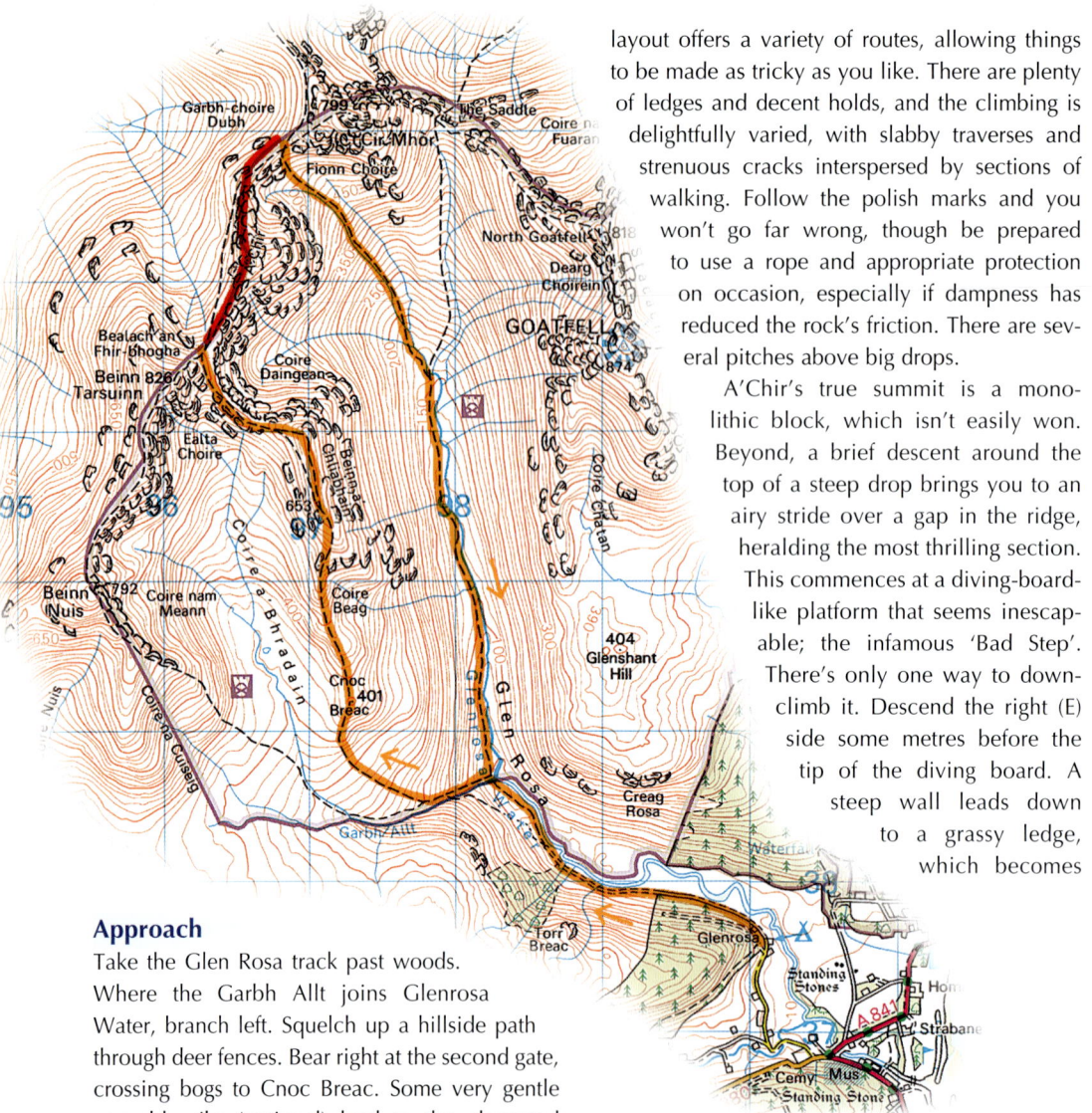

layout offers a variety of routes, allowing things to be made as tricky as you like. There are plenty of ledges and decent holds, and the climbing is delightfully varied, with slabby traverses and strenuous cracks interspersed by sections of walking. Follow the polish marks and you won't go far wrong, though be prepared to use a rope and appropriate protection on occasion, especially if dampness has reduced the rock's friction. There are several pitches above big drops.

A'Chir's true summit is a monolithic block, which isn't easily won. Beyond, a brief descent around the top of a steep drop brings you to an airy stride over a gap in the ridge, heralding the most thrilling section. This commences at a diving-board-like platform that seems inescapable; the infamous 'Bad Step'. There's only one way to down-climb it. Descend the right (E) side some metres before the tip of the diving board. A steep wall leads down to a grassy ledge, which becomes

Approach

Take the Glen Rosa track past woods. Where the Garbh Allt joins Glenrosa Water, branch left. Squelch up a hillside path through deer fences. Bear right at the second gate, crossing bogs to Cnoc Breac. Some very gentle scrambly ribs (optional) lead to the elongated summit of Beinn a'Chliabhain. Go N along the rocky spine. As cavernous Coire Daingean opens below, swing left to the col below Beinn Tarsuinn. On beginning to ascend again, split right on a turfy path that traces an atmospheric traverse (no difficulty) across the headwall of Coire Daingean.

Climb

You're now at a col beside A'Chir's knobbly dinosaur back. The ridge is not a keen knife-edge, but rather a succession of squat towers made of bulbous overlapping granite slabs. The complex

a rock gangway cutting diagonally towards a welcoming col. The last bit is a horrid polished chimney, which is likely to feel harder than Moderate in descent; it's more like VDiff, if truth be told. If in doubt consider abseiling the whole Bad Step from an in-situ peg backed up with a sling around an obvious flake further back. To avoid annoying rope retrieval problems make sure your anchors are extended, so that too much rope doesn't drag over rough slabs at the lip; this means leaving some tat behind. After this

1 – A'Chir Traverse

Mind the gap – the 'airy stride' near the summit of A'Chir

31

Arran and the Southern Highlands

Near the southern end of A'Chir

there's plenty more fun, with difficulties gradually easing all the way to the Cir Mhor col.

Descent

If all that wasn't enough, the keen could readily continue over the magnificent spike of Cir Mhor (see Route 3) and on to Goat Fell, to make a full round of Glen Rosa. Most people will be happy just to descend into the glen, which stretches long and easy back to Brodick.

Abseiling the Bad Step on a drizzly day

Route 2 – Pagoda Ridge, A'Chir

Grade	240m Severe
Distance	12km
Ascent	680m
Time	8 hours
Start/finish	Glenrosa campsite (NS000377) – limited car parking beside the track
Map	OS Landranger (1:50,000) 69
Accommodation	See Route 1
Sleeping out	It's possible to wild camp in Coire Daingean. However, the ground is mostly damp and tussocky.
Public transport	See Route 1
Seasonal notes	From the available guidebook literature it's not certain that Pagoda Ridge has yet received a winter ascent. Bearing in mind the featureless slabby sections and the tricky overlaps in between, V,5 would seem a fair guesstimate. The current ethical mood is set against the practice of scratching up classic rock climbs with crampons and axes however.

Named for its fancied resemblance to an Oriental tower, the overlapping slabs of Pagoda Ridge provide a charismatic and unusual climb in an impressive setting high above the lonely bowl of Coire Daingean. The rough slabby granite is superbly sound, protection is good where it matters and each pitch has real character – what more could you ask? Ambitious teams seeking a full day out can use this route to access the traverse of A'Chir (Route 1). Because it's less than 2km from the Rosa Pinnacle, Pagoda Ridge also makes an ideal last-minute stand-in for the much harder South Ridge Direct (Route 3), should conditions turn a bit iffy on the walk-in.

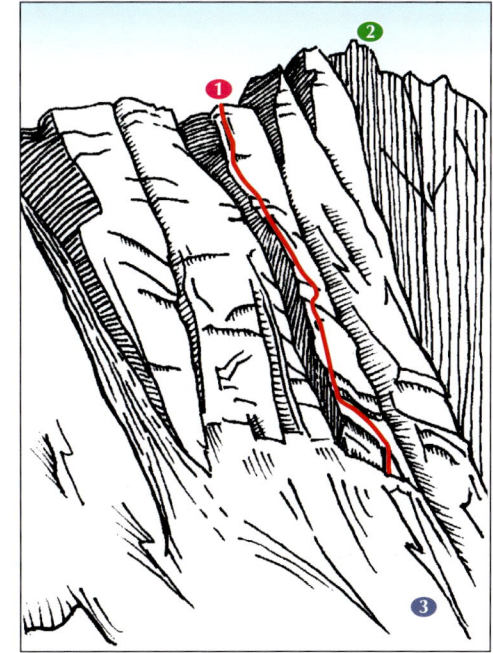

Pagoda Ridge

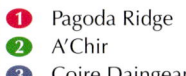

❶ Pagoda Ridge
❷ A'Chir
❸ Coire Daingean

Approach

Start as for the A'Chir approach, but instead of turning off the main Glen Rosa path, stay with it along the valley bottom, branching left as the angle steepens at the head of the glen to climb a path close to the burn that runs out of Fionn Choire. Above the 350m contour turn hard left, crossing the stream to cross very rough heather and boulders into Coire Daingean. If there is a path in any definite sense of the word, it has hitherto failed to identify itself to the author.

Head for the big wall at the back right side of the corrie, where a series of buttresses and gullies

33

Arran and the Southern Highlands

Climb

Pagoda Ridge 240m Severe

Pitch 1, 25m
Climb the heather seam to reach a short sharp flake crack. This point can be reached by a 4a variant by padding up the slab immediately right of the heather. Both variants are initially unprotected. From a small ledge at the top of the flake, pad up to place a runner under an overlap, before stepping back down again. Then move delicately left across a dimpled slab to reach a substantial heather ledge. Proceed left along this to belay below a big overlap.

Pitch 2, 25m
Head diagonally left to gain and follow a long slabby shelf, running between the big overlap and another overlap below. Do not go straight up from the belay – this leads to a tricky unprotected slab pitch that's necky for both leader and second (perhaps HVS 4c?). From the left end of the shelf

flank the knobbly crest of A'Chir. A wide tongue of vegetated slabs comes low, almost to the corrie floor. Left of this is an ill-defined grassy gully; left again is a clean buttress made up of slabs and overlaps, home to several worthy routes. Pagoda Ridge follows the left edge of the slabs. Prominent on the skyline high up this buttress is a big leaning block, best described as a cello case – a useful identifying feature. Skirt left of two detached slab tiers to reach continuous rock at the top of a heather slope. A flake leans against a clean slab, and is bounded on its left by a seam of heather. The initials PR and the name Mosque (an adjacent route) are scratched conveniently in the rock.

climb straight up to belay on a vegetated ledge. This point can be reached without climbing the first two pitches by entering from the grassy gully on the left – an inferior choice.

Pitch 3, 50m
Follow the edge of the slabs directly above the gully on the left, enjoying a couple of short sharp overlaps and easier slabby sections in between.

2 – PAGODA RIDGE, A'CHIR

Crossing the slab on pitch 1

20m of nice climbing leads to a large heather patch; walk straight up this to belay below a steep wall formed by yet another overlap.

Pitch 4, 20m
Juggy flakes lead out right onto an exposed nose, from where smaller holds allow you to surmount the overlap, gaining the slab above. Climb a concave scoop on brilliant rock to reach a spike belay on a sloping ledge directly below an intimidating blank-looking wall.

Pitch 5, 25m
It is possible to swing right using the top of the spike as a high handhold (don't try to mantelshelf it), and then traverse delicately right on an undercut slab, linking pockets and pockmarks to reach a shallow scoop – an exciting option for the bold. Alternatively descend right from the belay down an easy-angled slab, before making a hard pull up using a rounded flake on the wall (medium cam) to reach the same spot – a strenuous option for the strong. Now follow the line of least resistance back up and left to gain a slabby ramp cutting off hard left under yet another imposing overlap (medium/large cam). Belay at the far edge of the ramp, above the gully on the left.

Pitch 6, 35m
Step left onto the wall of the gully, and make a tough move up a short rounded crack to get established on the slabby crest above. Follow this in a magnificent position on impeccable rock, laying away off the sharp edge with your left hand.

35

Arran and the Southern Highlands

Traversing left, pitch 2

2 – PAGODA RIDGE, A'CHIR

Stepping onto the exposed nose, pitch 4

Reach a distinct steepening, where a thuggy lunge (or a sneaky hand jam) leads to easy ground above. Belay from threads at the 'cello case'.

Pitches 7 and 8, 60m
60m ropes allow this section to be run into one pitch. Follow the edge above the gully, soon entering a short offwidth in a shallow corner before reaching easier ground. Occasional steep steps prolong the interest to the end, though watch out for a prominent poised block that requires careful handling. Further blocky terrain then leads without incident to the saddle at the S end of the A'Chir ridge.

Descent
Given time and energy the A'Chir traverse (Route 1) makes a very satisfying continuation climb. The softer option is a rapid return to Glen Rosa via Beinn a'Chliabhain, as described in the approach to the A'Chir traverse.

ARRAN AND THE SOUTHERN HIGHLANDS

Route 3 – South Ridge Direct, Rosa Pinnacle, Cir Mhor

Grade	405m VS
Distance	13km
Ascent	779m
Time	10½ hours
Start/finish	Glen Rosa campsite (NS000377) – limited car parking beside the track
Map	OS Landranger (1:50,000) 69
Accommodation	See Route 1
Sleeping out	Those spending more than one day climbing on Cir Mhor can spare themselves legwork by sleeping under the Rosa Pinnacle. There are grassy camping and bivvying sites by several large boulders near the base of the crag.
Public transport	See Route 1
Seasonal notes	A true winter ascent would be a mixed climbing challenge, not least for the rarity of full conditions. However many in the climbing community would take a very dim view of anyone selfish enough to damage such a well-loved summer rock classic with winter tools.

Quality and difficulty don't necessarily go together. It is just a happy coincidence then that the hardest rock climb described in this book also happens to be the best. Perfect rock, airy positions, varied pitches, character-building cruxes, an irresistible line and considerable length all unite to optimum effect on South Ridge Direct. This is one of the greatest mountain trips in Britain, a world-class mid-grade climb that everyone ought to do at least once in their lives; indeed, once probably isn't enough. Cir Mhor is a hugely impressive pyramidal rock peak, the centrepiece of Arran's magnificent ridge system. Piercing the flank of the mountain is the Rosa Pinnacle, a major crag by anyone's standards. South Ridge Direct climbs its full height. Sweeping slabs, steep overlaps and blocky walls give it the monumental character so typical of Arran granite. Faced with rounded cracks and a general lack of small incuts, newcomers to the area may find the climbing quite butch for the grade. Despite the granite's knuckle-grazing roughness, friction is poor in the wet. Three named pitches merit the VS grade – the rest are easier.

Approach

As for Route 2, but instead of contouring into Coire Daingean continue on the eroded mess of a path up to Fionn Choire. Cir Mhor has dominated the view for some time by now, and at close quarters it is particularly striking, the Rosa Pinnacle doing its best impression of a Chamonix Aiguille. A climber's path branches off right to reach the foot of the crag at the base of an area of scrappy slabs. Allow about 2½ hours from the campsite.

Climb

South Ridge Direct 405m VS
Pitch 1, 50m
Climb easily from the lowest patch of rock, following a crack up a slab, and then a series of slabby ribs and vegetated sections by a line of your choice – bold but easy.

Pitch 2, 50m
Run out another ropelength up this straightforward ground, bearing slightly right to climb a short steepening via a little chimney, and then belaying on a slabby terrace below a bulging wall.

Pitch 3, 35m 4a
Sidle right along a horizontal crack, then up a slabby rib to the base of the wall where it is broken into big blocks/flakes. Pull strenuously up these, then foot traverse left along an obvious break to belay on a ledge below the famous S-Crack.

38

3 – SOUTH RIDGE DIRECT, ROSA PINNACLE, CIR MHOR

A welcome positive hold on the S-Crack, pitch 4

ARRAN AND THE SOUTHERN HIGHLANDS

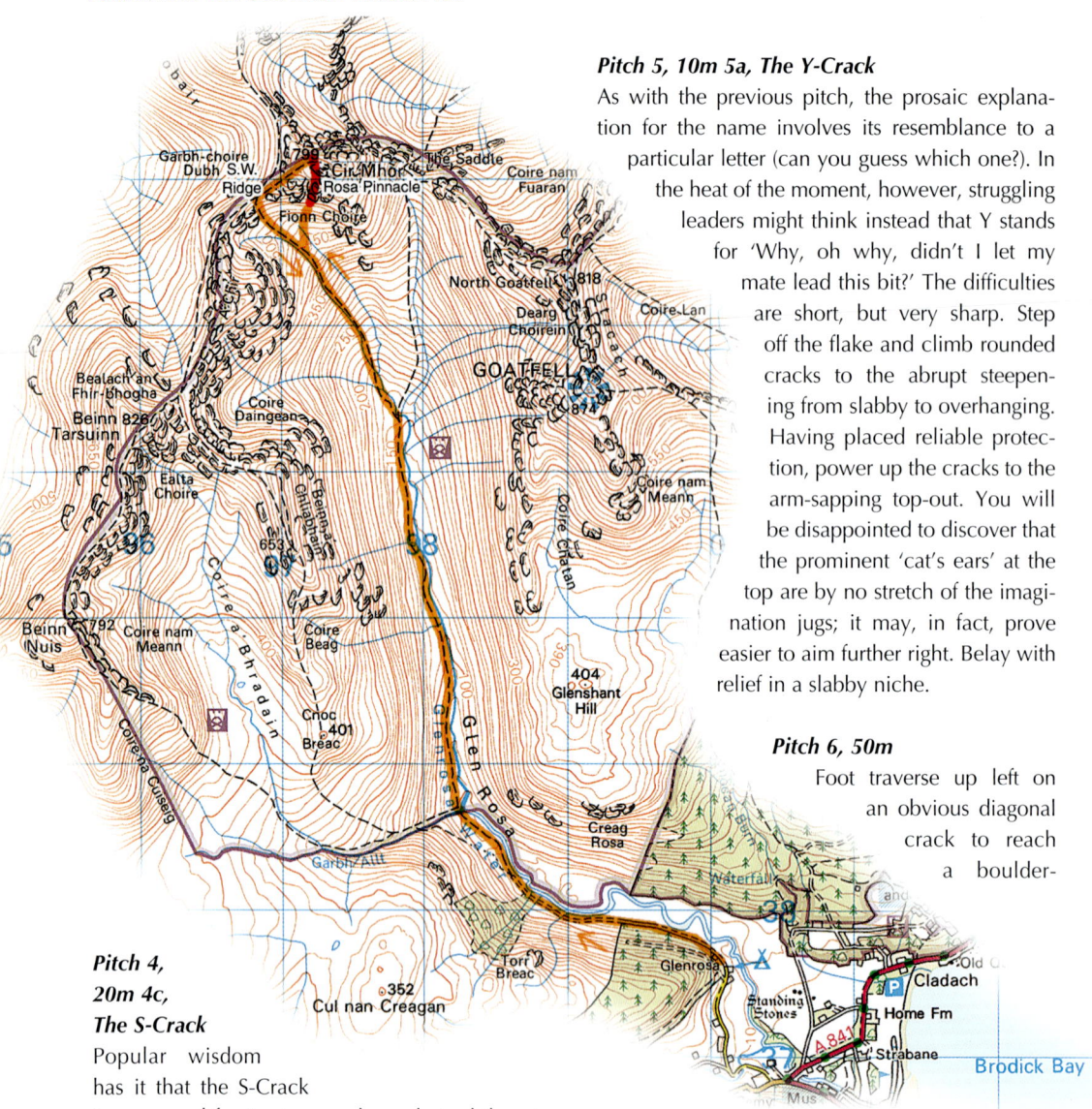

Pitch 5, 10m 5a, The Y-Crack

As with the previous pitch, the prosaic explanation for the name involves its resemblance to a particular letter (can you guess which one?). In the heat of the moment, however, struggling leaders might think instead that Y stands for 'Why, oh why, didn't I let my mate lead this bit?' The difficulties are short, but very sharp. Step off the flake and climb rounded cracks to the abrupt steepening from slabby to overhanging. Having placed reliable protection, power up the cracks to the arm-sapping top-out. You will be disappointed to discover that the prominent 'cat's ears' at the top are by no stretch of the imagination jugs; it may, in fact, prove easier to aim further right. Belay with relief in a slabby niche.

Pitch 6, 50m

Foot traverse up left on an obvious diagonal crack to reach a boulder-

Pitch 4, 20m 4c, The S-Crack

Popular wisdom has it that the S-Crack is so named for its sinuous shape; but while getting to grips with its curves you could be forgiven for thinking that S signifies 'sustained'. Fight your way up the relentlessly steep crack – jamming, bridging and laybacking. There are few positive holds, but plenty of runners – the challenge is not to hang around placing extraneous bits of protection and getting pumped. A surprise bucket hold provides a welcome jug before the strenuous top-out. Move left onto a sloping shelf to belay from a big perched flake (hint: it's worth arranging an upward-pulling anchor under the flake in case the leader fluffs the next pitch).

covered ledge.
Move around a blunt rib, and make a long, easy traverse along the top of a huge sweep of slabs. Belay at the far end just below the next steep tier, where it is breached by a deep right-angled corner.

Pitch 7, 25m 4b, The Layback Crack

Gain the right-angled corner crack, which is climbed by strenuous laybacking. Leaders with strong arms can continue all the way up the crack (hard work), but it is customary to quit it after a few metres, where a raised seam cuts off rightwards.

3 – SOUTH RIDGE DIRECT, ROSA PINNACLE, CIR MHOR

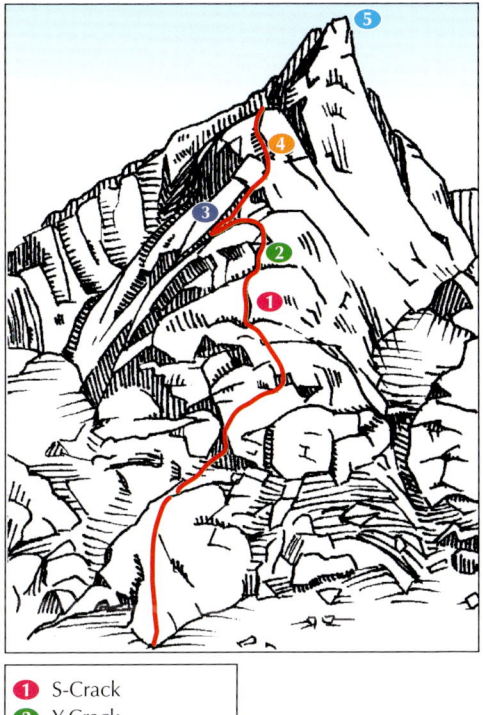

① S-Crack
② Y-Crack
③ Layback Crack
④ Three-Tier Chimney
⑤ Upper Pinnacle

Starting up the crux of the Y-Crack, pitch 5

Follow this, swinging extravagantly from jug to jug across the slabby wall with smears for your feet. This is bold, unless you've a very small cam. The seam leads to another blocky corner, where there's good gear. More laybacking, then gains a block-covered ledge.

Pitch 8, 30m 4a, Three-Tier Chimney
A good old-fashioned struggle that will leave the bouldering/climbing-wall fraternity at a loss. Climb the chimney system above the ledge, three steep steps with brief rests in between. The chockstone at the top is a welcome positive handhold, though it feels a little impermanent. Move right up to the ridge crest to belay.

Pitches 9 and 10, 60m
Continue easily in a grand position, moving left at one point to stay with clean rock on the arete to reach The Terrace.

Possible descent
This grassy diagonal rake marks the end of the VS climbing, and is a useful means of descent in failing daylight; climb it until safe ground leads off left above the crag to reach the path down Cir Mhor's South West Ridge. From here Glen Rosa is easily regained.

Continuation
The Upper Pinnacle, 75m VDiff
This great wedge forms the spire of the Rosa Pinnacle, as seen from a distance. It is set slightly to the right of the lower crag, immediately above The Terrace. Though it can be avoided, it shouldn't be. Ascend it in three pitches, starting up the W flank from The Terrace.

Climb a little wall onto a slab, which is followed until a chimney leads onto a grassy belay platform. Walk left along the platform to another short chimney; climb slabby ground just to its

41

At the top of pitch 7

3 – SOUTH RIDGE DIRECT, ROSA PINNACLE, CIR MHOR

On pitch 9, with the Upper Pinnacle yet to come

right, onto the ridge crest. Cross to the Pinnacle's E face, traversing airily rightwards into a corner. This leads to a belay stance. A brief climb up a last corner and slab wins the top of the Pinnacle.

Scramble down W to the grassy gap below Cir Mhor's craggy summit. The mountain is quickly dispatched by a slabby scramble up its left flank to the fine pointed peak.

Descent
Follow the South West Ridge path, as above.

ARRAN AND THE SOUTHERN HIGHLANDS

Route 4 – Glen Sannox Horseshoe

Grade	2/3 scramble as described (harder or easier variations are possible)
Distance	15km
Ascent	1700m
Time	8½ hours
Start/finish	Car park at Sannox (NS016454)
Map	OS Landranger (1:50,000) 69
Accommodation	See Route 1
Sleeping out	There is a wonderful grassy meadow near the river and shipping beacons in the mouth of Glen Sannox – camp sensitively.
Public transport	Buses run between Brodick and Sannox (and on to Lochranza) several times a day.
Seasonal notes	This makes a superb winter round, very long but escapable at several points. Cioch na h-Oighe and Caisteal Abhail's East Ridge provide sections of I/II by the easiest line; the Witch's Step direct would be very much harder.

Circling the northern half of Arran's mountains, the Glen Sannox Horseshoe is one of the best scrambling ridge walks in Scotland. The views and positions are memorable, and the rock for the most part impeccable. Technical difficulties can be varied at will, with some very good optional clambers. The Witch's Step direct is a different ball game from the rest of the route, a short but meaty Difficult climb for which a rope is advised. Avoiding it, as described here, gives a more consistent outing without need for climbing gear. Even skirting around the hardest sections is a hefty undertaking, with plenty of ascent and tough terrain throughout.

Approach

Follow the track up Glen Sannox, past the white beacon towers. At the mine workings branch left on a fainter path heading towards Coire na Ciche. The imposing mass of Cioch na h-Oighe looms above, a huge broken face with one very steep clean wall, home to some big rock climbing numbers. The scrambling route breaches the mountain's nose by a surprising line of weakness.

Climb

At the lip of the corrie bowl turn hard right on a good path that traverses the face on a heathery terrace between broken crags to reach the blunt N rib. The path then turns left up the rib, threading through slabby outcrops. There's some brief unavoidable grade 1/2 scrambling, though things can readily be made more interesting still.

The Witch's Step from The Saddle

44

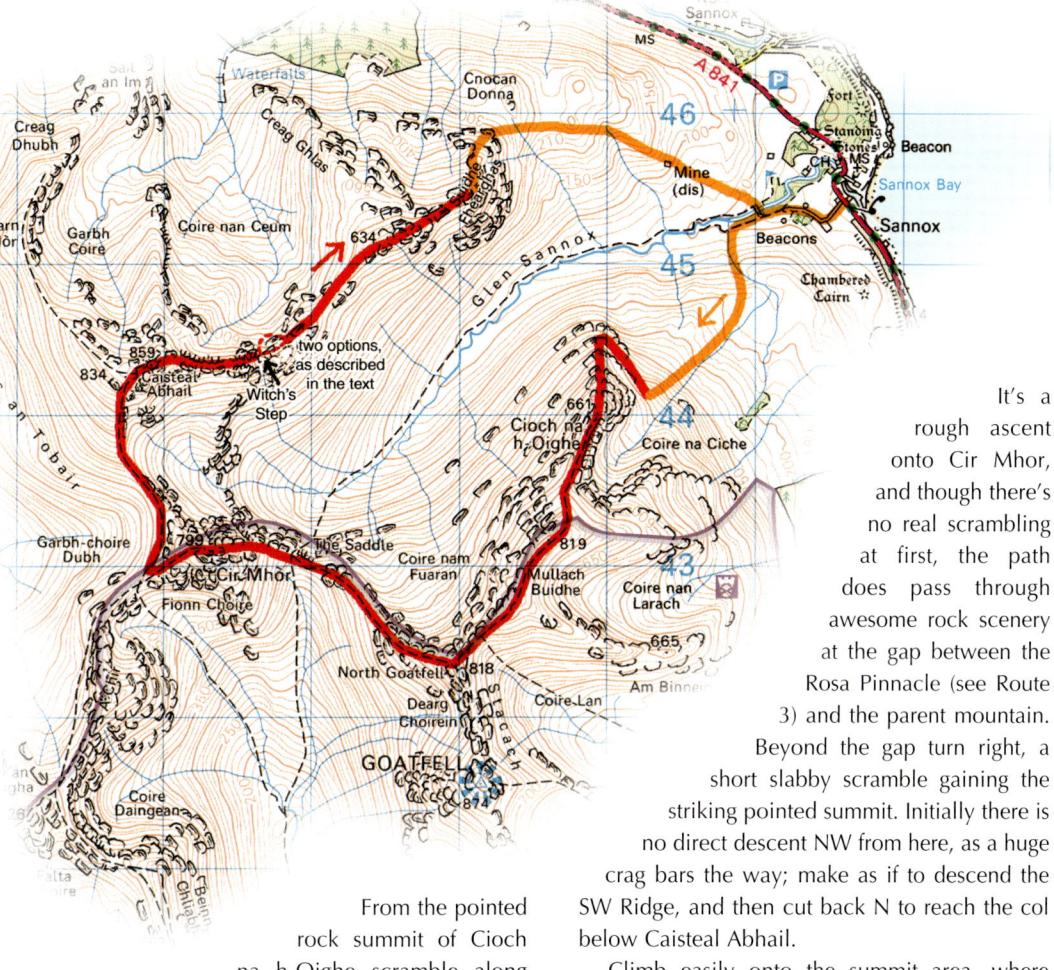

4 – Glen Sannox Horseshoe

From the pointed rock summit of Cioch na h-Oighe scramble along the wonderful crenellated crest (grade 2) over a couple of airy little tops, ignoring the unnecessary path lower down on the W flank. Then stroll over Mullach Buidhe and on to North Goatfell. Being close to Arran's highest summit this short section is often thronged, while more interesting peaks in the rest of the range are all but ignored; there's nowt so queer as folk, as they say.

The steep WNW descent from North Goatfell requires a modicum of care, the path having been eroded into a mess of gravel by the plodding hordes. At one point a pinnacle sits astride the ridge; it's fine to clamber onto this (grade 2), though you cannot continue directly off the far side. The long descent eventually reaches The Saddle, having lost you half your hard-won height gain.

It's a rough ascent onto Cir Mhor, and though there's no real scrambling at first, the path does pass through awesome rock scenery at the gap between the Rosa Pinnacle (see Route 3) and the parent mountain. Beyond the gap turn right, a short slabby scramble gaining the striking pointed summit. Initially there is no direct descent NW from here, as a huge crag bars the way; make as if to descend the SW Ridge, and then cut back N to reach the col below Caisteal Abhail.

Climb easily onto the summit area, where there are several chunky granite tors. The highest point is the easternmost of the two main lumps; follow an obvious grade 2 scramble up big blocks on its W side to the flat top. Walk off the far side to begin descending the complex E ridge, a descending row of pointed towers. It's possible to skirt the main obstacles on an obvious path, but better – as always – to take them head on, with a few passages of at least grade 2/3. Not far short of undemanding ground, a steep pinnacle bars the way; climb it from the left, with a couple of reachy lunges (grade 3). Descend carefully from the summit into the tight V-notch of the Witch's Step, beyond which rises a final spire; a short slabby groove provides the only appreciable scrambling on the way down. There are two alternatives from here:

45

Descending into the Witch's Step

Cioch na h-Oighe from the Mullach Buidhe ridge

Witch's Step direct, 45m Difficult
The complex face of the spire can be breached direct by roped parties. From the neck of land in the base of the V-notch, a short chimney groove leads to a slab set in a left-slanting diagonal corner. The crux is low down, and involves surmounting a weird bulging step onto the holdless polished slab. It's an off-putting little passage, and not recommended in the wet. Above, follow a vegetated fault and then a chimney formed between the monolithic blocks of the sharp, forked summit. This is perhaps the most dramatic spot on the entire round.

Witch's Step avoided, grade 2/3 scramble
Unroped teams would be wise to descend N from the neck down an earthy gully bed, until a well-worn line can be picked up to flank the tower: a brief scramble to exit the gully gains a path looping back towards the main ridge crest beyond the tower, at the end of all difficulties. It's a shame to miss out on the excitement however. Adventurous souls will soon quit the flanking path to climb a slabby line up the tower's N flank (grade 2/3), moving left around the final huge summit blocks to come at them from the E. Descend E, following signs of wear and a few nice scrambly bits to reach easy ground. The broad ridge now continues onto Suidhe Fhearghas, the last top of the day.

Descent
A steep, rough descent from here gains a boggy shoulder, from where a path heads down into Glen Sannox near the old mine workings. Cross the footbridge to meet the approach track.

Route 5 – Traverse of South and Centre Peaks, the Cobbler

Grade	Difficult
Distance	8km
Ascent	900m
Time	5 hours
Start/finish	Car park at the head of Loch Long (NN295049)
Map	OS Landranger (1:50,000) 56
Accommodation	Crianlarich Youth Hostel is fairly near for those with a car (0870 004 1112). Or try the Forest Enterprise campsite at Arrochar (01301 702 293).
Sleeping out	There's a howff of sorts under the Narnain Boulders, and many tent pitches in the surrounding area.
Public transport	Train or Citylink bus from Glasgow to Tarbet, or a local bus to Arrochar
Seasonal notes	Though it's neither the highest nor most reliable venue, the Cobbler's popularity in winter is justified by a wealth of classic climbs. The route described becomes a wonderful, though fairly stiff, winter grade III.

The derogatory expression 'a load of old cobblers' must refer to something else entirely; this particular Cobbler is anything but. It is instead the most strikingly quirky mountain in the southern Highlands, its three sharp peaks of folded mica schist forming a distinctive toothed skyline high above the head of Loch Long. With a rich cache of quality routes from the tweedy and traditional to the outrageously overhanging, the Cobbler is one of Scotland's showpiece climbing hangouts. Being barely an hour north of Glasgow ensures enduring popularity. Though it doesn't attract the crowds, the traverse of the South and Centre Peaks links a number of routes to create an old fashioned mountaineering line with grand situations and plenty of interest.

Approach

From the lochside car park near Arrochar cross the road and head straight up an uncompromising hill of recently felled forestry, on a well-used path that often doubles as a stream. At a T-junction turn left and contour round to join the Allt a'Bhalachain at a small dam. Cross the burn and climb a grassy sponge to gain the left-bounding ridge of the corrie. Follow this past outcrops to the base of the SE Ridge of the Cobbler's South Peak.

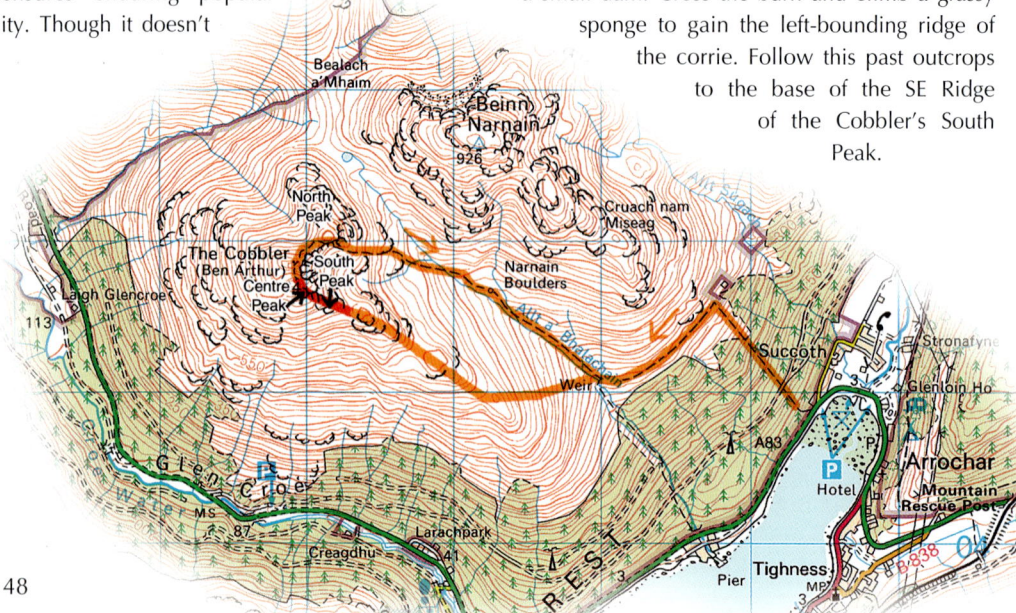

5 – Traverse of the South and Centre Peaks, the Cobbler

The Cobbler from the east. Left to right: South Peak, Centre Peak, North Peak and Beinn Ime in snow

South Peak
Climb
SE Ridge, 105m Moderate

Though at least 50% grass, the rock when you encounter it is excellent mica schist typical of the Cobbler. In the wet or wind it's best to climb the ridge in four roped pitches. The steep terminal nose is bypassed on the left. Gain the ridge just above this via a series of vegetated slabby ledges. An airy step right takes you out onto the ridge's vertical right wall for a few moves before regaining easy ground on the blunt crest. Climb foliage onto a minor bump, then teeter over a bridge of boulders to the neck beyond. A short slabby passage gains further vegetation; follow the path up to a steep cracked wall. This is made of lovely stuff, though sadly it's short lived. Simple vegetated scrambling then gains the dramatic tilted summit.

Descent
Original Route, 25m Moderate

A polished descent with death-fall potential – rope advisable. From the summit slab's far left corner, downclimb an awkward smooth crack to a small ledge. Step right (facing out) and clamber down jugs to a lower ledge. It's possible to rig an abseil here. Otherwise, at the far end of the ledge is a well-marked line down a groove, leading to a narrow earthy path. Traverse this path above a sizeable drop until a smooth step down leads to easy ground at a col.

The Cobbler

1. South East Ridge
2. South Peak
3. The Arete
4. Centre Peak
5. North Peak

49

Nearing the top of the South East Ridge of the South Peak

Centre Peak
Climb
The Arete, 70m Difficult
Walk a little way up the eroded hillwalker's path, and then quit it for a prominent cracked wall on the right. Following the crack proves an absorbing short pitch; some leaders may question the grade. Big chocks and/or friends are invaluable. Belay on the knobble above. You can summit in one further 50m ropelength. Cross a bridge of boulders to the final spike, which from this angle loosely resembles Skye's Inaccessible Pinnacle (see Route 48). Gain a shallow niche on the right, and then climb the crest on good rock all the way.

Descent
Doorway Route, 15m grade 3 scramble
This was a legendary test of manhood for Campbell chiefs of old, though thankfully these days girls are allowed to do it too. From the precariously bijou summit descend a steep little cleft to an exposed ledge on the S side, leading to a cave-like through route onto easy ground. It is a bad place to shelter in a thunderstorm.

Now merely walking, head briefly NE around the rim of the corrie, descending an eroded path below the impressive North Peak (bagged by a short detour) onto the corrie floor. The path threads through outcrops, meeting the Allt a'Bhalachain and passing the chunky Narnain Boulders before rejoining the approach route.

Pitch 2 of The Arete, nearing the summit of Centre Peak

Arran and the Southern Highlands

Route 6 – Coire Gaothach Circuit, Ben Lui

Grade	Easy I
Distance	18km
Ascent	950m
Time	8 hours
Start/finish	Car park at Dalrigh, just off the A82 (NN343292)
Map	OS Landranger (1:50,000) 50
Accommodation	Crianlarich Youth Hostel (0870 0041112), Bridge of Orchy Hotel Bunkhouse (01838 400 208)
Sleeping out	The valley of the River Cononish is a bleak and breezy spot, but if you really want to camp out then try the vicinity of the little stone enclosure (NN282273) or even the floor of Coire Gaothach.
Public transport	Trains on the Glasgow – Fort William line stop at nearby Crianlarich and Tyndrum, while buses plying the A82 should drop you anywhere you like.
Seasonal notes	Positioned in the lee of the prevailing westerlies, and topping out on one of the highest peaks in the Southern Highlands, Coire Gaothach holds snow well. When stripped of its winter covering this is no more than a scrambly hillwalk, though it still remains the best route to the summit.

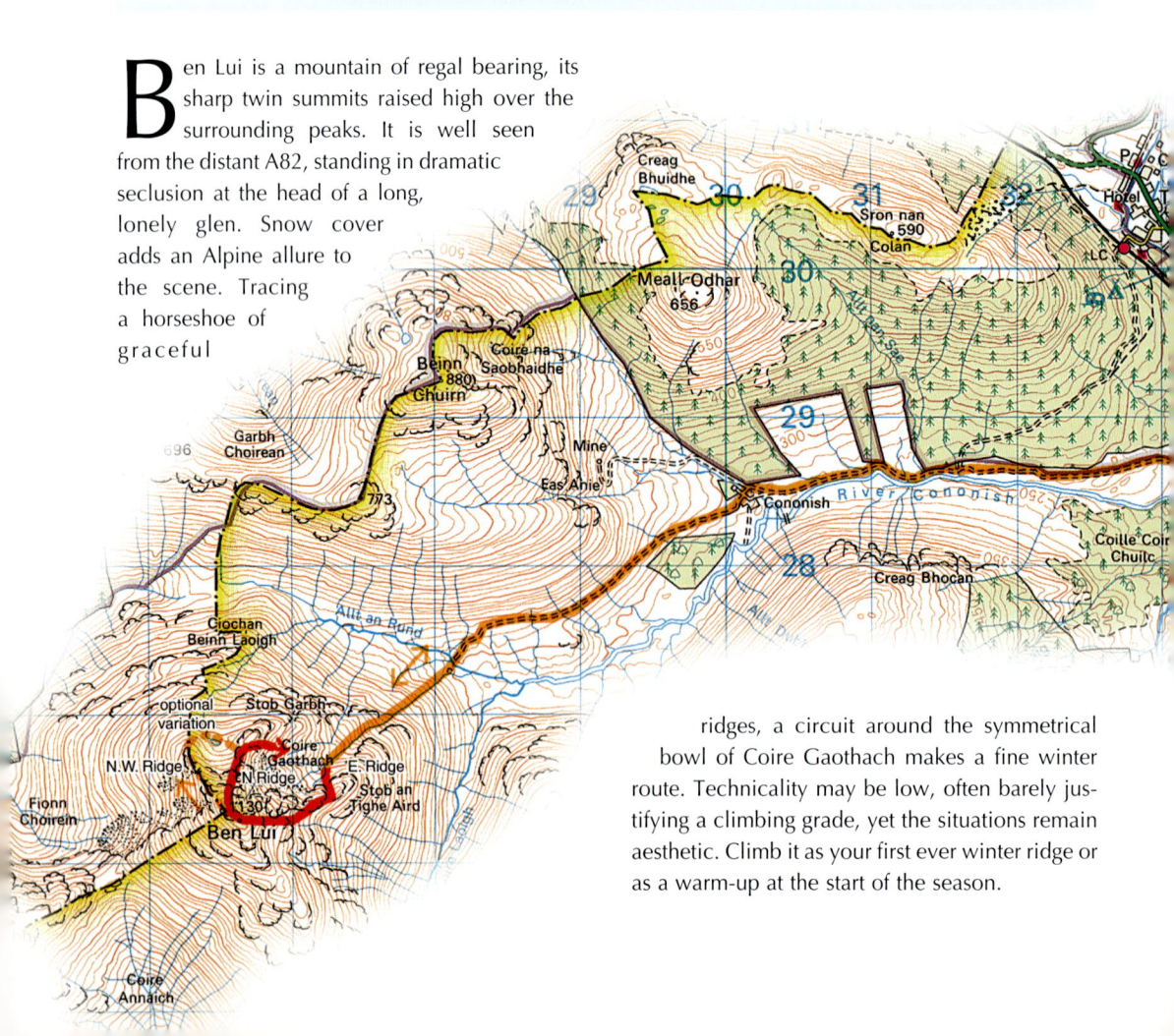

Ben Lui is a mountain of regal bearing, its sharp twin summits raised high over the surrounding peaks. It is well seen from the distant A82, standing in dramatic seclusion at the head of a long, lonely glen. Snow cover adds an Alpine allure to the scene. Tracing a horseshoe of graceful ridges, a circuit around the symmetrical bowl of Coire Gaothach makes a fine winter route. Technicality may be low, often barely justifying a climbing grade, yet the situations remain aesthetic. Climb it as your first ever winter ridge or as a warm-up at the start of the season.

6 – COIRE GAOTHACH CIRCUIT, BEN LUI

The open arms of Coire Gaothach from the Cononish track

Approach

It is a long slog of nearly 7km from the car park to the base of the mountain on a stony vehicle track all the way. People have been known to drive as far as Cononish, though to do so you'd need to secure permission from the farmer. Drivers without a 4WD would be happiest using someone else's car. A mountain bike is a more sensible option.

From the car park head just right of a small group of houses, turning right for a bridge over a burn. Keep on the track through a stand of trees and under the railway line to reach open ground beside a forestry plantation. The track now follows the N bank of the wide River Cononish to lonely Cononish farm. From here it leaves the riverbank, climbing gradually with a small mine and the impressive waterfall of Eas Anie on the right. Two kilometres later the track descends slightly to rejoin the river. Ford this to reach an old stone-walled enclosure.

A muddy path now climbs steeply towards Coire Gaothach, following the course of its outflow. Pass between the twin gable ends of Coire Gaothach's enclosing ridges to reach the sloping corrie floor. Here a group of large boulders provides shelter for a breather. The headwall looms ahead, a sweep of rock and snow rearing to Lui's twin summits. First done way back in 1891, the classic Central Gully goes straight up the middle of this face at an amenable grade I. The route is all on snow, starting easily and building to a pleasantly exposed climax. Compared even with this relatively gentle route, the difficulties of the corrie circuit seem modest.

Climb

Turn left, climbing vegetation and little outcrops to get established on Ben Lui's East Ridge. Follow this, keeping just left of the corrie rim. At first it is

53

Starting up the crux section of the East Ridge. Frozen turf makes things easy, though deep snow would be less so.

broad and grassy, but the ground soon rises to a jagged little false summit. Stay on an easy slope just left of the first major rock mass. Above is a short band of steep broken crag, bounded on the right by the drop into Coire Gaothach. In summer this is a scrambly mixture of vegetation and loose rock; when frozen solid or snow covered it's rather more pleasant. It is unavoidable and moderately exposed, though the difficulties are short lived; weave up an obvious line of weakness a little left of the cliff edge. The continuation ridge to Lui's true (SE) summit is much gentler. From the main top take the narrow crest to peak number two, with a couple of scrambly rock steps. This short, level arete can be heavily corniced on the corrie side.

Descent

To complete the second half of the horseshoe descend direct from peak two down the N rim of Coire Gaothach. The descent is initially steep and craggy, though it soon eases. Poor visibility, icy snow or a large cornice may all render this option unattractive.

The best **alternative** is to continue pleasantly down Ben Lui's short NW Ridge instead. This forms the back of another, shallower corrie. At the first safe opportunity cut back right to the floor of this second corrie, passing just right of a tiny lochan (sometimes buried by snow) to gain the N rim of Coire Gaothach at a slight saddle below the awkward upper section of the ridge. Descend direct into the corrie from here, on steep snow and/or scree, to regain the approach path.

6 – Coire Gaothach Circuit, Ben Lui

On the crux of the East Ridge

LOCHABER

The self-proclaimed Outdoor Capital of the UK enjoys unrivalled year-round popularity among climbers and hillwalkers, with the greatest concentration of mountaineering routes in the country on some of the biggest and most impressive mountains. Ben Nevis is, of course, the biggest and baddest of them all. It is a beast of a hill, hosting climbs of Alpine scale and setting. Winters on the 'The Ben' are good enough to draw regular climbing pilgrims from the continent, and its summer climbs are just as illustrious. The jagged peaks rimming cavernous Glen Coe provide an arena of similar quality. In terms of ridges, Ben Nevis, the Aonachs and Glen Coe are the obvious hotspots, though the graceful Mamores and lonely Ben Alder have attractions of their own.

On the Garbhanach–Gearanach crest, Ring of Steall (Route 14). Behind, the Carn Mor Dearg Arete (Route 20) rises to Ben Nevis.

Route 7 – Sron na Creise, Creise

Grade	3 scramble
Distance	12km
Ascent	1000m
Time	5 hours
Start/finish	Layby beside Blackrock Cottage on the access road to Glencoe Ski Centre (NN268530)
Map	OS Landranger (1:50,000) 41
Accommodation	Glencoe Youth Hostel (0870 004 1122), Glencoe Farm Bunkhouse (01855 811 906), Red Squirrel Campsite – beware the mighty midge (01855 811 256), camping by Kingshouse Hotel, Bridge of Orchy Hotel Bunkhouse (01838 400 208)
Sleeping out	Level ground in Cam Ghleann tends to be sodden. Perhaps the best bet for wild camping is down in Glen Etive.
Public transport	Public buses running between Glasgow and Fort William will drop you on the A82 close to the King's House Hotel and the Ski Centre.
Seasonal notes	Perfectly feasible as a winter route, though the ridge crest doesn't seem to hold snow as readily as the face to its left. Estimated grade III; however, most difficulties can readily be skirted. The rock on the technical slabby bits is compact, and might prove hard to protect. Watch for cornices on Creise and hurtling skiers on Meall a'Bhuiridh.

Across the mouth of Glen Etive from Buachaille Etive Mor (Route 9 and 10) stands the Blackmount range, a clutch of rugged high peaks. Outside the winter months the group offers limited climbing interest, though it's a nice venue for a wild wander. Sron na Creise, the north ridge of Stob a'Ghlais Choire, is one of the few noteworthy summer scrambles. It's too short and disjointed to rate as a classic, but it is still surprisingly good, taking a logical line up patches of very decent rock. Being fairly non-serious it makes a worthwhile backup option when your plan A in Glencoe has crapped out in rain or snow. To avoid a feeling of anti-climax the ridge is best considered a prelude to a fine hillwalking circuit over Creise and Meall a'Bhuiridh.

Approach

Pass just left of Blackrock Cottage, taking any of a number of faint paths that skirt W below Creag Dhubh over moorland of remarkable bogginess. Almost invisible until you unexpectedly stumble across them, the peat hags, spongy sloughs and malevolent black watercourses make progress a

Stob a'Ghlais Choire from Rannoch Moor. Sron na Creise is the right-hand skyline; Inglis Clark Ridge follows the broad buttress left of centre.

hit-and-miss affair. The best line traverses the hillside just above the marshy levels. Rise gently into the mouth of Cam Ghleann. Fording or boulder-hopping a burn (care in spate), climb steep grass towards the right end of Sron na Creise, which forms the skyline dead ahead.

Climb
Once established on the grassy nose of the buttress you're faced with two choices: either deliberately seek out the difficulties, or weave through them on an unpleasant mixture of scree, soil and vegetation. Let's face it, there is only one decision. Take the first rock patch direct. Some holds are wobbly, and it steepens appreciably with height. Back on straightforward terrain, bear slightly left as you ascend, reaching a collection of monster boulders beneath a slabby mass. Gain the slabs via a steep left-leaning groove. Pad delicately up the rough-skinned rock, following some fairly small holds back onto easy ground.

You soon encounter a second, and rather bigger, slabby buttress. Again it starts steeply, with a tricky little wall. It's quite serious for a few moves, though the holds are all there if you take time to find them. Above it's gentler, and an obvious groove debouches onto a grassy levelling to the left of a chossy little gully. Ascend a short way, then cross

the gully. The crag forming its right wall seems pretty mean at first, but you'll soon spot a tenuous-looking rightwards traverse across a sloping ledge. A couple of careful moves along this gain more substantial holds, which lead up to broken ground. A few final fun bits and the scramble's in the bag.

Descent
If you're desperate to get off the hill the quickest descent is down the loose stuff skirting what you've just climbed, but it's not pleasant. Alternatively, to increase the time spent scrambling try descending the NE Ridge of Stob a'Ghlais Choire (see Route 8).

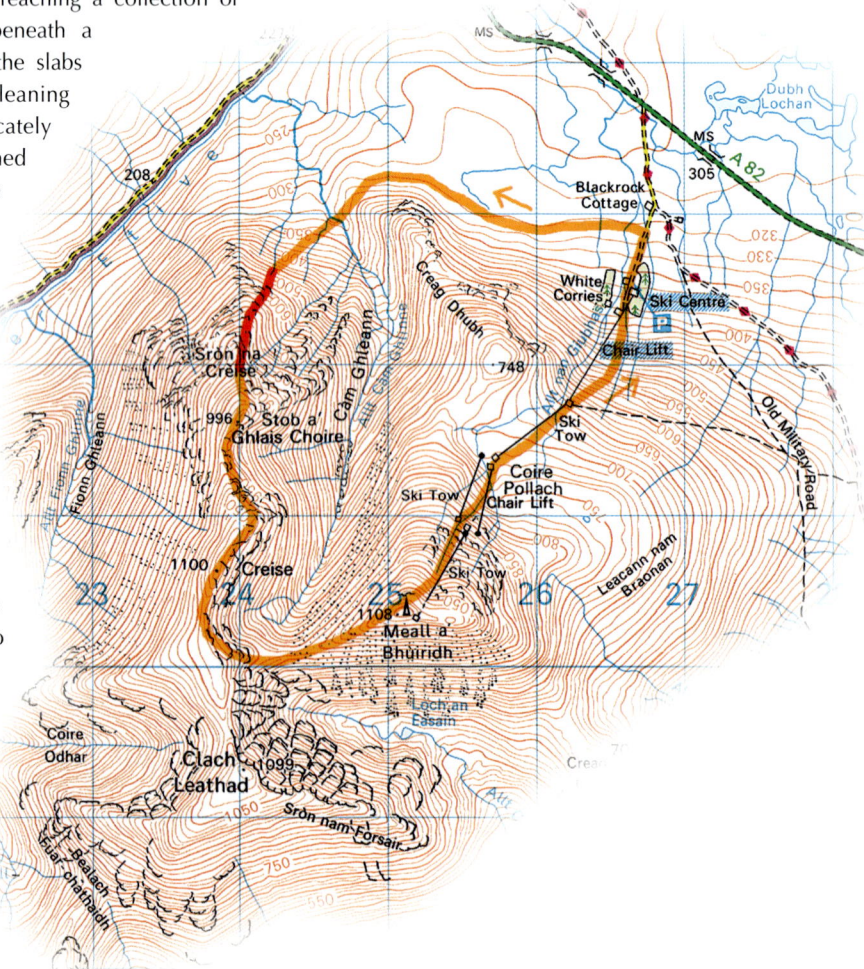

7 – Sron na Creise, Creise

Buachaille Etive Mor from Sron na Creise

On the slabs above the 'monster boulders'

Creise from Stob a'Ghlais Choire, under late spring snow

Continuation

The most satisfying option is to make an extended walking circuit. Continue to the minor summit of Stob a'Ghlais Choire, then climb around the rim of Glas Choire onto the summit of Creise. The precipitous slopes to your left can hold a lot of snow well into spring/summer, and are often quite severely corniced. Continue roughly S for about 600m, to the point marked as spot height 1070m on the 1:25,000 map. In clear visibility the ridge leading down and then back up to Meall a'Bhuiridh is plain to see, though finding and effecting a safe descent to its foot can cause pause for thought in snow. A cairn marks the drop-off point down a small broken crag to the col at pretty much the only natural break in the cornice. On then, up the blunt crest to the day's last summit, before descending all the way to the road beneath the tows of the Glencoe Ski Centre – a welcome guide in mist.

Route 8 – Inglis Clark Ridge, Creise

Grade	160m III
Distance	8km
Ascent	720m
Time	7½ hours
Start/finish	Layby beside Blackrock Cottage on the access road to Glencoe Ski Centre (NN268530)
Map	OS Landranger (1:50,000) 41
Accommodation	See Route 7
Sleeping out	See Route 7
Public transport	See Route 7
Seasonal notes	This is a (justifiably?) neglected summer Difficult, originally done way back in 1903 by husband-and-wife team Dr and Mrs Inglis Clark. This climbing couple were later involved in building the CIC hut under Ben Nevis, named in memory of their son Charles. Clumps of greenery en route might be made up for by stretches of decent clean rock – though beware the odd loose block. Bear in mind its orientation in the lee of the prevailing winds, as windslab and cornices can be an issue in winter.

Framed by Sron na Creise (Route 7) the shallow NE-facing corrie below Stob a'Ghlais Choire is made up of a number of parallel buttresses and gullies, well seen from the Glen Coe road. Though it scarcely breaches the 900m contour, the back wall of this corrie can hold large quantities of snow and ice, ideal ground for mid-grade climbers. Many routes must have been put up here over the decades, yet few have been recorded for posterity. Despite its accessibility, this general air of neglect adds to a certain exploratory feel. The best and most popular line here is Inglis Clark Ridge, a wonderful mixed climb with difficulties on both rock and ice.

Approach

As for Sron na Creise (Route 7) into the mouth of Cam Ghleann. Cross the main burn below a little gorge and waterfall, and head up steeply into the scoop bounded on the right by Sron na Creise, staying on a blunt rocky rib (some simple scrambling) between the two watercourses draining the corrie.

Although Inglis Clark Ridge is almost dead centre in the corrie bowl, this is not apparent in close-up, when only the right-hand half of the corrie is seen properly. The route climbs the bulkiest buttress in sight, a broad mass of rock, tapered at its foot and crowned with a blunt tower. A prominent icefall cascades down its lower reaches,

Lochaber

The icefall crux, pitch 1

constituting the first pitch. It is the best passage on pure ice described in this book.

Cross some slabby ice flows to gain the snow gully running up to, and then right of, the buttress. Climb snow to the tongue of rock just below the obvious icefall. All the gullies in this vicinity look to be straightforward grade Is, but the twin parallel rock ribs immediately right of Inglis Clark Ridge might offer interesting mixed climbs.

Inglis Clark Ridge

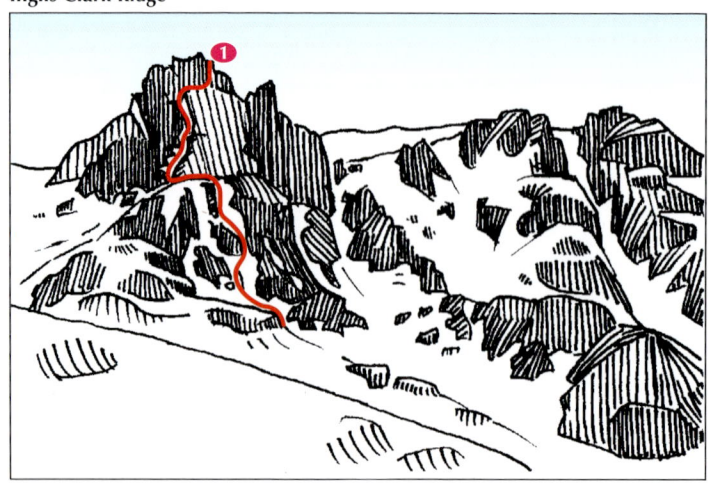

Climb
Inglis Clark Ridge, 160m III
Pitch 1, 55m
According to the SMC Glencoe Guidebook this pitch is only 35m long, though this may come as news to those who find themselves running short of rope at just the wrong moment. The length clearly depends

❶ Inglis Clark Ridge

Interest increases, approaching the belay ledge on pitch 3

on where the first belay is set up, and how banked-out the base of the route is. If belayed from a little crack in the tongue of rock just under the icefall (the logical place), then 50m ropes will not be sufficient to do the pitch in one. In this eventuality it's possible to take an intermediate stance about two-thirds of the way up, in a little niche below and right of the crux step.

Climb an ice-choked groove over a steepening and onto a slabby step where a rib of rock might poke free, dividing the icefall into two strands. Continue quite steeply up the left-hand strand, stepping right across the rock rib to belay in the niche if necessary. Above the groove, the icefall rears up to a climax, a very decent bit of grade III climbing bringing you to a boulder belay at a big terrace.

Pitch 2, 30m
Follow a little turfy groove just left of the main rock mass before moving right onto a second terrace.

Pitch 3, 35m
Step right to ascend mixed rock and turf steps with interest, a palpable sense of exposure provided by the sudden imminence of the gully bounding the right side of the ridge. As the rocks become steeper and more continuous move left onto a ledge below a clean vertical wall.

Pitch 4, 40m
One of the finest mixed pitches described in this book. Sidle left along the ledge, climbing a sloping shelf below the wall in a wonderfully airy position. Dispatch the wall by moving up square-cut rock steps at its left end. Now head back diagonally right over chunky blocks to gain a little right-angled corner. This is trickier than it looks, but soon leads to easier ground, a final sloping continuation groove spitting you out onto the level top of the tower, the end of the technical climbing.

A broad, bouldery neck connects the ridge with the main mountain. The exit slopes can be profoundly corniced; if in doubt stay roped until safely on level ground. Walk left to the minor summit of Stob a'Ghlais Choire.

Descent
NE Ridge Stob a'Ghlais Choire, grade 1 scramble / I
Though the quickest and most straightforward descent, this is still a scramble, and it's worth ensuring sufficient daylight is kept in hand to see your way to *terra firma*. The ridge starts broad and easy angled but soon steepens appreciably, dropping down several slabby rock steps that look daunting from above. Given daylight the safest line isn't hard to follow, though take care in icy conditions. Keep slightly left of centre down each successive steep band until, just before reaching safety, you come up against the final step, a disconcerting vertical crag. Move right along the grassy terrace at its lip to gain safe grass and scree slopes running down below the crag into Cam Ghleann. Stay with the high ground on the rib that follows on from the base of the NE Ridge to regain the main burn in the valley near the waterfall and little gorge.

Route 9 – Curved Ridge, Buachaille Etive Mor

Grade	3 scramble
Distance	5km (optional 14km)
Ascent	750m (1100m)
Time	5 hours (8 hours)
Start/finish	Lagangarbh layby off the A82 (NN221562)
Map	OS Landranger (1:50,000) 41
Accommodation	See Route 7
Sleeping out	Discreet wild camping close to the road is feasible in Glencoe.
Public transport	Scottish Citylink buses between Glasgow and Fort William run through Glencoe, and can pull over where you like.
Seasonal notes	Although it holds snow less readily than some neighbouring peaks Buachaille Etive Mor can provide fantastic winter climbing. Curved Ridge is an excellent grade II/III, possible in most conditions. However beware avalanche risk on the slopes immediately below the ridge, and from the top of the ridge proper up to the summit of Stob Dearg. In descent note too that Coire na Tulaich is a notorious avalanche black spot; if in doubt here follow the corrie's west-bounding ridge (with care) instead of the usual path.

Few Scottish mountains hold a candle to Buachaille Etive Mor, a huge buttressed pyramid spitting scree over its heather skirts. Rearing implausibly over the watery waste of Rannoch Moor, this great stone sentinel dwarfs traffic on the A82, turning the head of every passing motorist. It's surprising there aren't more collisions beneath the gatehouse of Glencoe. Tiredness can kill, but so too can startling mountain views. With a number of major buttresses and gullies, the North and East faces are both confusing and very daunting. However, there are sneaky breaches in the Buachaille's formidable defences – and Curved Ridge is one. It is a high quality scramble in a thrilling position.

Approach

The route can be identified from the roadside E of Lagangarbh. Curved Ridge forms the left wall of Easy Gully, which in turn lies left of and below the obvious detached mini-summit of Crowberry Tower. Cross the footbridge, pass whitewashed Lagangarbh hut and shortly bear left, taking a rising traverse on a path beneath the Buachaille's formidable ramparts. Ascend just left of the obvious Waterslide Slab – you can't miss it. Zigzag steeply up soil and ribbons of scree. Being just one among many impending bastions the ridge is ill-defined from this angle; it's left of the unmistakeable Rannoch Wall/Crowberry Ridge. Follow the erosion gradually right towards a little scree gully and a slabby wall.

Lochaber

Curved Ridge slants right to left below the towering Rannoch Wall of Crowberry Ridge (Route 10)

Buachaille Etive Mor

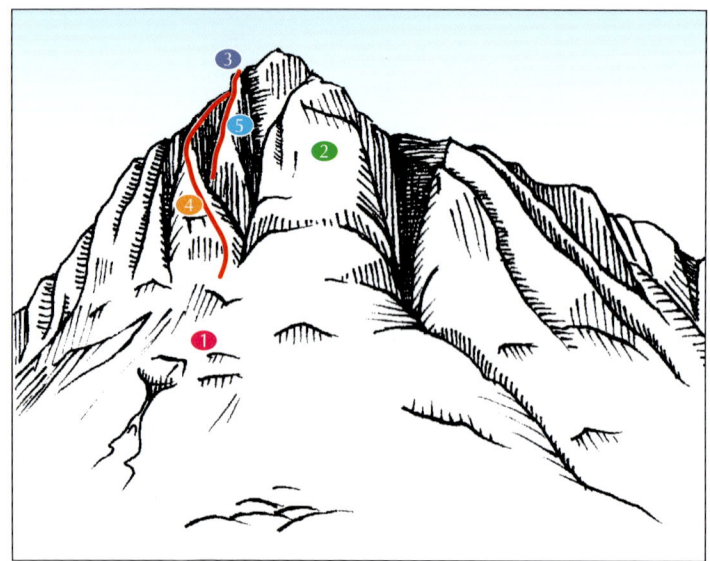

Climb

The polished groove up this wall makes a suitable intro, though it feels harder than anything above. This can be outflanked with minimal difficulty by a zig left and a zag right. More scree and an unavoidable rock step follow. Directly above is a steep rock rib – both exposed and thought-provoking. The rock is well worn, and incut holds are plentiful. An easier section soon leads on up the rounded crest. With Rannoch Wall hanging stupendously overhead to the right, and drops increasing on either hand, the situation is magnificent. Another steepening provides further interest. The rubbly gully on the right is split at this point by a rock mass; climb the cleaner rock on the left, via an exciting series of abrupt steps. The hardest of these is a smooth groove. With Rannoch Moor stretching away below your bootsoles it pays to go slow, though decent holds do come readily to hand. Above, difficulties gradually ease until a small cairn marks the point where Curved Ridge merges into the broken mountainside.

Rannoch Wall is now below, and Crowberry Tower (see Route 10) directly overhead. It's possible to pick your way up a broad scree gully (sometimes snowfilled) and on to Stob Dearg, the main peak. Far better, though, is to climb Crowberry Tower en route. A rough path traverses rightwards under the tower on shattered rock above a formidable drop. Once on the crest of Crowberry Ridge, turn left and scramble fairly easily (though airily) onto the detached summit. This is a wonderful position. Return a few metres the way you came, until a ledge curves leftwards around the summit block. Descend a short rock step to the neck

1. Waterslide Slab
2. North Buttress
3. Crowberry Tower
4. Curved Ridge
5. Crowberry Ridge

Spacious views from high on Curved Ridge

between Crowberry Tower and the main mountain. Stob Dearg is now just a stony scramble away.

Descent
The quickest return is to head roughly W from the summit cairn along a short stretch of summit ridge, and then down well-scuffed ground to the saddle at the head of Coire na Tulaich. Then take the standard hillwalker's path into the base of the corrie, and so to Lagangarbh. The initial descent into the corrie is all earthy bits and grinding scree, and makes you sorry for non-scramblers who come up this way. Bear left, though, and you'll soon discover a brilliantly engineered path that eases what was once an unpleasant descent.

Continuation
Those with spare enthusiasm might instead prefer to make a long day of it by continuing SW along the Buachaille's gentler spine, to climb Stob na Doire and Stob Coire Altruim, ending on Stob na Broige right above the deep trench of Glen Etive. Not half bad. Return to the col between Stob Coire Altruim and Stob na Doire and descend on grass into the Lairig Gartain. A path heads back to the A82 close to Lagangarbh.

Route 10 – Crowberry Ridge via the Rannoch Wall, Buachaille Etive Mor

Grade	Severe (as described), followed by grade 3 ridge scramble
Distance	5km
Ascent	750m
Time	7 hours
Start/finish	Lagangarbh layby off the A82 (NN221562)
Map	OS Landranger (1:50,000) 41
Accommodation	See Route 7
Sleeping out	See Route 9
Public transport	See Route 9
Seasonal notes	The practice of climbing out-of-nick classic summer rock routes with winter tools scratches the rock and tends to be disfavoured. For the record, January Jigsaw is said to be at least grade IV, though this may well be an underestimate. Naismith's Route or Shelf Route are winter alternatives. The continuation along Crowberry Ridge and over the tower is II/III.

Fancy two routes for the price of one? Though entirely different in character, this climb is directly adjacent to Curved Ridge (Route 9); they even share a start and finish (for map, see Route 9). Both can be done in a day. Rising steeply to the bold Crowberry Tower, Crowberry Ridge looks demanding. Though exposed, the crest itself is easier than appearance suggests. However, reaching it is another matter. The left flank of Crowberry Ridge is the famous Rannoch Wall, a vertical sheet of rhyolite with superb multi-pitch climbs leading to the ridge and tower above. Poised 2000ft above the tawny tundra of Rannoch Moor, even the easiest lines offer a wild 'space walking' experience. Though 'just' a Severe, January Jigsaw gives you the sort of buzz you'd normally only get from Es. OK, so it's nothing like a ridge; but it does lead to one, and for

Evening light on Buachaille Etive Mor, seen from Lagangarbh

An unknown climber starts up Agag's Groove, adjacent to January Jigsaw

something this special it's worth stretching a few definitions. The historic Direct Route provides a worthy substitute to the route described here, at a similar standard.

Approach
As for Crowberry Ridge until above the first rib of that route. From here bear right into scree-filled Easy Gully and clamber over to the base of Rannoch Wall. Start just left of the obvious left-curving line of Agag's Groove, below a detached flake. Agag's itself makes a great alternative at VDiff, though slightly less sensational than January Jigsaw.

Climb
January Jigsaw, 79m Severe
To struggle fully-laden, or to climb blissfully unencumbered and then have to retrieve the bags later? – the dilemma is as old as cragging itself. Since Curved Ridge offers a convenient descent, routes on Rannoch Wall lend themselves to the latter approach.

Pitch 1, 25m
Up a grassy bit until behind the detached flake. Follow a short straight crack to a succession of steps leading slightly left. Protection is spaced, and there's an immediate sense of verticality, with the mountain falling away below. At a ledge and flakes traverse briefly right to belay near a spike. This doesn't appear to be attached, so perhaps don't make it your sole anchor.

Pitch 2, 20m
From the top of the spike step onto a wall and climb easily via thin ledges straight up to a huge block belay, shared with Agag's Groove.

Pitch 3, 15m
Spectacular! Use the block as a natural runner for your left rope, then step from it onto the slightly undercut wall over Agag's Groove. Traverse right on decent holds, taking a fairly high line. There's no gear until you reach a shallow groove. Once you've got a couple of relieved runners in here, get your belayer to unhook the left rope from

Rannoch Wall

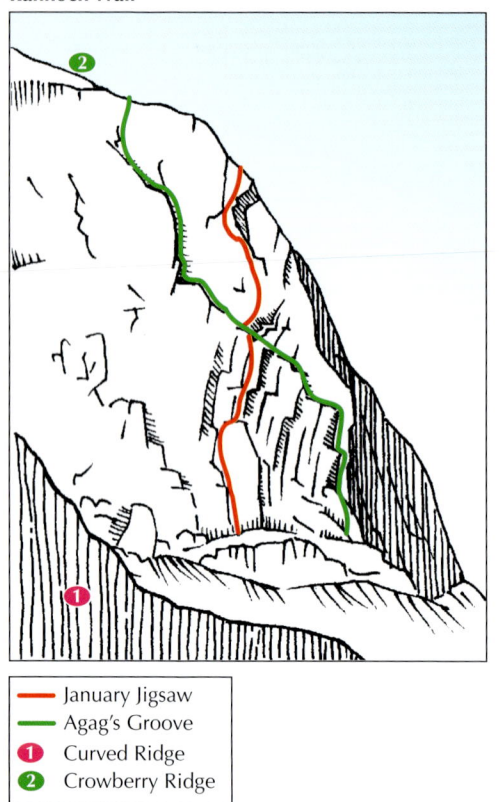

— January Jigsaw
— Agag's Groove
❶ Curved Ridge
❷ Crowberry Ridge

behind the belay block – or the drag will get you down. Follow the groove into a little niche ('The Haven') then traverse a tad left to reach a minimalist stance below an overhung crack. The belay includes a curious antique peg, which needs backing up.

Pitch 4, 19m
Climactic! Climb diagonally right, most improbably, to gain a groove. Organise protection. Ascend for a move or two, then step bravely left and commit to a vertical wall. This is the crux, tricky and quite run-out at the grade. Catch your breath on the ledge above, then gain salvation up a short groove.

You are now on the sloping terminal nose of Crowberry Ridge. The apex is convex rather than knife-edged, yet still very exposed. Scramble up slabby, rubbly ground for some way, until an

10 – CROWBERRY RIDGE VIA THE RANNOCH WALL, BUACHAILLE ETIVE MOR

exciting path heads left of the crest. This passes directly above the gulf of Rannoch Wall, so be careful to avoid knocking either stones or your partner onto climbers below. A short easy-angled slab and a stretch of path lead to a steep corner, for which it's worth roping up. An in-situ peg suggests that others have done likewise. Broken ground then leads to the base of Crowberry Tower. If you've struggled all the way up January Jigsaw with a rucksack, your consolation comes now – just carry on up the tower and on to Stob Dearg, as described for Curved Ridge.

Descent

Alternatively, with Curved Ridge as an exciting descent route retrieving your sack is no chore. Traverse left under the tower to the cairn marking the top of Curved Ridge. Now descend this carefully. In reverse it is entertaining, and best done in rock shoes. Only the crux groove gives pause for thought, and this is easily abseiled from a handy block. Once reunited with the bags, either carry on down or head back up Curved Ridge to bag Stob Dearg via Crowberry Tower. For those who've not climbed the Buachaille before, the latter is particularly worthwhile.

The belay on pitch 1 of January Jigsaw

LOCHABER

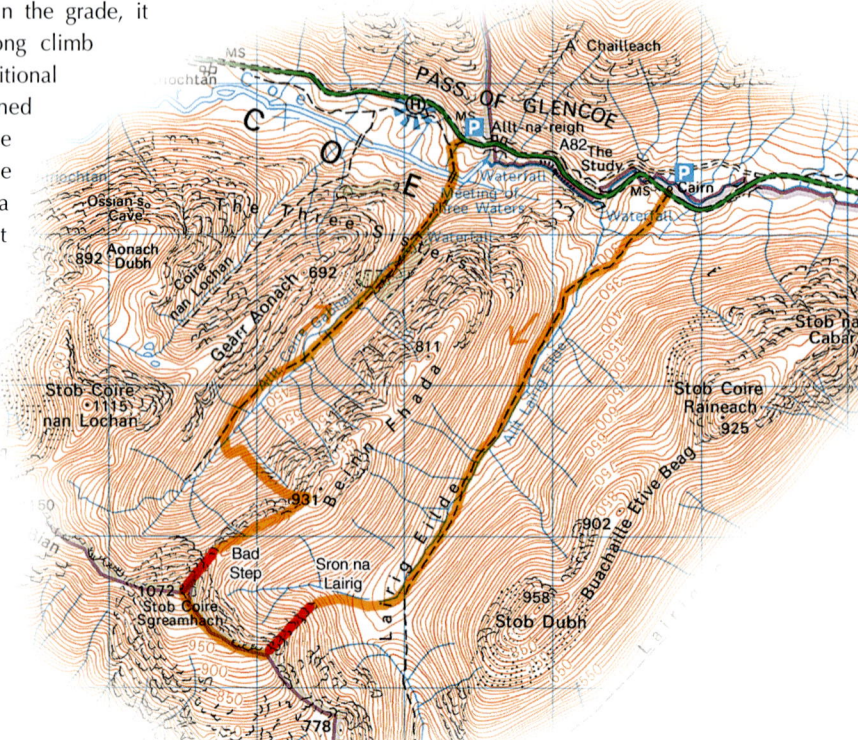

Route 11 – Sron na Lairig, Stob Coire Sgreamhach

Grade	300m II
Distance	10km
Ascent	910m
Time	7 hours
Start/finish	Car park beside A82 (NN187563) near an odd beehive cairn, just E of a newly engineered stretch of road.
Map	OS Landranger (1:50,000) 41 and Explorer (1:25,000) 384 – recommended
Accommodation	See Route 7
Sleeping out	The moraines at the head of the Lairig Eilde provide sheltered wild camp sites
Public transport	See Route 9
Seasonal notes	In summer Sron na Lairig is a scrappy but worthwhile grade 2/3 scramble, with the main difficulties on good rock found low down, and easier turfy ground higher up.

The words 'seclusion' and 'Glencoe' are not often seen together, but if any part of this teeming area can be considered isolated it must be the Lairig Eilde. Tucked away at the head of its barren glen, the grand ridge of Sron na Lairig throws down an obvious gauntlet, a line that's compellingly visible even from the road. Other routes hereabouts are obscure, but such a fate will never befall this much-loved classic. Although low in the grade, it is a magnificent long climb with a stirring, traditional ambience. Combined with Stob Coire Sgreamhach and the crest of Beinn Fhada it makes a brilliant ridge circuit.

Approach

The approach from Dalness in Glen Etive may be shorter, but the extra ascent renders this alternative unpopular. Most hike in from Glen Coe. From the car park on the A82 a signposted path heads SW up the Lairig Eilde – crossing, and a while later re-crossing, the burn. By local standards this is an appreciable walk-in, though less strenuous than most. Just before the path reaches its high point split off right, passing close to some moraine hummocks to reach the base of the ridge.

72

11 – Sron na Lairig, Stob Coire Sgreamhach

Sron na Lairig (left) and Stob Coire Sgreamhach (right) from the Lairig Eilde

Climb

From close quarters the onward route is hard to spot. The bottom is broad, as is the case with many sorts of bottoms (I am told), and initially the line is open to much variation. Climb just about anywhere at an uncomplicated II; ideal terrain on which to move together, though in friendly conditions confident parties might leave the rope coiled for a while. The slabby rib at the lowest point of the buttress is the customary entrée, though the big broken face to its left can also be fun if the snow and/or turf are firm. Zigzag up pleasant mixed ground, passing right of a steep band to reach a broad platform. Above, the ridge becomes narrower and more rocky. The easiest onward line is obvious. First go left to right up a little icy groove, and then weave back left over occasional entertaining steps onto a level crest.

A rocky arete rears up steeply ahead; stick to a turfy line just to the left of this, climbing with increasing exposure onto a grassy mini-summit, like a smaller and more vegetated version of the Ben's Great Tower.

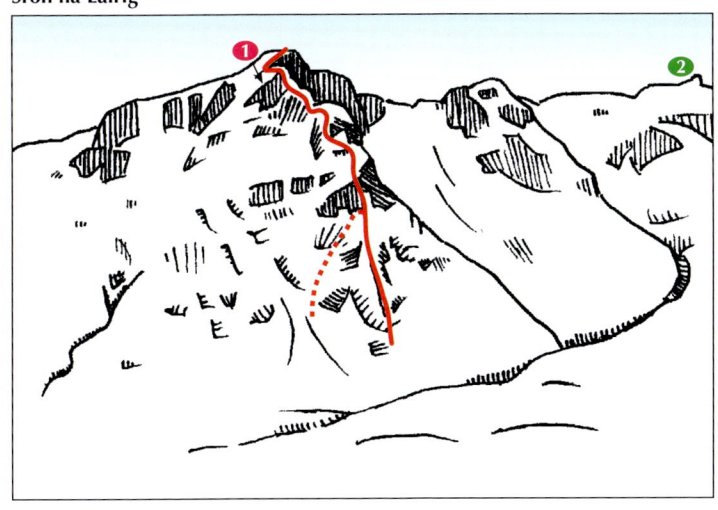

Sron na Lairig

❶ Tower
❷ Stob Coire Sgreamhach

73

On the level crest below the tower, Beinn Fhada behind

On descending from this the ridge pinches down to a thin neck, where a boulder provides a firm anchor. Because of the death-fall potential the next bit is perhaps best climbed with a fixed belay. Move up just left of the crest to reach a levelling after about 30m, and further possible belays. Beyond is a second narrow neck, with a spike on its far side. Teeter across above an unnerving void, traversing right of the spike onto less exciting ground. Bear right up easy snow, past a rock outcrop (spike belay) to meet the stony SE Ridge of Stob Coire Sgreamhach.

Possible descent
The quickest way off is SE to the first col. From here regain the Lairig Eilde on reasonably angled slopes, moving left lower down to avoid steep ground in a burn.

Continuation

For the full-on classic experience it's best to stay out a while longer, though bear in mind that this alternative involves intricate downclimbing and route finding. First climb onto the graceful summit of Stob Coire Sgreamhach. Intriguingly, this translates as 'Peak of the Loathsome Corrie', though mountain fans will find nothing to loathe here. Descend the NE Ridge towards Beinn Fhada. Initially this is unproblematic. Just before the obvious col progress is slowed by a tricky little crag band, called the Bad Step by some, a brief section of grade II. In soft snow a rope is recommended. Downclimb scrambly rock to gain a short ledge running right, onto the E side of the ridge. Once on the E side, descend little steps and ledges until a traverse line leads back left below the crag to the col.

Scanning the onward route from the tower

Now stride along the knobbly spine of Beinn Fhada, scrambly though nowhere difficult. Because it's steeply rimmed on all sides, choosing a safe descent off this ridge is tricky, and in poor visibility those new to the area should pay attention. Of many potential choices, perhaps the least problematic is to quit the ridge earlier than seems ideal, a good way before its terminal nose. Clamber over an elongated crest to reach a little gap around 800m distance beyond the first col. As a guide to identification: on the 1:25,000 map the gap is marked as spot height 876m; on both the 1:25,000 and 1:50,000 sheets the subsequent unnamed summit is given a height of 931m.

Descent

From the 876m saddle it's possible to descend either right into the Lairig Eilde or left into Coire Gabhail (the Lost Valley). Both options require care under snow. Coire Gabhail seems marginally easier, and may be less avalanche prone given the prevailing winds (don't just take my word for it, however). For this complex route finding the 1:25,000 map is recommended. Skirt right around a patch of steep ground to reach a strip of slope with rocky outcrops to each side. Descend roughly WNW, keeping slightly left of a burn in a steep-sided ravine. Just short of the valley floor a final patch of crag should be avoided to left. Below is the Allt Coire Gabhail, beyond which is the path back to Glencoe. Meet the road a little way W of your layby.

Lochaber

Glen Etive hills from the top of Sron na Lairig

Buachaille Etive Beag from the tower

Route 12 – Dorsal Arete, Stob Coire nan Lochan

Grade	120m II,3
Distance	6km
Ascent	990m
Time	5–6 hours
Start/finish	Layby on A82 (NN168569)
Map	OS Landranger (1:50,000) 41
Accommodation	See Route 7
Sleeping out	The upper shelf of Coire nan Lochan is an idyllic wild camping venue, though the convenience of being well placed below the route is offset by the likely arduousness of such a high winter camp.
Public transport	See Route 9
Seasonal notes	The lower reaches of the route are probably too turfy to make a pleasant summer scramble, though the crux rock section would provide a few interesting moments at around Moderate.

Dorsal Arete is short but sweet. Thanks to its low grade and prime location in Glencoe's most reliable winter corrie it is something of a trade route, often draped in ropes from top to bottom. On a fine weekend leave any hopes of solitude behind, and come expecting the atmosphere of a high street in the sales season, with mandatory queuing, as in the Alps. Excessive popularity cannot diminish the appeal, however; indeed, it should be taken as a sign of quality. Though the climbing is largely a breeze, it would be unfair not to mention the awkward crux, where exposure and technicality combine for a few sweat-inducing moves. At this point spinelessness is not an option, in keeping with the route's name.

Approach

If a deep freeze is gripping the lower slopes, the Zigzags (grade I) up the nose of Gearr Aonach make a rewarding prelude, adding some welcome length to the mountaineering component of the day, on what is otherwise a rather diminutive climb.

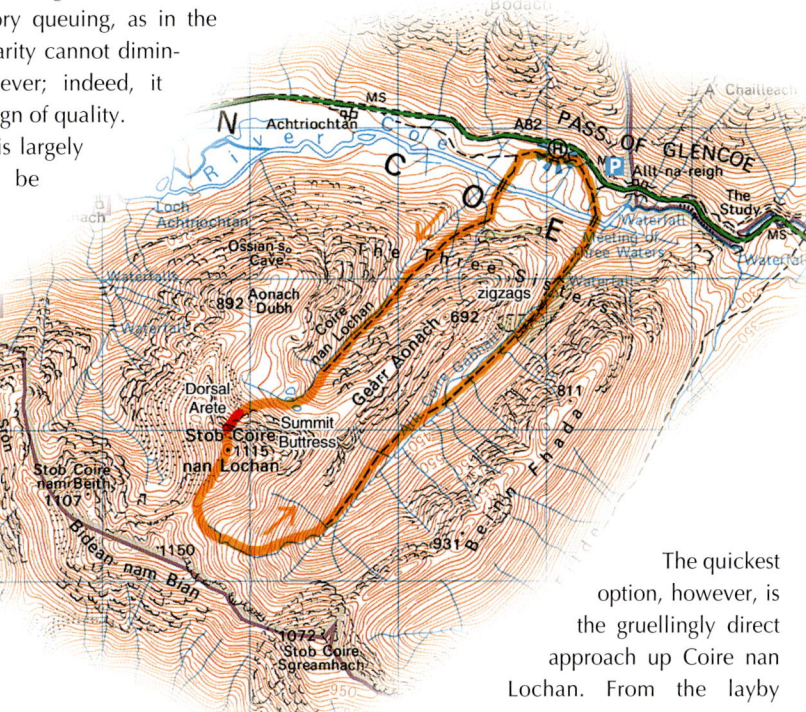

The quickest option, however, is the gruellingly direct approach up Coire nan Lochan. From the layby

LOCHABER

The cliffs of Coire nan Lochan; Dorsal Arete is on the far left, half hidden behind Summit Buttress

follow a path down to the River Coe, over a bridge and up steeply between Gearr Aonach and Aonach Dubh, sticking to the E bank of the burn. Turn a little slabby headwall either to the right or left to emerge onto the lochan-studded shelf of the upper corrie. Dorsal Arete is the slight-looking rib, set between the much more massive crags of Summit Buttress and South Buttress. The skirt of snow beneath the routes can be prone to windslab avalanche if the snow has been carried on south-westerlies.

Climb

Start just in the mouth of Broad Gully, the trench to the left of Dorsal Arete. Move up and right onto a platform, a comfortable belay. The crest at

Dorsal Arete

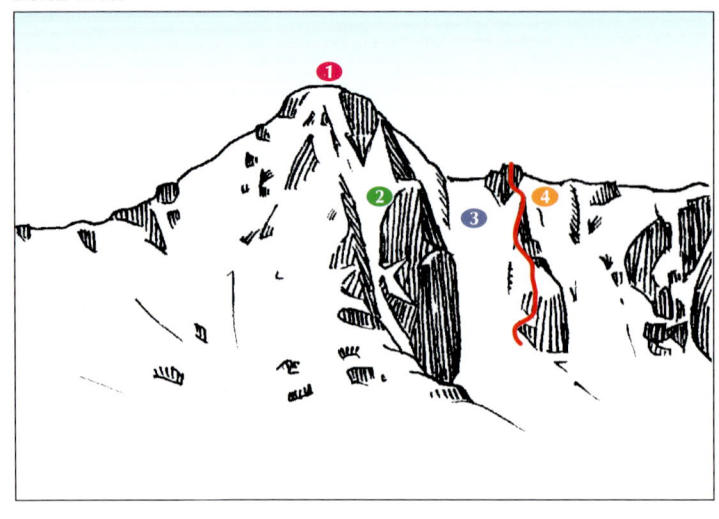

❶ Stob Coire nan Lochan
❷ Summit Buttress
❸ Broad Gully
❹ Crux fin

78

Poised on the crux fin

this stage is rather broad and indistinct, allowing you to vary the line and belay stances at will. The ground is a mix of low-angled snow, frozen turf and little rock patches. The competent might solo, while beginners may appreciate fixed belays; many parties initially opt to move together with running belays.

After a couple of (short) ropelengths the crest begins to narrow, breaking into a collection of small pinnacles. Thread through these with some interest (good rock protection) to belay just below a prominent narrow fin on the skyline. This is the crux, which briefly attains technical grade 3 and is best treated as a proper pitch. Unless it's blanketed in unstable snow, the slope below and left of the fin is easily traversed, thus avoiding all the excitement. Try to resist this temptation.

For a bigger buzz attack the fin direct. Gain and climb small rock steps on the crest, being sure to place a sling over a handy spike in passing. On the crux step the exposure is suddenly spectacular. Make an awkward mantel onto a flat-topped block. Hint: try using a sneaky sidepull with your right hand and a firm placement in a crack behind the block with your left axe. At this point balletic grace is off the agenda, and most climbers will at best manage an undignified beached whale manoeuvre to end up straddling the block *à cheval*. Easier ground leads along a ledge to the right of a sharp upper fin to reach a short, steep rock groove. This offers cracks for protection and

LOCHABER

Aonach Eagach (Route 13) from Stob Coire nan Lochan

axe torquing, though with crampons grating and rope drag tugging at your harness you might feel stirred, if not shaken. Pull through with some difficulty to belay on the saddle beyond. A final easy groove now leads to the top.

Descent
Those poor misguided souls with a cragging mentality can descend N from here, following the rim of Coire nan Lochan to reach a broad saddle behind Aonach Dubh, soon regaining the approach path. Alternatively, given safe snow Broad Gully makes an exciting glissade or a more pedestrian downclimb.

Continuation
However, this is a mountaineering guide, and I can't help but recommend bagging a summit or two. Stob Coire nan Lochan is yours for a measly five minutes' work. From here it's nice to drop SSW to the col below Bidean nam Bian, at which point a descent into Coire Gabhail (the Lost Valley) is quick and simple. Given time and enthusiasm Bidean can also be climbed via its narrow NE spur. From its summit descend ESE, taking care around the head of Lost Valley Buttress, to reach the Bealach Dearg, another route into Coire Gabhail.

Route 13 – Aonach Eagach

Grade	II
Distance	10km (plus possible 6km on road to retrieve your car)
Ascent	1150m
Time	6 hours in summer, but significantly longer under snow. Winter benightments are common.
Start	Layby on the A82 near Allt-na-reigh cottages (NN174567)
Finish	Minor road just short of Glencoe village (NN112585)
Map	OS Landranger (1:50,000) 41
Accommodation	See Route 7
Sleeping out	See Route 9
Public transport	See Route 9
Seasonal notes	Aonach Eagach is a much gentler beast in summer, but no less worthwhile. The difficulties on this grade 2 scramble come in short sections with easier ground in between. There are one or two tough moves, particularly in the wet, and hillwalkers who aren't inured to this sort of scrambling will really feel the unrelenting exposure. Climbers who want to catch the ridge in memorable mood should wait for winter. With icy rocks and delicate cornices the difficulties of the 'Notched Ridge' move up a few extra notches, and even bits you'd normally stroll along blindfold may be pretty gripping. In full winter conditions the pinnacles can be a time consuming top-end grade II, for which most teams will need a rope and a small rack of gear (several slings and half set of nuts will do). Treat it as an alpine route and move efficiently to get off the hard ground before dark.

Looking west along the pinnacles from Meall Dearg

Lochaber

Aonach Eagach is possibly the most famous ridge in mainland Britain, and has put the willies up generations of hillwalkers. It forms the devilishly steep north wall of Glencoe, sweeping to a narrow crest that's weathered into a formidable array of spines, offering several kilometres of inescapable scrambling above a yawning gulf. Though it's only a grade 2 summer scramble some sections are quite intimidating, and the overall seriousness belies the grade somewhat. In snowy garb Aonach Eagach looks and feels truly Alpine, and rates as one of the best winter mountaineering expeditions in the UK. Because it's so remarkable in such conditions, this is how it is covered here, though the route description applies in summer too, minus the obvious references to snow.

Approach

It is usually tackled from E to W. There are two customary routes onto the crest. Most climb Am Bodach direct from the Allt-na-reigh layby via a well-scuffed path, staying W of the Allt Ruigh before bearing left and steeply zigzagging with some easy scrambling onto the summit of Am Bodach. This is the recommended winter approach. Alternatively, to start the day with a bang ascend from the road at The Study, 1km E of Allt-na-reigh, and climb the craggy S face of A'Chailleach seeking out the best scrambling. This culminates in an exciting grade 3 pitch up the rightmost of three grooves in the steep yellow band at the top. Then walk 2km over an intermediate peak onto Am Bodach. This is a satisfying summer option if time and weather allow, though it adds distance and ascent to the route stats given here. For full details of A'Chailleach see *Scrambles in Lochaber* by Noel Williams (Cicerone).

Climb

Winter traversers should gear up on Am Bodach, keeping the rope handy. The first difficulty is encountered soon after leaving the summit, when the narrow ridge ahead abruptly drops off at your feet. Sloping ledges on the right (N) side of the nose lead down in an exposed position to a stance at a boulder beside a small detached tower. A short chimney descends left to easier ground. In dodgy snow this whole section should be trodden cautiously, and consider an abseil from the boulder. Continue to descend a short slab (worth abseiling if icy), then follow the easy crest, passing the odd rusty fence post. At a small top listed as spot height 924m on the OS 1:25,000 map, bear right down eroded ground to a small col above a deep gully; insecure snow adds spice to this brief descent. The broad top of Meall Dearg comes soon after.

A tough pitch on the pinnacles, with Stob Coire Leith waiting beyond

Stuck in a rut? Deep snow on the pinnacles west of Meall Dearg

The onward view promises great things, a bristling array of pinnacles beckoning all the way to Stob Coire Leith. Within the next 1km there are several substantial rock masses, subdivided into a host of smaller spikes and notches. This is the best bit of the day, often so narrow it seems that a slip could land you on the A82. In soft snow or verglas expect a protracted and insecure struggle. Comprehensive metre-by-metre descriptions of this section tend to confuse rather than illuminate. In terms of overall direction route finding is unproblematic, since you can only go either forward or backward. Simply follow the signs of polish (or the trough in the snow) along the crest, ticking off the tough bits as you go. Clamber up and over the larger pinnacles and thread around many of the smaller ones, with some of the most exposed ground coming near the end. There's nothing harder than a grade 2 scramble or winter II, though you might feel like adding an extra numeral for atmosphere.

A col marks the end of substantial difficulties; in summer the ascent onto Stob Coire Leith demands only a little basic scrambling, though it's more exciting under snow. A gentle stroll then leads without further incident to Sgorr nam Fiannaidh.

Descent

I know one experienced hillgoer who prefers to about-face on the summit of Stob Coire Leith and retrace his steps back to the car. Since you get to enjoy the whole scramble again in reverse, minus the end-of-day car retrieval trek, this seems a viable decision for a long summer evening.

From Am Bodach westwards there is NO safe way down into Glen Coe for several kilometres. If you're caught on the pinnacles at nightfall, keep going. This can't be over-emphasised. The direct descent S from Sgorr nam Fiannaidh and the dangerously eroded 'path' on the W bank of Clachaig Gully are both occasionally recommended, but neither is a safe bet in darkness, poor visibility or deep snow. It's far better to put in some extra mileage on foot at this point than risk either of these short cuts. Stay on the ridge instead,

13 – AONACH EAGACH

Looking back east at Meall Dearg

heading W from Sgorr nam Fiannaidh to the slight rise some 750m further on. Then bear NW down a broad shoulder towards the col below the Pap of Glencoe. From here trend WSW to join a clear path zigzagging down to the road between the Youth Hostel and Glencoe village. Regain your car via a hefty schlep on tarmac, or better a sneaky hitch. Best of all abandon the car until morning and beeline to the Clachaig Inn.

LOCHABER

Route 14 – Ring of Steall

Grade	I winter
Distance	15km
Ascent	1500m
Time	8 hours
Start/finish	Car park at the head of the Glen Nevis road (NN167692)
Map	OS Landranger (1:50,000) 41
Accommodation	Glen Nevis Youth Hostel (0870 004 1120), Ben Nevis Inn (01397 701 227), Calluna bunkhouse Fort William (01397 700 451), Glen Nevis campsite (01397 702 191)
Sleeping out	With almost uniquely impressive surroundings, the flood plain at Steall would be the perfect wild camp spot, were it not a sodden sponge beloved of midges.
Public transport	Bus or train to Fort William, from where a local bus service runs up Glen Nevis.
Seasonal notes	In summer the Ring of Steall is only a ridge walk, pleasingly narrow at times but with minimal scrambling challenge, a couple of short stretches of grade 1. The circuit is feasible in almost any seasonal conditions.

The graceful curving ridges of the Ring of Steall provide one of the finest low-grade winter mountaineering days in the country. In the heart of the magnificent Mamores, with the Glencoe peaks to one side and the Nevis range to the other, the setting could hardly be bettered. Although largely non-technical, two sections give a lot of entertainment under snow. These are the

Sgurr a'Mhaim from Golden Oldie (Route 21)

86

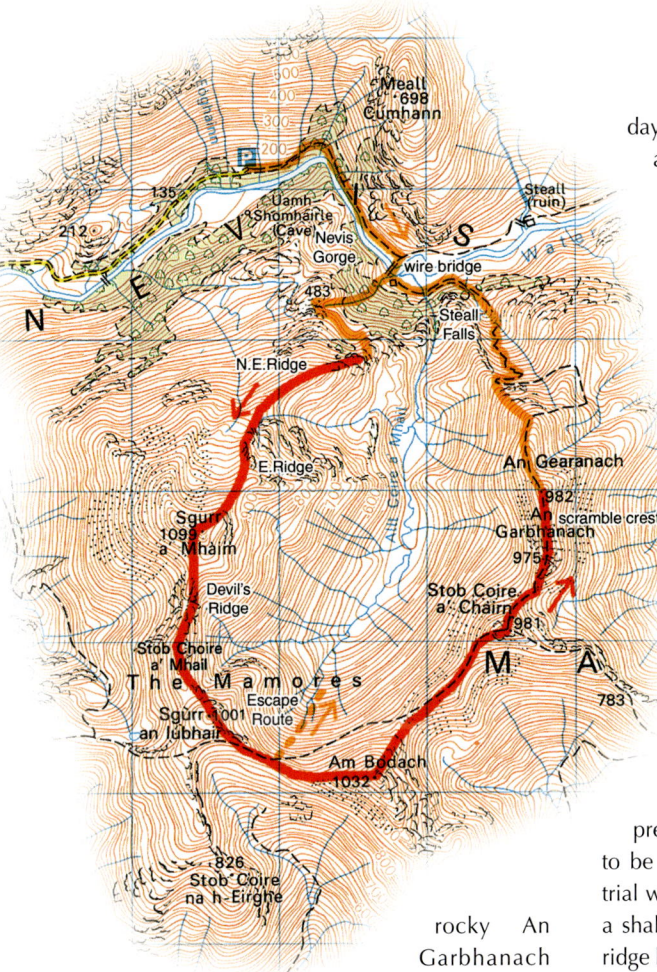

14 – Ring of Steall

day's excitement commences at a wire bridge, a wobbly crossing with the frisson of a potential dunking. From the (private) Steall hut head WSW through precipitous birch woods, following the line of a burn to emerge at an open bowl not far below spot height 483m (marked on the OS 1:50,000 map). Turn hard left to traverse below a line of crags until a steep little scrambly section brings you to a level shoulder on the left-hand skyline formed by Sgurr a'Mhaim's NE ridge. Under new snow, when all traces of path are obliterated, this approach can be a challenge in itself.

Climb

Some commentators advocate heading from here onto the E ridge for some basic scrambling. However, when the hills are in winter nick and daylight is at a premium the fastest ascent onto the Ring has to be best. Climb the knobbly NE ridge, a sore trial when the snow is deeply drifted. Soon reach a shallow corrie/saddle at a point where the NE ridge broadens and turns abruptly left towards the E ridge. Climb scree and boulders to reach the E ridge at a level crest. Now tackle the imposing summit pyramid of Sgurr a'Mhaim, sticking to the arete until barred by a craggy step. Here move slightly right, before climbing obvious ledges back to the crest (grade I) and then easily to the summit cairn.

A stony path zigzags down S to the start of the Devil's Ridge. Here the ground narrows to form an exposed arete. A clear path snakes along the crest. Thanks to prevailing winds this can often be uncovered while the E side is hung with thick cornices. Unconsolidated, untracked snow provides without doubt the most challenging experience. In most conditions roping up isn't necessary, though the wise will come equipped for that possibility.

Begin easily, descending into a tight notch, exited up a slabby rock step. A while later, pass a shattered pinnacle via a short groove on the

rocky An Garbhanach – An Gearanach spine, and the evocatively named Devil's Ridge, an aesthetic, sinuous crest. It is hard to write about this route without gushing superlatives; even the approach up Glen Nevis deserves a glowing report. Though it's feasibly done clockwise with an easy descent at the end down the NW spur of Sgurr a'Mhaim, the anti-clockwise circuit described here provides a more adventurous approach.

Approach

Few Scottish valleys are as spectacular as Glen Nevis, which looks as though it belongs more to the Rockies or the Alps than the lowly Highlands. This is really big country. Follow a well-made path up the boulder-choked Nevis Gorge to emerge onto a hidden plain framed by walls of crag and wood, down which roars the 100m Steall falls. Hop bogs to the Water of Nevis. The

Struggling with soft snow on the Devil's Ridge, with Sgurr a'Mhaim behind

14 – Ring of Steall

right – possible direct, though it can prove tricky. The arete then wends its airy way over a tightrope wedge-shaped high point, before sweeping on a little further to terminate at a wide saddle. Climb stony slopes onto Sgurr an Iubhair, from where an easy descent gains a major bealach.

Possible Descent
If nightfall is now closer than the end of the route, this is a good place to bail out NNE into Coire a'Mhail, thus completing only the Semicircle of Steall rather than the full Ring. Down in the corrie, follow the right bank of the burn, crossing several perpendicular streams until reaching a broadening in the glen a little way beyond the foot of Sgurr a'Mhaim's E ridge. The direct route downvalley from here would send you over the Steall falls; instead climb NE over a shoulder to reach a cairn marking the descent path from An Garbhanach (as described below).

To continue with the Ring, climb easily up a broad stony ridge onto the summit of Am Bodach. The subsequent descent NE is steep and rocky, and can prove treacherous when icy or heavily snow laden – roping up may not be out of the question here. A minor unnamed top follows and then the rounded peak of Stob Coire a'Chairn, where the main Mamores ridge is quitted for the E arm of the Steall horseshoe. Descend to a bealach.

The ragged fang of An Garbhanach now sits squarely in your path, an intimidating sight on a wild day. Ascend steep rough slopes immediately left of the true crest to reach the knife-edge peak.

At the northern end of the Devil's Ridge, with great things yet to come

LOCHABER

Still plenty to do – looking at the eastern half of the Ring from the col below Sgurr an Iubhair

The blocky arete slung between here and the final summit of the round, An Gearanach, is the second highlight of the Ring and, arguably, the technical crux. The sense of space is considerable, especially if you stick to the very top, although the difficulty can be reduced a little by keeping slightly right. All too soon the excitement abates on the summit of An Gearanach.

Descent

Carry on down the grassy N ridge until overlooking the headwall of the mountain's shallow N corrie. At this point the OS maps mark a path looping off to the right, then back left to a cairn on a little shoulder. Preferably, a more direct descent can be made down a steep NW path to reach the same point. Now zigzag down the corrie all the way to the floor of Glen Nevis. Slosh through the bogs below Steall Falls, staying far left for the driest line, to recross the wire bridge.

Route 15 – Castle Ridge, Ben Nevis

Grade	275m Moderate
Distance	11km
Ascent	1150m
Time	6 hours
Start/finish	North Face car park, near Torlundy (NN145764), or car park in Glen Nevis (NN123730)
Map	OS Landranger 41
Accommodation	See Route 14
Sleeping out	Beneath the N face of Ben Nevis there are several flatish camping spots. Try just E of the Allt a'Mhuilinn near the CIC Hut. Other sites can be found just towards Coire na Ciste, above the slabs beside the hut. Given the number of people passing (various things) this way, it's wise to treat your drinking water.
Public transport	See Route 14
Seasonal notes	With its altitude, Alpine-scale north face and typically fiendish weather, Ben Nevis in winter can be seriously mean. In fact, snow can fall here in any season; even snowy plods up the tourist track shouldn't be underestimated. Castle is one of the easiest of the Ben's winter ridges, graded III. The steep mixed pitches are short lived, and difficulty is not sustained throughout. It is possible in a variety of conditions, though beware avalanche danger on the approach slopes. Situated relatively low on the mountain it is in nick less often than the other Nevis routes described.

The Mamores and misty Glen Nevis from the Tourist Track

LOCHABER

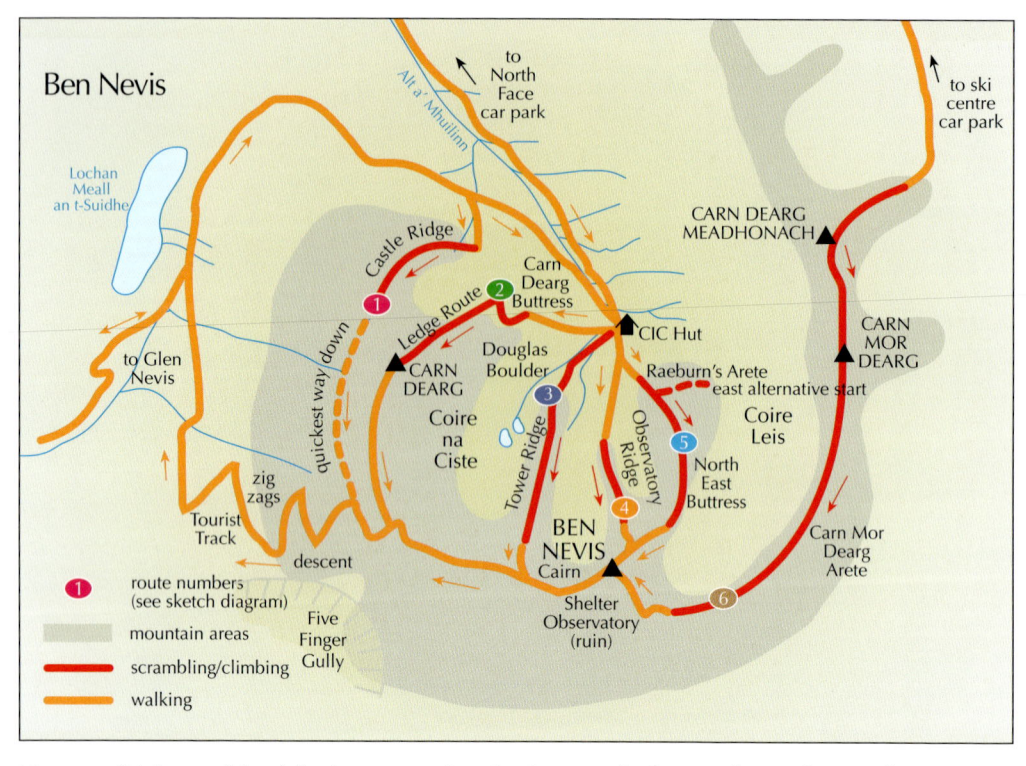

Map now slightly out of date following construction of a short stretch of new path at Lochan Meall an t-Suidhe

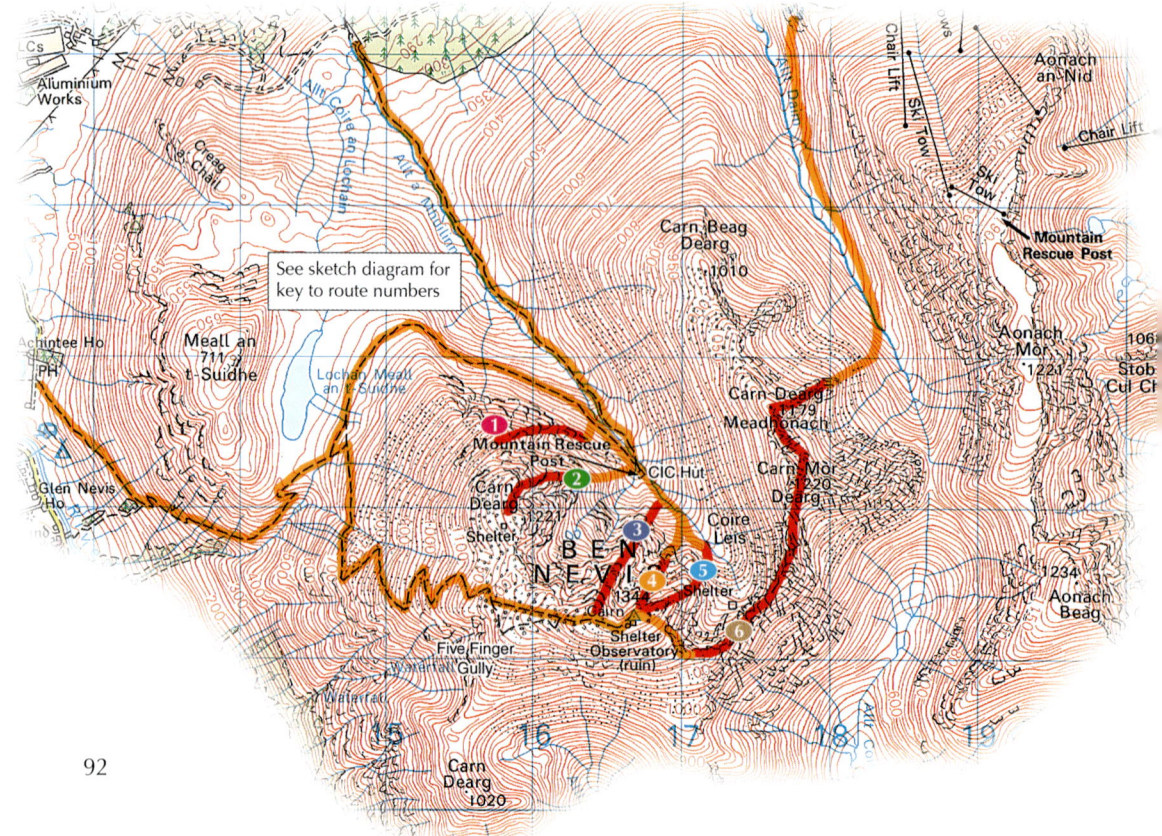

92

15 – Castle Ridge, Ben Nevis

Ben Nevis

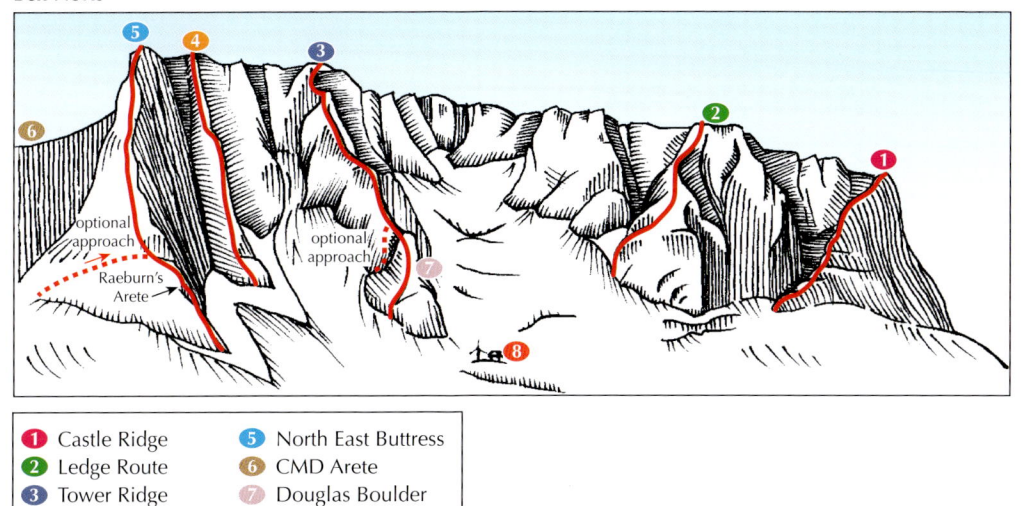

- ① Castle Ridge
- ② Ledge Route
- ③ Tower Ridge
- ④ Observatory Ridge
- ⑤ North East Buttress
- ⑥ CMD Arete
- ⑦ Douglas Boulder
- ⑧ CIC Hut

Castle Ridge gets less attention than it deserves. Though the shortest and least aesthetic of the Ben's big four (the others being Tower Ridge, Observatory Ridge and the NE Buttress) it still has many attractions. Not least of these is quick access and descent. Since Castle Ridge is one of the first major features passed on the walk-in, you can be well established on the route while parties bound for higher objectives are still plodding towards the CIC Hut. Because the difficult steps are very brief, Castle Ridge is a suitable place for aspirant mountaineers to practise their rope skills, and a reasonable summer solo objective for the competent. Crowning a vast rambling north wall, this slabby crest offers a grand line up a relatively neglected part of the mountain.

Approach

There are two common approaches to the north face. One takes the Tourist Track from Glen Nevis, turning off at a sharp bend just below the mind-numbing zigzags onto a new path that runs towards the outflow of Lochan Meall an t-Suidhe (not yet marked on maps in January 2010); before reaching this burn branch right on an eroded old path that contours around the NW shoulder of Carn Dearg to meet the Allt a'Mhuilinn near the CIC Hut. The alternative approach up the Allt a'Mhuilinn from the 'North Face' car park near Torlundy tends to be more popular with climbers. The old route ascended a series of muddy slopes that wouldn't have looked out of place on the Somme; these are now bypassed by an excellent path that climbs diagonally through plantations to connect with a forestry track by an intake on the Allt a'Mhuilinn. Just uphill is a car park used by local guides, and a gate and stile. Beyond this the path continues its old course up the Allt a'Mhuilinn; parts of this stretch have also been repaired.

The Glen Nevis approach is the most convenient for Castle Ridge. Follow the path under the huge North Wall of Castle Ridge, passing the boulder known as the Lunching Stone. From here it's possible to make a direct assault on the slabs above to get established on the ridge. However, route finding is much easier if you keep to the path for a couple of hundred metres, before climbing steep grass and scree to reach the right flank of a shallow gully descending from Castle Corrie.

Climb

Climb slabby steps and grass ledges, staying just right of the gully all the way into a scoop

Castle Ridge from below; the route follows the obvious left–right diagonal

in the mouth of Castle Corrie. The steep wall of Raeburn's Buttress rears up on the left, with the pinnacled mass of The Castle straight ahead. A large sloping grass terrace runs horizontally from the left between bands of crag to meet you at this spot – this is an alternative approach from near the CIC Hut and a useful escape route if weather conditions suddenly deteriorate. Cross a stream to reach the broad slabby crest of Castle Ridge.

The lower ridge throws down a succession of little slabs and walls, some of which can be tricky when wet. There is a choice of possible lines; the easiest and most popular follows a series of shallow grooves and ledges, marked by polish and crampon scratches. A clean-cut, left-slanting corner gives the first short Moderate pitch, soon leading to an easier angled patch of boulders and further slabby sections.

A tricky corner marks the start of the crux section, which tackles the prominent blunt tower on the skyline. Above this corner, traverse right across a small slabby ledge to reach a steep nose poised over the North Wall. The drop suddenly seems hungry, and many climbers will rope up. Climb a steep cracked groove, with a long reach to good holds and a comforting ledge. Easier ground then gains the final obstacle, a short smooth chimney leading to the upper ridge. Stroll along the rubbly crest, crossing a short, clean arete, then a tilted slab, to reach the stony summit slopes of Carn Dearg.

Descent

It's not necessary to reach any summit, making Castle Ridge the best choice for a short day. One possibility is to descend to the approach path beside Lochan Meall an t-Suidhe; traverse briefly SW to safely avoid the North Wall, then head for the lochan's S end. This is, however, an unpleasantly steep boulder field. A knee-saving alternative is to head towards the summit of Carn Dearg, carefully skirting the gullies that flank The Castle. Begin to contour S just above a band of broken crags at 1150m. It's rough underfoot, but even in poor visibility navigation is simple, since the Tourist Track eventually bisects your course (if you did overshoot, Five Finger Gully could serve as a terminal collecting feature). Descend the zig-zags back to Glen Nevis.

15 – CASTLE RIDGE, BEN NEVIS

Tilted slab near the top of the ridge, looking to Carn Mor Dearg (Route 20)

LOCHABER

Route 16 – Ledge Route, Ben Nevis

Grade	450m grade 2 scramble
Distance	12km
Ascent	1300m
Time	7 hours
Start/finish	North Face car park, near Torlundy (NN145764), or car park in Glen Nevis (NN123730)
Map	OS Landranger (1:50,000) 41
Accommodation	See Route 14
Sleeping out	See Route 15
Public transport	See Route 14 for the Glen Nevis approach; for the North Face car park approach, various local bus services stop at Torlundy.
Seasonal notes	This is the best grade II winter route on Ben Nevis, and one of the most popular climbs of its grade in the country. In benign conditions it might feel like a soft touch, though it often sports passages on ice in the lower half and exposed mixed climbing above, so it's not a trip for novices to take lightly. Number Five Gully holds a lot of snow, and has a habit of avalanching. It can remain snow filled into summer, complicating the approach for scramblers.

Ask most people to list the Ben's classic ridge climbs, and it's a fair bet they'd omit Ledge Route. Perhaps that's because the name is hardly redolent of all things ridge-like. And yet its upper half is a grand arete, not to be missed. Ledge Route is a perennial classic, a great climb at any time of year. A firm favourite with winter mountaineers, it also happens to be the best easy summer scramble on Ben Nevis. It is not particularly tough for the grade in either season, though its length compensates for this, making it ideal for those who fancy a major mountaineering line without excessive technicality. Given that most big rock features on the savage side of the Ben can seem daunting to the uninitiated, Ledge Route comes as something of a compensation. Though amenable, it is not without interest. The highlight is a narrow square-cut gangway like the top of an immense garden wall, a memorably airy passage in summer or winter.

Approach

As for Route 15 (using either approach variant; see map Route 15), but continue further to reach the CIC Hut. Now double-back W, keeping well left of a row of dank crags, zigzagging up steep scree and grass to reach the left side of the foot of the magnificent Carn Dearg Buttress. With clean overlapping slabs split by the unmistakeable soaring corner line of Centurion, this is home to some of the most exciting mid-grade rock climbing in Britain. Continue left beneath the crag into the mouth of Number Five Gully.

Climb

Ledge Route is considered a grade 1 scramble by some. But, compared with benchmark grade 1s such as Snowdonia's Crib Goch, its length, route finding and exposure are more in keeping with grade 2, albeit a gentle one. In summer it is often used as a climbers' descent, though that's only advised to those who already know the way.

Hard snow can linger late in Number Five Gully, and an axe may be useful in early season. It is often possible to skirt right of any snow patches on wet slabs. Clamber up the bouldery (or snowy) gully bed for a short way until a slabby ramp cuts diagonally rightwards between steep rock bands. Head up this with care; it is invariably slimy and scattered with loose chips. In sub-zero conditions expect plenty of ice hereabouts. Keep following the ramp rightwards on seeping rock above a sizeable slabby drop. Below is the line of The Curtain, a classic IV,5 ice climb

16 – Ledge Route, Ben Nevis

Teetering up the 'gangway'

– even seepage has its uses, in the right season. Beyond the worst of the water trickles you find yourself on a slanting ledge system. An exciting dead-end detour follows this out right for a while over the huge main wall of Carn Dearg; remember that any rocks you dislodge might really spoil some climber's day.

But I digress. Return to the site of the slime. Here, a vegetated scoop (I hesitate to call it a gully) strikes up left to a point overlooking the middle reaches of Number Five Gully. Move rightwards using another sloping shelf system, a mixture of outcrops, vegetation and loose bits underfoot. The 'gangway' section of the route is now directly overhead, crowning a vertical wall. Keep heading right to reach the buttress crest, with unfolding views to the N.

Variation

This same point can be reached by a less exciting and more roundabout line that avoids the bottom of Number Five Gully altogether – a good bet if snow patches still clog the start of the normal line. It begins well left of Moonlight Gully Buttress, climbing easy ground to traverse the mid-height break on the buttress, and then continuing in much the same line over the middle section of Number Five Gully to meet the route as described above. For details consult Scrambles in Lochaber, *Noel Williams (Cicerone).*

Either way, once on the crest the climb improves immeasurably, and route finding is a breeze. Follow the ridge up leftwards to the start of the 'gangway'. Though it's feasible to skirt it on

Looking down from the summit plateau in winter – Ledge Route is the rightmost sunlit edge

the right, this is far less aesthetic. The clean-cut arete may look intimidating, but other than the palpable drop on the left it's all pretty straightforward. Balance gracefully upwards until, at its end, a short vertical downclimb gains easier ground. Then continue pleasantly up the less airy ridge crest beyond, a long, gradual wind-down. The rock is of variable quality in places, but there are several interesting steps and a wide panorama out over Lochaber. You're eventually deposited onto the bouldery table near the subsidiary top of Carn Dearg. The summit of Ben Nevis is now just a stroll away.

Descent

When it's blowing a hoolie and the clag is down, getting off the Ben is no joke. The summit plateau is ringed on virtually every side by steep ground and deeply incised by gullies, often hugely corniced. Regular accidents occur when people loose their bearings in poor visibility and simply walk off the edge. The easiest and most direct descent to Glen Nevis follows the hillwalker's path, or Tourist Track, the course of which has recently been made more obvious with the construction of a column of large cairns marching over the plateau. If these are invisible under snow take these exact bearings: from the summit trig point head on 231° grid for 150m, watching out for the head of Gardyloo Gully on your right; carry on descending on a bearing of 281° grid for a further 1km, or more to be sure. This gets you onto the zigzags of the Tourist Track between the Red Burn on your right and Five Finger Gully on the left. Steer well clear of the latter – it claims lives. The notoriously rubbly stretch of path down to Lochan Meall an t-Suidhe is currently being renovated (January 2010).

Route 17 – Tower Ridge, Ben Nevis

Grade	600m Diff (800m VDiff including Douglas Boulder)
Distance	13km
Ascent	1300m
Time	8 hours
Start/finish	North Face car park, near Torlundy (NN145764), or car park in Glen Nevis (NN123730)
Map	OS Landranger (1:50,000) 41
Accommodation	See Route 14
Sleeping out	See Route 15
Public transport	See Route 16
Seasonal notes	Tower Ridge in winter is one of Scotland's best-loved mountaineering routes, and no ordinary grade III. Because of its unusual length and the variable conditions-related difficulties that may be met, it needs to be taken seriously by even the most accomplished teams. Powder snow and verglas add considerably to the challenge, and benightments are common. A summer visit is just as recommendable – if less demanding – and helps build familiarity for a future winter attempt.

Tower Ridge has all the cachet and atmosphere of a truly classic climb. With an obvious line, superlative length and magnificent situations it ranks among the grandest routes in Scotland. Rising in a series of rocky steps from the massive conical buttress of the Douglas Boulder right up to the Ben's summit plateau, its profile is compelling. The summer climbing is largely easier than you might expect, making Tower Ridge a fitting choice for aspiring mountaineers.

Wintry Tower Ridge rises from the Douglas Boulder (low down, centre frame), seen from high in Coire na Ciste. Behind is Carn Mor Dearg, and the peak of Aonach Beag behind the CMD Arete (Route 20).

Camp beneath the Douglas Boulder, with the Great Tower prominent high above

17 – Tower Ridge, Ben Nevis

Confident groups will remain unroped for much of the time. Others will opt to move together, save for the few short cruxes. The trickiest sections are also the most spectacular, and here fixed belays tend to be deemed sensible. Snowy or no, this brilliant route should grace everyone's ticklist.

Approach
As described in Route 15 to the CIC hut (see map in Route 15). Behind the hut, on the left side of Coire na Ciste, rears the striking mass of the Douglas Boulder, marking the foot of Tower Ridge.

A level section on the ridge below the Great Tower

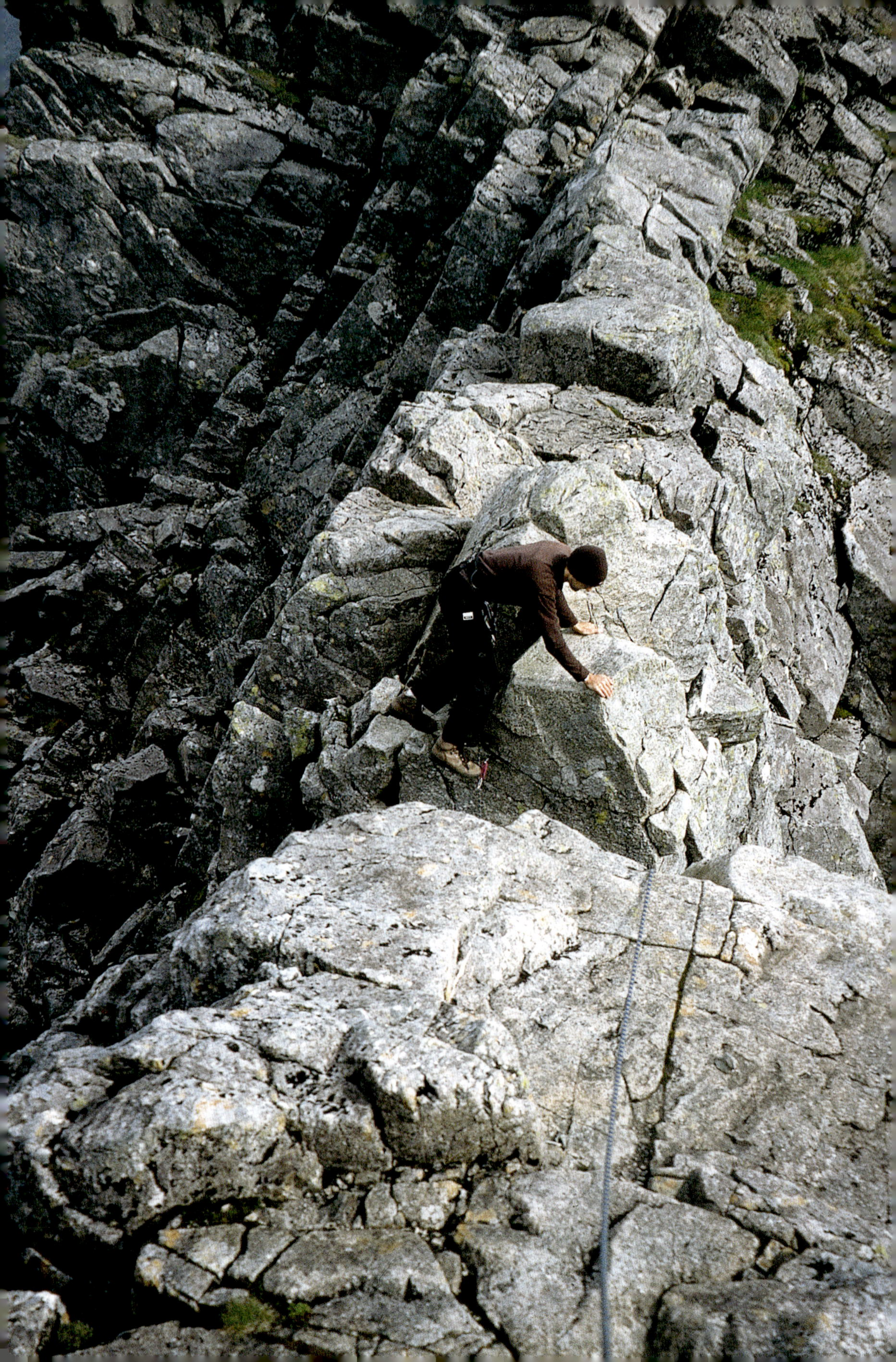

17 – TOWER RIDGE, BEN NEVIS

Climb
Most parties seem content to bypass the Douglas Boulder, but its ascent at around VDiff is a suitable prelude, and recommended. Though the ground is of the go-anywhere variety, it's worth following one of the established climbs. Try Direct Route, 215m VDiff: a prominent groove cleaves the NE face. Start at the lowest toe of the buttress, below and to the left of a clean-looking slab. Climb easily into a vague scoop to reach the deeper chimney groove above. Two pitches up this gain a pronounced shelf. Traverse briefly right, then climb steeply to the summit. To reach the Douglas Gap at the start of the route proper, downclimb on the right (facing down) or abseil.

For those not wishing to indulge in the above, this point can also be reached by walking around the base of the Boulder, then scrambling up scree, rock and grass in a shallow bay below its E side to enter East Gully (loose and often slimy), which soon leads to the Gap.

Smoothed by decades of use, a 20m chimney is the key to the ridge crest. It can be tricky in the wet, and might be worth climbing as a roped pitch. Follow signs of wear along the broad grassy ridge above, over two slight dips and some steeper steps. The Little Tower is the next distinctive feature. It's more of a bump than a tower, but provides an absorbing scramble, at first up flakes of lovely rock on the crest (possible variations are less good). Head right up a tricky slanting ledge, and back left up an indistinct corner to the top of the 'tower'. This is exposed, and a rope usually seems sensible. A long flatish section follows, bringing you to the base of the unmistakeable Great Tower.

Scrambly steps lead to the tower's intimidating vertical nose. Peel off left around the corner on a short path known as the Eastern Traverse – often steeply banked out in winter, but easy in summer. This gains a deep cleft crowned by a massive boulder. Clamber out through the roof of the cave and tackle steep rock on the right, leading airily to the top of the tower.

Even if you haven't needed to thus far, it's definitely wise to rope up while crossing the infamous Tower Gap. Descend briefly from the tower onto a short thin crest, with a giddy void to either side. The smooth downclimb into the gap feels insecure, though it's short lived. At the time of writing it was 'graced' with a bit of fixed tat to help with quick protection and/or aid. Clamber more easily up the far side of the notch to belay on straightforward ground above. Much gentler scrambling ensues as the ridge – vegetated and loose in parts – begins to merge with the mountain's flanks. A final steep wall is turned by a rightwards ledge traverse, followed by a couple of rubbly steps onto the summit plateau. Now strike a few macho poses for the benefit of ogling walkers.

Descent
There are a variety of options to suit different conditions. For the easiest descent, see Route 16. Winter climbers often use Number 4 Gully, though the cornice can be large. In summer it's a touch on the unpleasant side. When snow free, Ledge Route (Route 16) is a better option, though the exit gully from this route can harbour a big snow patch until well into summer.

With several hours daylight to spare, by far the most enjoyable summer 'descent' is to make a circuit over the famous CMD Arete (Route 20). Having done this, from the summit of Carn Dearg Meadhonach either hold much the same line in descent to meet the Allt a'Mhuilinn path close to the forest edge, or (less pleasantly) veer left down steep rough slopes to gain the glen about 1km downstream of the CIC Hut.

Descending into Tower Gap

LOCHABER

Route 18 – Observatory Ridge, Ben Nevis

Grade	420m VDiff
Distance	14km
Ascent	1300m
Time	9 hours
Start/finish	North Face car park, near Torlundy (NN145764), or car park in Glen Nevis (NN123730)
Map	OS Landranger (1:50,000) 41
Accommodation	See Route 14
Sleeping out	See Route 15
Public transport	See Route 16
Seasonal notes	At a pretty stiff grade IV,4 this is generally considered to be the Ben's hardest winter ridge, particularly under powder snow. In such conditions it's possible to avoid the upper section by heading left into Zero Gully.

Tucked into a corner between the enclosing arms of Tower Ridge and the NE Buttress, Observatory Ridge remains largely hidden from a distance. Newcomers might wonder what the attraction is, until it finally hoves into view. Seen end-on its lower half looks exposed and unrelenting. This feeling only increases when you get on the route. Observatory Ridge may be shorter than neighbouring Tower Ridge, but it is both harder and more sustained. Rain reduces the rock's friction to that of Vaseline, giving the polished crux sections a certain memorable edge. When wet, the only gripping thing about this climb is its atmosphere. In benign conditions, however, Observatory Ridge is one of the most enjoyable routes around.

Approaching the North Face of Ben Nevis. From left to right: North East Buttress, Observatory Ridge and Tower Ridge rising from the Douglas Boulder to the Great Tower

18 – Observatory Ridge, Ben Nevis

Unroped climbing on the lowest rock band; the ridge is the imposing lump above

Approach
As for Tower Ridge (Route 17, East Gully start) around the foot of the Douglas Boulder, continuing slightly leftwards up scree past where the Tower Ridge route branches off right (see map in Route 15). Cross the bottom of Observatory Gully and climb rubbly outcrops to the base of the steep rock.

Climb
Just left of the toe of the ridge is an easy 50m rock band leading to a sloping grass shelf. Climb direct to a shallow groove, which is followed to the bottom end of the shelf. This initial tier seeps readily, in which case it's probably wise to rope up.

From the right end of the grass the broad crest above may look easy angled, but appearances can be deceptive. Once committed it is actually quite exciting, with several tough steps. Those who aren't keen to solo VDiff should rope up before proceeding. Moving together is a good option for the competent – in the dry – though the first few pitches are both tricky and bold on occasion, and fully earn their grade. Follow the slabby crest with fairly limited protection. A short shallow corner at about 40m will give pause for thought. It is strenuous, polished and evil in the wet. Belay not far above, immediately under a substantial steepening.

Break out right below the steep wall, with an airy feeling under your boot soles. Follow a series of grooves up hard steps and right-slanting ledges, taking the line of least resistance below and right of the true crest, outflanking the steepest section of the ridge. After a couple of rope lengths you'll find yourself moving left onto the arete proper at a grassy levelling.

Follow the crest up a succession of slabby sections, interspersed with patches of scree and

Outflanking the steep bit

the occasional harder obstacle. Some of these mini-cruxes are quite demanding; luckily the rock is sound and adequate protection is always forthcoming. The best line up each steepening is well marked by polish and crampon scratches, the easiest option tending to be found to the right – though not always. The climbing feels quite strenuous at times, with many big step-ups; it goes on a bit, too. Difficulties gradually ease off, however, as the ridge becomes increasingly indistinct and begins to merge with the face behind. Immediately to the left is the damp open groove of Zero Gully, a celebrated winter ice climb. Stay just right of this all the way to the summit boulder field.

Descent

You're now just near the top of the NE Buttress. Walk right a short distance to reach the mountain's summit. See routes 16 and 17 for the options from here.

Regaining the arete at the grassy levelling

Route 19 – North East Buttress via Raeburn's Arete, Ben Nevis

Grade	Raeburn's Arete 230m Severe; NE Buttress 300m VDiff
Distance	14km
Ascent	1300m
Time	10 hours
Start/finish	North Face car park, near Torlundy (NN145764), or car park in Glen Nevis (NN123730)
Map	OS Landranger (1:50,000) 41
Accommodation	See Route 14
Sleeping out	See Route 15
Public transport	See Route 16
Seasonal notes	At grade IV,4 this is a highly regarded winter mountaineering route of the same stature as Observatory Ridge and Tower Ridge. Belays are secure, and the ridge can be tackled in a variety of conditions, but the major difficulties are met high up; the Mantrap and the 40-Foot Corner can prove extremely awkward.

With quality rock and fine situations, the North East Buttress it is every inch a classic. The original line accesses the buttress by outflanking its northern toe and then doubling back along a terrace system; better, though, is to reach the same point via the clean nose of Raeburn's Arete, a quality trip in its own right. The onward route then follows a broad crest bounding the top of the Minus and Orion faces, famous for some of Scotland's best climbs. For the most part the ground is easy enough to comfortably move together on, except perhaps for a couple of short hard crux sections. Because these occur high on the ridge, at a point from which retreat would be complicated, beginners should be cautious in bad conditions. When wet or icy, the polished Mantrap lives up to its reputation.

Approach

As for Observatory Ridge (Route 18) and Tower Ridge (Route 17, East Gully start) until past the foot of the Douglas Boulder (see map, Route 15). From here, instead of continuing up scree, contour E to the bottom left-hand end of a clean slabby N-facing buttress which sits at the foot of the prominent NE Buttress. Although not immediately apparent from directly below, the left side of these slabs is framed by a clean arete. Beyond this to the left is a deep corner and then more broken

Pitch 2 of Raeburn's Arete

Nearing the Mantrap, with the Douglas Boulder (Route 17) in sunshine far below

ground. Start at a grass terrace just below and right of this deep corner.

Climb

Raeburn's Arete, 230m Severe
This is one of the best routes of its grade on Ben Nevis, and combines superbly with the NE Buttress. The rock on the first couple of pitches is of the 'go anywhere' variety, with plentiful holds and gear. The line is fairly obvious. 60m ropes allow you to run shorter pitches together.

Pitch 1, 55m
From the lowest rocks, climb right of a damp little overhung bay to gain a grassy ledge at about 20m (possible belay for those with 50m ropes). From the left end of the ledge step up and left to gain a shallow groove. Move left out of this onto the blunt arete, which is followed to a little stance in a corner with a flat muddy floor.

Pitch 2, 60m
Move delicately right along a sloping shelf for a few metres before curving up and left to rejoin the arete. Follow this to where the angle eases in a wide bay. Again, it's possible to belay sooner if need be.

Pitches 3 to 5, 115m
At the top of pitch 2 the crag on the left cuts back in a deep slabby corner, running into vegetated grooves above the untidy-looking E face – the top section of Newbigging's Route Far Right Variation, an underused VDiff. This is not the correct line, but it does eventually lead to the same place. It is a viable alternative, though not in the same class as Raeburn's. For Raeburn's, bear right from the belay to tackle rather steeper rock leading back to the clean arete above and right of the decoy corner. There are no further route-finding dilemmas – simply continue up this in a

19 – North East Buttress via Raeburn's Arete, Ben Nevis

After the 40-Foot Corner comes an easy ridge scramble. Behind are the Carn Mor Dearg Arete (Route 20) and Aonach Mor (Route 21).

Typical North East Buttress ground, below the Second Platform

wonderful position for three more lovely pitches to reach broken ground at the First Platform.

North East Buttress, 300m VDiff
From the rubbly First Platform, gain and follow a short section of level arete leading to a mass of steep rock. This can be climbed direct at VDiff (approx 60m), though it is customarily avoided by taking a shallow and somewhat grubby gully on the left. Signs of wear then show the way gradually right up a series of steep little walls and grooves, leading to a marked sloping ledge – the Second Platform. For a while the ridge crest has been broad and ill-defined, but from here it narrows again. Follow it for some way – largely quite amenable, with occasional tricky bits to maintain your interest – to the foot of a steep wall barring onward progress. This can be tackled direct, although it is quite hard. Most parties choose to outflank it just to the right up a series of big rounded steps – lovely climbing. Above, the crest bears very briefly left before easy blocky ground leads on up to the base of the unmistakeable Mantrap.

This is only a short step, but polished and quite strenuous for a couple of moves. In imperfect conditions it can be unpleasant, though thankfully protection comes readily to hand. The Mantrap can be avoided either to left or right, but neither variation is as good, nor really significantly easier. Soon after comes the 40-Foot Corner. Bridge elegantly to the top, enjoying the plentiful holds and gear. Easier scrambling leads to a last steepening, climbed with a delicate step left along a sloping ledge. Then, quite abruptly, you are on the boulder field at the top. Turn right to stroll to the summit.

Descent
See routes 16 and 17 for descent options.

Route 20 – Carn Dearg Meadhonach East Ridge and Carn Mor Dearg Arete

Grade	II
Distance	18km
Ascent	1000m
Time	9½ hours
Start/finish	Nevis Range ski centre car park (NN172773)
Map	OS Landranger (1:50,000) 41
Accommodation	See Route 14
Sleeping out	This long wandering route doesn't lend itself to a round trip based on a wild camp; just as well, since the Allt Daim is a bleak spot to sleep in winter.
Public transport	Local bus service from Fort William to the Nevis Range ski centre
Seasonal notes	In summer the E Ridge of Carn Dearg Meadhonach is a rather scrappy grade 1 scramble, though worthwhile for its position and scenery. The easier continuation along the CMD Arete is one of the top scrambly hillwalks of Britain and rightly popular.

Winter ridges on the big bad Ben tend to have a well-deserved stiff reputation, something that will rightly give lower-grade climbers pause for thought. They needn't steer clear at the first flurry of snow, however. Ledge Route (Route 16) is one fairly undemanding winter option; the other is the famous Carn Mor Dearg Arete, an elegant swooping rooftop that makes for the finest (OK, only) extended circuit on the mountain. Though providing nearly 1.5km of sustained scrambling interest, the CMD Arete is straightforward in all

Carn Dearg Meadhonach's East Ridge catches the sun; Carn Mor Dearg's Arete scythes up onto Ben Nevis. As seen from Aonach Mor (Route 21)

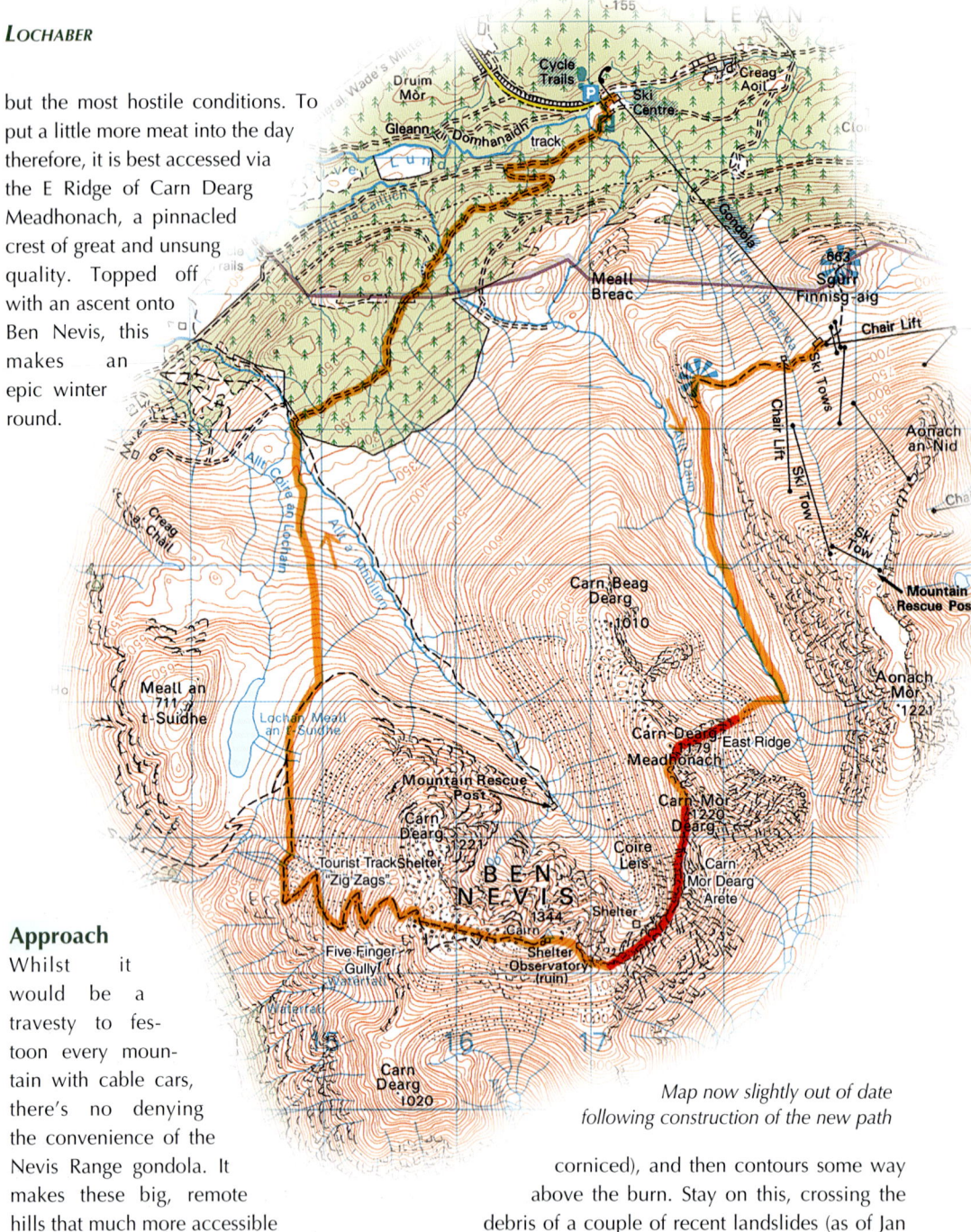

Lochaber

but the most hostile conditions. To put a little more meat into the day therefore, it is best accessed via the E Ridge of Carn Dearg Meadhonach, a pinnacled crest of great and unsung quality. Topped off with an ascent onto Ben Nevis, this makes an epic winter round.

Approach

Whilst it would be a travesty to festoon every mountain with cable cars, there's no denying the convenience of the Nevis Range gondola. It makes these big, remote hills that much more accessible to winter day-trippers. Suppress the pangs of guilty complicity, and ride in comfort to the station at 650m. Walk W along a track, passing the chairlift used by climbers bound for Aonach Mor's E face, to reach a point overlooking the trough of the Allt Daim. Head S over broken ground on a faint path that briefly descends steeply (occasionally

Map now slightly out of date following construction of the new path

corniced), and then contours some way above the burn. Stay on this, crossing the debris of a couple of recent landslides (as of Jan 2005). Three parallel buttresses jut towards the valley, dropping at right angles from the main Carn Dearg Meadhonach – Carn Mor Dearg spine. Yours is the middle one. Once beneath the most imposing section of Aonach Mor's gully-riven W face (see Route 21), cross the Allt Daim and ascend steep grass (and/or snow) to reach a

112

20 – Carn Dearg Meadhonach East Ridge and Carn Mor Dearg Arete

As seen from Aonach Mor. Left to right: Carn Mor Dearg, Ben Nevis and Carn Dearg Meadhonach – the route takes the obvious pinnacled ridge

patch of gently angled granite slabs at the base of the E Ridge of Carn Dearg Meadhonach.

Climb

Carn Dearg Meadhonach East Ridge, 300m (approx elevation) II

Pad pleasantly up the slabs. If verglassed or snow-draped, they can be skirted on the left. Above is a broad bouldery shoulder – a chore when icy. Trudge up this with gradually increasing steepness and exposure. In places the rocks are a tad tottery, requiring careful handling. Reach the top of the first 'pinnacle', which is effectively a big scree heap rather than a distinct summit. Now the proper climbing begins. If you haven't already done so, it's worth donning a harness here.

Cross a small neck of snow/broken boulders above gullies dropping to right and left. Ascend pleasant mixed ground, enjoying several interesting bouldery steps – a pleasure if the turf is frozen.

As the angle relents the crest begins to pinch in, steep drops falling away on either side. At a little levelling the onward route becomes visible, an impressive rank of teeth with sharp spines and sheer N faces. The main tower looks particularly intimidating. Thankfully the appearance is somewhat deceptive. Given safe conditions most difficulties can be bypassed on snow slopes to the left, though sticking with the true arete is better. While confident groups may solo, at this stage roping up is likely to appeal to many. There are ample spikes and cracks for protection.

Clamber over granite blocks on the crest to reach an airy minor summit. Descend briefly to the narrow saddle beneath the main tower. The tower is climbed on mixed terrain, steering a little left of the steepest ground. From the summit follow the lovely arete onto the next saddle. This same point can be reached by traversing leftwards below the tower on easy snow until a shallow

On the summit plateau of Ben Nevis, looking back over the Carn Mor Dearg Arete to Aonach Mor (Route 21). On the right is the NE Buttress (Route 19).

gully leads to the arete. Beyond, an uncomplicated ascent gains the cairned summit of Carn Dearg Meadhonach. Walk easily onto Carn Mor Dearg.

Possible descent
If menaced by the clock or the weather it's possible to bail out down the E Ridge of Carn Mor Dearg; nowhere hard, though requiring care.

Carn Mor Dearg Arete, 1.5km (horizontal distance) I
With its pure curving line and airy situations, few winter routes of this modest grade can match the CMD Arete. Low technicality makes it genuinely feasible for mountaineers of all abilities. Bear in mind though that deep fresh snow, iced-up rocks and high crosswinds can all pose an unanticipated challenge.

Scrambling interest commences soon after leaving the summit, the crest narrowing as it drops S to provide much entertainment on sound, blocky rock. Initially the difficulties are best turned on the right, should the urge to bypass them arise. As the line swings rightwards around the head of Coire Leis, steep crags develop on the right, and the easiest route correspondingly moves to the left of the crest. A dip at the arete's low point offers some respite from the clambering, beyond which there's a good deal more ridge-top fun as the route reascends, finally meeting the shoulder of Ben Nevis at a high saddle.

Possible descent
There is no safe descent off the CMD Arete itself. From the point where it terminates it's feasible to descend N into Coire Leis, staying just left (facing down) of the broken line of old abseil posts. There may be a considerable avalanche risk here, while at other times this deceptively steep slope can be extremely icy. In the latter

End the day on the roof of Britain; now all you've got to do is get down. Glen Spean from the summit plateau of Ben Nevis

eventuality two axes and a cautious front-pointing downclimb are advised – this can be more exciting than anything on the preceding climb.

Continuation

Given sufficient time a quick trip over the Roof of Britain rounds things off nicely. An hour and a half of daylight should be enough to cross Ben Nevis summit plateau and gain the safety of the Tourist Track zigzags; less is cutting things fine. A large part of the descent will almost inevitably be in the dark. The ascent is a butch, bouldery slog of around 300m vertical elevation. Take care of the crags rimming Coire Leis – the safest line stays just left of an intermittent row of sawn-off posts. The summit sports all sorts of old tat including a ruined Victorian meteorological observatory.

Descent

Continue down the Tourist Track (as per Route 16) to an acute bend just above the Halfway Lochan. Branch right here on a new path that runs to the outflow at the N end of the lochan, where the engineered route abruptly ends (not yet marked on maps in January 2010). From here continue in the same well-trodden line, fast becoming established as an unofficial path, to descend a boggy slope just E of the Allt Coire an Lochain to reach the Allt a'Mhuilinn. Cross the burn via a deer fence at the forest edge and hop over a stile to the guides' car park. There's now the option of the new path to Torlundy, but to return to the ski centre follow the forest track as used by guides and centre groups, which soon cuts right into the woods. These privileged few can drive the track while the rest have to slog the final 4km on foot; keep right at the first junction, left at the second and right at the third.

115

LOCHABER

Route 21 – Golden Oldie, Aonach Mor

Grade	400m (approx) II
Distance	7km
Ascent	740m
Time	6½ hours
Start/finish	Nevis Range ski centre car park (NN172773)
Map	OS Landranger (1:50,000) 41
Accommodation	See Route 14
Sleeping out	The Allt Daim in winter is a bleak spot to kip; the gondola provides such quick access that a wild camp is redundant.
Public transport	See Route 20
Seasonal notes	Golden Oldie translates into a grade 2 summer scramble on largely sound granite blocks. It is described as the 'West Ridge' in *Scrambles in Lochaber* by Noel Williams (Cicerone).

Thanks to the Nevis Range gondola, Aonach Mor is that rare beast, an easily accessible Scottish winter-climbing venue. At the first sign of a freeze ice warriors invade Coire an Lochain en masse, swamping many of the best lines. The W flank feels altogether wilder, a vast array of parallel gullies and rambling rock ribs in a secluded setting. Though this magnificent face was once neglected, its mountaineering potential is now widely recognised, and on a pleasant day it, too, can become almost busy. Of several fairly similar granite ridges running direct to the mountain's summit, Golden Oldie is the easiest, the most popular and arguably the finest. It is a route of character, with an Alpine scale and ambience.

Approach

As for Route 20 into the valley of the Allt Daim. Staying fairly close to the Allt Daim is the easiest course – traversing further uphill involves crossing ravines running down from the W Face; these can be arduous in deep snow. Once opposite the E Ridge of Carn Dearg Meadhonach climb leftwards towards the steepest and most compact area of the face, a group of rocky ridges and gullies set up high directly below Aonach Mor's summit. In this huge and confusing spread of mountainside it is hard to locate the correct route among dozens of potential lines. Given poor visibility, newcomers to the area may find this an impossible task! Golden Oldie is the leftmost in a close-packed group of four ridges, with a prominent steep middle section. Note that the two gullies that flank either side of the ridge meet up below the crag at about the 710m contour. Another aid to identification is the fact that everything to the left of Golden Oldie is less steep and less well-defined.

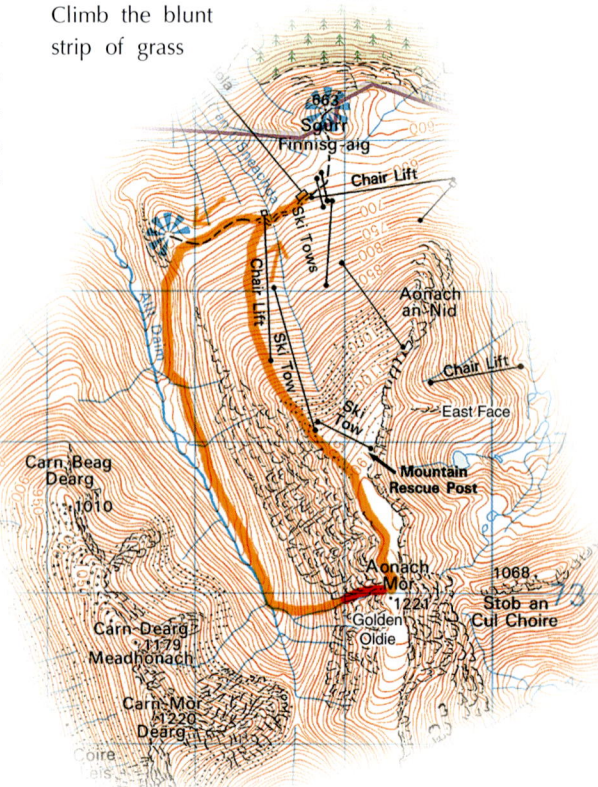

Climb the blunt strip of grass

21 – GOLDEN OLDIE, AONACH MOR

Ben Nevis (left) and Carn Mor Dearg (Route 20) from Aonach Mor's summit plateau

and outcrops between the two gullies to reach a gearing-up point on the right, at the foot of the first steep band. Stamp out a platform here if the snow is deep.

Climb

Though belays are good when needed, runners can be conspicuously absent if the ridge is wreathed in snow. In this situation, and considering the length of the route, taking time to excavate flared granite cracks may not always be a gamble worth taking. Carry several long slings (240cm) to make best use of the many big blocks found en route.

Directly above the first belay ledge is a shallow icy groove, an entertaining start. Climb this with joy to gain straightforward ground. Now zigzag up for some way without further difficulty – an opportunity to save time by climbing together on a short rope. The ridge soon begins to steepen, throwing down the odd interesting move, until you come up against the next major step. It's probably worth pitching this bit, belaying from a handy little spike/flake on the right wall. Climb the step via another shallow groove line. This is steeper than it looks from below, and in poor conditions can feel challenging for the grade.

From a sound nut belay at the top of the groove clamber more easily through blocky terrain to end up in a square-cut chimney on the right. From the top of this there's a heady perspective across the right-hand gully to Western Rib (II/III), the adjacent ridge. Move left, threading through and over rounded blocks on the crest, with an exhilarating sense of air to each side. At the next major crag band head for yet another shallow groove, overlooking the right-hand gully. Climb the groove to a small chockstone – place runners on the left wall. Given unfrozen turf or soft snow to pull up on, surmounting this is most definitely the crux. Above is a ledge and spike belay on the right. Step back left from here, up a right-angled continuation corner, to belay on more level ground. As speed is of the essence on this Alpine-scale route, moving together may be a wise choice from here on.

The crest now becomes narrower and blockier. Weave and clamber, with much amusement and considerable ridge-top exposure, passing a number of

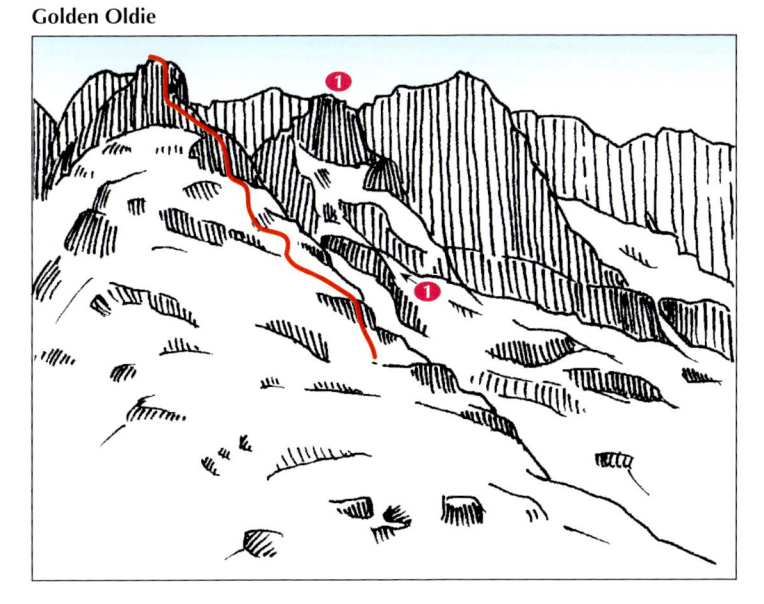

Golden Oldie

❶ Western Rib

The square-cut chimney

21 – GOLDEN OLDIE, AONACH MOR

Hacking up the crux groove

On the upper crest

minor steps and thin notches. Just when you're beginning to think that surely it must all be over soon, comes the sting in the tail. The ridge pinches down, levelling out onto a tight rock crest with precipitous snow slopes plunging away on either hand. Walk the plank with trepidation, being sure to organise some sort of protection along the way. Both climbers must be prepared to launch off left if their friend falls right (and vice versa), though such a terrifying textbook contingency ought to be avoidable with care. At the end of the arete a strange rock boss serves as runner and handhold for a long step down to the right. Traverse back onto the crest, which becomes steadily broader and less steep until it merges into the mountainside. Plod up an easy snow slope to gain the plateau a short way N of the summit cairn.

Descent

This is one of the quickest descents in the book, though in poor visibility beware cornices rimming the E and W faces. Head N, following the elongated summit plateau to reach the top ski tow. Stay just left of the ski fences to regain the foot of the chairlift at around 640m, as mentioned in the approach section. With luck you'll be in time for the last gondola down. If not, prepare for the walk of shame down the MTB trail and through the forest to the car park.

119

LOCHABER

Route 22 – North East Ridge, Aonach Beag

Grade	450m Difficult (possible variation at Moderate)
Distance	10.5km
Ascent	1195m
Time	7 hours
Start/finish	Nevis Range ski centre car park (NN172773)
Map	OS Landranger (1:50,000) 41
Accommodation	See Route 14
Sleeping out	Cavernous An Cul Choire is a little-used wild camping spot, and difficult to access. There are many suitable sites throughout this huge corrie complex – a grassy area near a waterfall N of the base of the ridge looks ideal.
Public transport	See Route 20
Seasonal notes	Grade III under snow, but not to be taken lightly. For quality and challenge this route in winter is comparable to the big Ben Nevis ridges. The crux (as in summer) is short and sharp, and though the rest of the climbing is less difficult, its remoteness makes this a considerable undertaking.

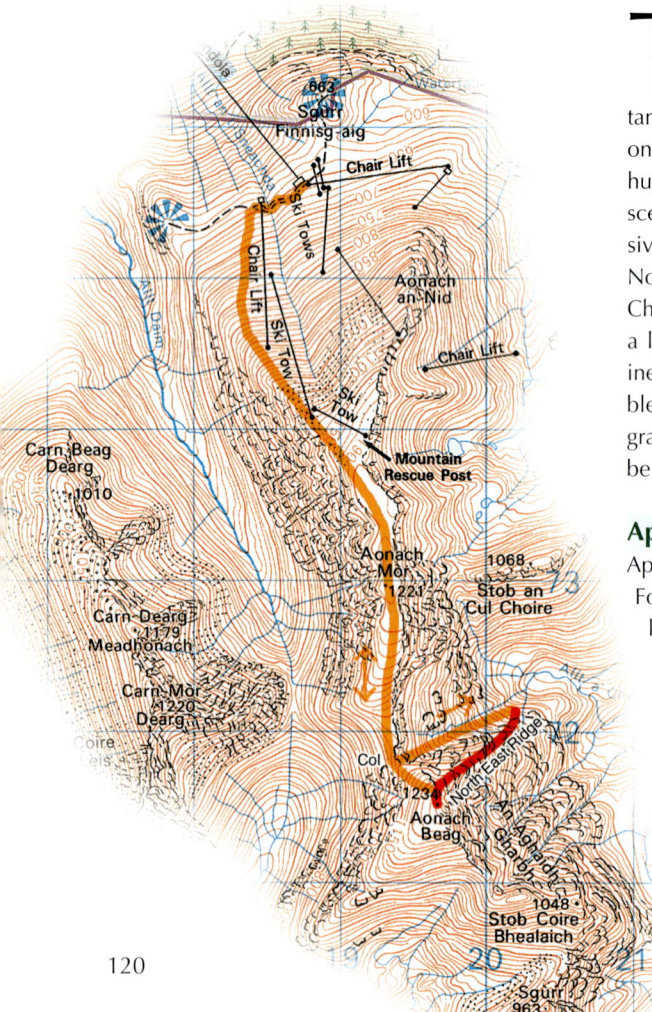

The Ben swarms with climbers; ant-like processions of hillwalkers crawl over Carn Mor Dearg; and Aonach Mor has been tamed by the ski tow. Of Lochaber's 4000ft peaks, only Aonach Beag remains aloof. The mountain's huge eastern corrie complex harbours Highland scenery on an epic scale, a setting as impressive and out of the way as any in Scotland. The North East Ridge rises out of the depths of An Cul Choire, a big and very distinguished route with a line so obvious that its relative unpopularity is inexplicable. Though largely an exciting scramble, two short crux pitches boost the technical grade, meaning that this route can only sensibly be recommended to roped mountaineering teams.

Approach

Approaches from Glen Nevis or the Leanachan Forest may be satisfying, but they are also lengthy. As for Route 20 and 21, the Nevis Range gondola provides the most convenient access. From the top of the gondola continue up the ski fields. A vague path stays just W of the ski tows, though once the resort has closed for the season any route is fair game. Continue S along Aonach Mor's curiously extended summit plateau, descending easily to the col before Aonach Beag. Views of Carn Mor Dearg and Ben

22 – North East Ridge, Aonach Beag

Aonach Beag's North East Ridge and the Grey Corries, seen from the Aonach Mor / Aonach Beag col

Nevis are inspiring, as is the perspective on the North East Ridge, seen here in full profile.

The lip of An Cul Choire is guarded by scrappy crags, and may carry large cornices even when it seems from the valley that all snow has melted for the summer. Hard against the N face of Aonach Beag a strip of easier ground runs down into the corrie, and though this too may be corniced it provides the only sensible line. Descend steep mossy scree with care. Continue down very rough ground under the mountain's N face. Just short of the floor of the upper corrie a grassy line leads onto the base of the ridge.

Aonach Beag NE Ridge

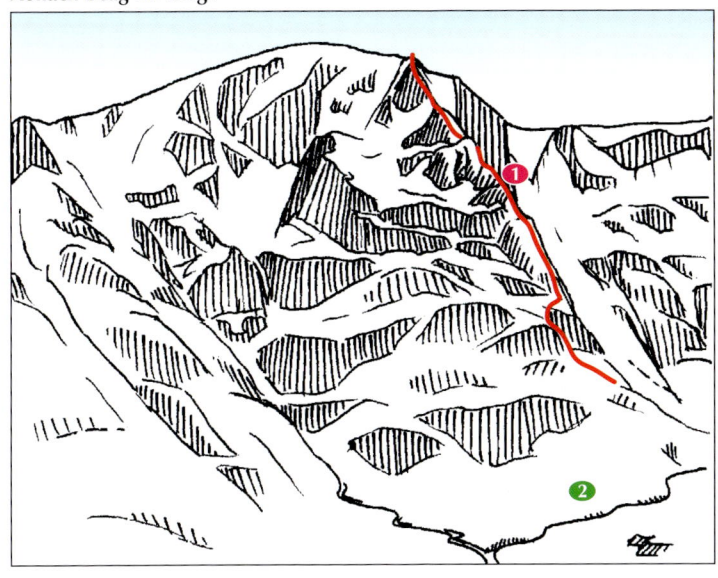

Climb

The ridge begins broad and vegetated. Climb patches of moss and grass, actively seeking out little outcrops of wrinkled schist towards the right edge to inject some light entertainment. Initially, easy ground is close at hand on the left. Gradually the sections of blocky scrambling become more frequent. As the ridge

❶ Crux Step
❷ An Cul Choire

121

Great scrambling, below the crux step

steepens appreciably there is a sustained stretch of scrambling above the growing drop of the N face. This leads to a little level section below an abrupt rock fin, beyond which rises the crux step.

The front face of the fin looks impregnable – to bypass it, cross a bouldery neck onto the right (N) flank. To avoid a direct ascent of the crux altogether, it is possible to continue along much the same line, traversing vegetated ledges beneath the crux step before climbing wobbly ground to regain the ridge crest beyond. This warrants Moderate, and it's fairly unpleasant.

Better, though harder, is a direct assault on the crux, dispatched in two pitches of Difficult climbing. Start just behind the rock fin at a good block belay.

Pitch 1, 15m
Climb steeply up stacked blocks in a shallow corner to a tight gap between the fin and the ridge proper. Continue up the juggy wall above onto a sloping ledge to the left of another little fin. Belay here to avoid rope drag.

Pitch 2, 35m
Climb a wide groove onto a bouldery ledge. Above is a cracked slab, leading to a short, sharp upper prow. Climbing this prow direct demands a couple of strenuous reachy moves, well above Difficult grade. Instead sidle right along a slippery, mossy ledge system. This is serious, and would be more pleasant in winter. A rusty peg protects the traverse. Make for a prominent acute-angled chimney/corner, which will be met with

22 – North East Ridge, Aonach Beag

Beyond the crux, and loving it

Airy excitement on the upper knife-edge

misplaced relief. Don't relax; this is the crux. The angle may be acute, but the climbing isn't at all cute. Udge up the corner, which proves to be an honest old-fashioned struggle – that is, dank, muddy and insecure. Clip another ancient peg and then go for it, making full use of a variety of inelegant techniques and some welcome positive flake holds. The top-out feels a tad loose. Pull carefully onto the ledge above.

The rest of the route can be tackled unroped. First up, a fantastic exposed knife-edge, best climbed by sticking to the crest. With good grade 3 moves and drops sucking at your heels, this is probably the most enjoyable part of the day. The difficulty soon begins to abate, broad vegetated patches dividing the steeper rock buttresses. But the position remains superb, the ridge forming a gangway between two huge complex faces. The rim of Aonach Beag's summit plateau is often corniced, and though the ridge tends to shed its cover first, there's a chance that your last few metres will be on insecure snow.

Descent

From the summit cairn, poised on the edge of the vast E face, follow the hillwalker's path NW. This zigzags down to the Aonach Mor – Aonach Beag col on a thin strip of safe ground between the mountain's precipitous N and W faces; take great care in mist. Climb back over Aonach Mor, descending beside the ski tows in time (ideally) for the last gondola down.

Route 23 – Long and Short Leachas, Ben Alder

Grade	I winter
Distance	42km
Ascent	930m
Time	11 hours with bikes or 14 hours on foot. Best done over two days.
Start/finish	Beside the railway in Dalwhinnie (NN634847)
Map	OS Landranger (1:50,000) 42
Accommodation	Newtonmore hostel (01540 673 3601); Loch Ossian Youth Hostel (0870 004 1139) makes an alternative base for those approaching Ben alder from the Glasgow – Fort William railway in the west.
Sleeping out	Culra bothy (NN523762) is ideally placed for this route. Thanks to the Mountain Bothies Association it is in a good state of repair, and even boasts cast-iron stoves. Bring coal or peat logs, picking up kindling in the forest en route from Dalwhinnie. There are only limited spaces in Culra bothy, so at busy times it may be worth carrying a tent.
Public transport	As Dalwhinnie is on the main road and rail line from Perth to Inverness, this route can be accessed on public transport. The only drawback is that bikes cannot be taken on buses, and even on trains they must be pre-booked.
Seasonal notes	In summer the Leachas Ridges are only very basic scrambles. Although too easy for inclusion in a mountaineering guidebook, they make a fine hillwalk. Under snow the circuit is a low-end grade I winter climb, feasible in almost any conditions.

Although the truly great climbs are memorable in and of themselves, less distinctive routes can still offer a deep and lasting satisfaction. This often has as much to do with their setting as with the quality of their climbing, in a move-for-move sense. In some cases 'It ain't what you do, it's the where that you do it', to bastardise an old song. Ben Alder's Leachas Ridges are a case in point. Although pleasant enough, they are hardly a technical challenge. Thankfully the surroundings more than compensate for any shortcomings. Ben Alder is a Highland giant, rugged, complex and magnificently remote. Climbing in this empty fastness is an adventure for mountaineers of any standard. Given mountain bikes and legs of steel the route can be completed in one mega-day, though most people will prefer the added ambience of an overnight stay.

Ben Alder (left) and the Lancet Edge (right) greet the dawn on the walk-in from Culra

Approach

Ben Alder is further from civilisation than almost any other peak in the Central Highlands. Despite its isolation, the journey in is not as arduous as it might be, thanks to good estate tracks. These aid progress without really scratching the veneer of remoteness. A mountain bike comes highly recommended, beating the footsore trudge hands down. From Dalwhinnie head for Loch Ericht, crossing the railway to pick up a rough tarmac private road along the forested N shore, which is followed for about 9km. Just before reaching the sinister-looking millionaire's hideaway of Ben Alder Lodge fork right on a stony unsurfaced track, climbing steadily onto a windswept moor. Descend towards Loch Pattack. About 500m short of the loch a path branches off left, making a beeline for Culra bothy. This is the walker's direct route – too muddy for comfortable cycling.

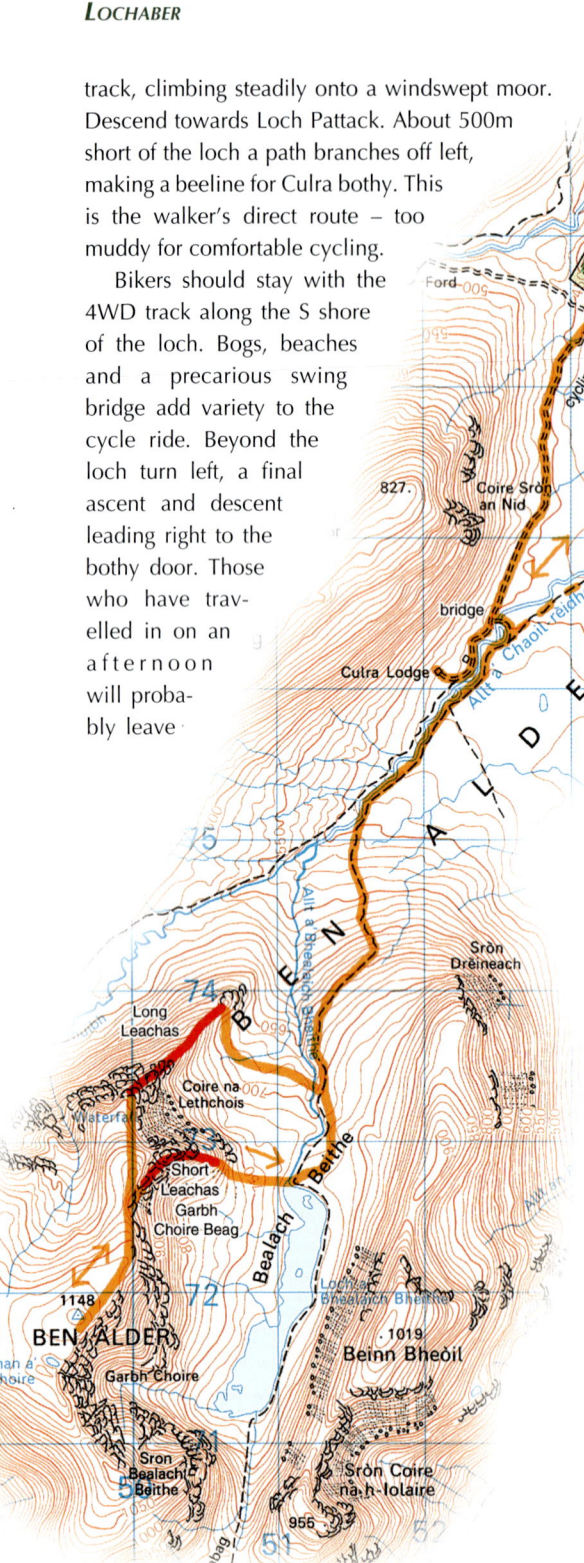

Bikers should stay with the 4WD track along the S shore of the loch. Bogs, beaches and a precarious swing bridge add variety to the cycle ride. Beyond the loch turn left, a final ascent and descent leading right to the bothy door. Those who have travelled in on an afternoon will probably leave the climb for next morning. Culra is an isolated spot, with a stirring outlook up the Bealach Dubh, a deep trench flanked on one side by Ben Alder and on the other by Sgor Iutharn's Lancet Edge. This dramatic prow provides a snow climb of similar difficulty to the Leachas Ridges.

From Culra retrace your steps a few hundred metres to cross the Allt a'Chaoil-reidhe on a swing bridge (it can be forded outside the bothy, though in winter only by the foolhardy). Head back SW along the riverbank, climbing towards the Bealach Beithe, with the Leachas Ridges looking more inviting with every step. Once parallel with Coire na Lethchois, the shallow scoop between the outstretched arms of the Leachas, head WNW, crossing a burn and a wide boggy section to reach a saddle at the base of the Long Leachas.

Climb

Long Leachas, Grade I

The ridge rises in a series of broken rocky buttresses, with easier grassy sections in between. The best climbing is had when the turf is frozen or pasted in firm névé. Stay more or less with the crest, weaving around the steepest obstacles using vegetated ledges and occasional little rock steps. Halfway up the second major steepening, a ledge

23 – Long and Short Leachas, Ben Alder

Nearing the top of the Long Leachas, looking back at distant Loch Pattack

Checking out the way down the Short Leachas, with the Long Leachas on the left and Lock Pattack in the distance

leads onto the N side of the ridge, from where a short loose gully cuts back up to the crest. The arete then narrows pleasingly. Negotiate blocky ground over a level section, and carry on up to a prominent little tower. Skirt either side of this, soon reaching the summit plateau. Where the Long Leachas meets the mountain, a gully cuts left into Coire na Lethchois. Though the cornice may be appreciable, this might be outflanked well to the right (facing out) to give an escape route should conditions on the plateau prove hostile.

The summit of Ben Alder is 1.5km to the S, following the E edge of the plateau past the Short Leachas (note landmarks for the return leg) and along the rim of the mountain's two big E corries. Because of the snow-catching potential of its extensive summit table, Ben Alder's cornices can be fearsome. The summit area is marked by a trig point and a surprising number of ruined shelters. As befits a major peak in such a central position, views range wide over the Southern Highlands, Lochaber and the Cairngorms.

Descent
Short Leachas, Grade I
Return to the Short Leachas, which is gained by a brief rocky descent from the plateau rim. Potential cornice issues here might be reason enough to carry a rope. Given unconsolidated snow the rocky upper section can feel a little tricky in descent, though all difficulties are short lived and the correct line is never in doubt. As you lose height the angle and technicality relent, leaving you on a broad grassy nose. Skirting right of some scrappy terminal crags, head for the outflow of Loch a' Bhealaich Bheithe to reach the Culra path.

THE CAIRNGORMS

Best known for their barren plateau scenery, bitten and gouged by great corries, the Cairngorms bask in a 'big country' atmosphere befitting Britain's only genuine sub-arctic wilderness. This is the largest unbroken stretch of high land in Scotland. It is a serious, forbidding place, but alive with wonderful features. Where else might you find semi-permanent snow beds, for instance, or Scotland's answer to the Yeti? To get the most from this range a long, self-sufficient expedition comes highly recommended, not least as it offers the best chance to meet Ben Macdui's fabled Big Grey Man. Ridge climbs are thin on the ground here, but those that do exist are awesome. Perhaps Mitre Ridge best exemplifies the special qualities of the area, a route on which thrilling isolation meets testing climbing to provide an awfully big adventure.

Cairngorm's snowy pate, as seen from Pygmy Ridge (Route 26)

THE CAIRNGORMS

Route 24 – Eagle Ridge, Lochnagar

Grade	240m (approx) Severe
Distance	15km
Ascent	770m
Time	7 hours
Start/finish	Glen Muick car park (NO309852)
Map	OS Landranger (1:50,000) 44
Accommodation	Braemar Youth Hostel (0870 004 1105), Blue Mountain Lodge Ballater (013397 56333)
Sleeping out	The floor of the North East corrie is rough and boggy – the best camping options are close to the NE shore of the lochan.
Public transport	Bus from Aberdeen to Ballater, followed by an optimistic hitchhike or a 13km tarmac trek up Glen Muick.
Seasonal notes	Oft crowned the Queen of Lochnagar's winter routes (also, incidentally, owned by a queen), Eagle Ridge is one of the big winter trips of Scotland. It is graded a hefty VI,6 in decent conditions, and is likely to feel harder still under fresh powder. A snow patch with mini-bergschrund sometimes lingers at the base well into summer.

Lochnagar's 'steep frowning glories' have been widely celebrated since Byron's day. Its yawning NE corrie is superlative, with a selection of climbs to match. Though the quality is most apparent in winter, Lochnagar's summer rock routes also have considerable appeal. Of these Eagle Ridge is most popular, rated by many among the best low-grade classics in Britain – and rightly so. The line is magnetic, the setting magnificent and the ground entertaining throughout. With a succession of perplexing, exposed little cruxes, the route keeps you guessing to the end.

Protection is good and the coarse granite is a joy, but bear in mind that Eagle Ridge is no soft touch at Severe, while in the wet it is closer to VS.

Approach

From the pay-and-display car park at the Glen Muick roadhead, pass the visitor centre and turn right on a track over the River Muick to reach a derelict lodge. Take a short path through trees to meet the 4WD track that climbs beside the Allt-na-Giubhsaich, following it to a high point at 700m. Here a well-used path splits off left, climbing easily to the col between Lochnagar and the outlying Meikle Pap. The buttressed cirque of the North East Corrie is well seen from here. Drop W

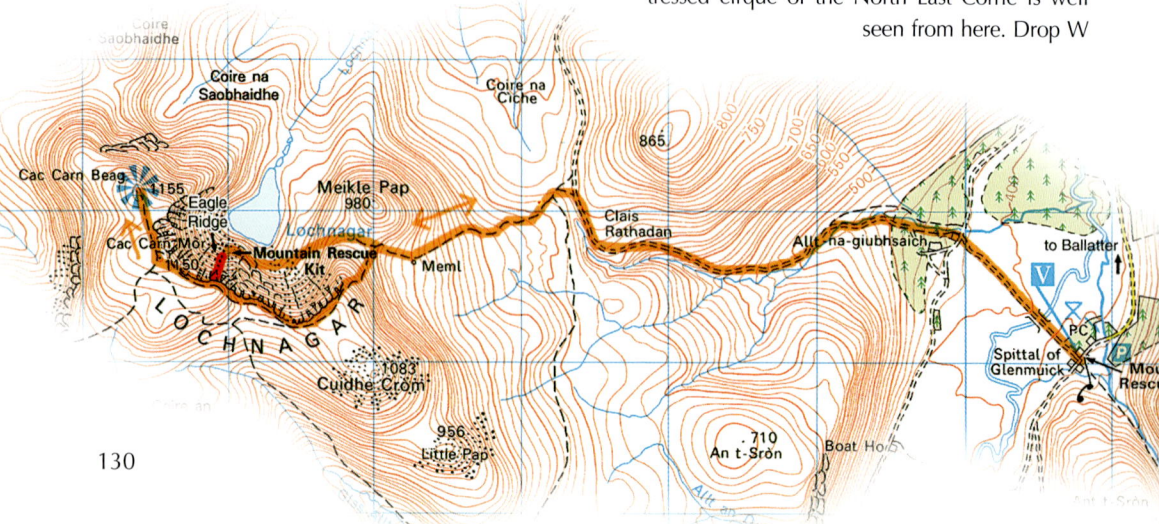

24 – Eagle Ridge, Lochnagar

Walking in to Lochnagar's magnificent North East Corrie

into the corrie down a steep bouldery hillside to gain a traverse path some way above the loch, leading to the mountain rescue box directly below the crags. Among all the mighty buttresses, Eagle Ridge may not be immediately obvious to the newcomer.

Scan your eyes left from the prominent rockfall scar on Tough-Brown Face, over Parallel Gully B to Parallel Buttress; left of this a vegetated inset area is taken by the winter route Parallel Gully A. Left again is a clean wedge of rock soaring the full height of the

Eagle Ridge

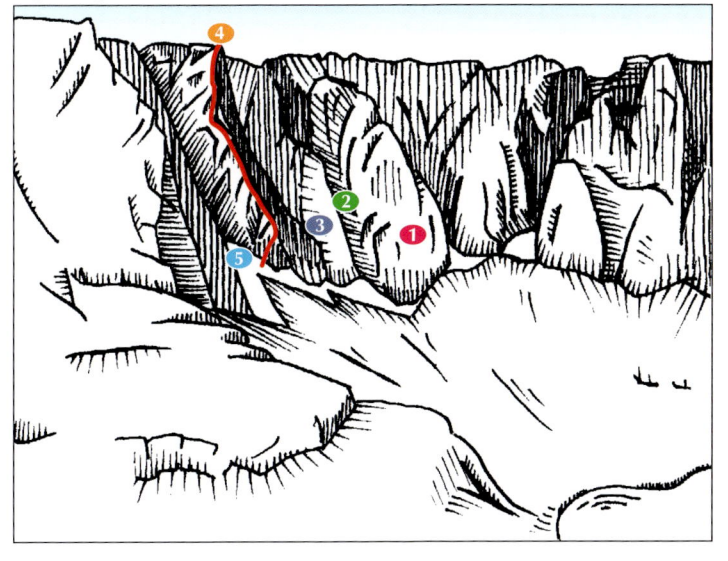

1. Tough-Brown Face
2. Parallel Gully B
3. Parallel Gully A
4. Eagle Ridge
5. Douglas Gibson Gully

131

The Cairngorms

In the gorgeous groove of pitch 1

24 – EAGLE RIDGE, LOCHNAGAR

The arete and slab on pitch 4

crag, with the deep cleft of Douglas Gibson Gully to its immediate left. This is the line – and what a line. Climb scree to the mouth of Douglas Gibson Gully, where a sizeable snow patch may linger long into summer – there's occasionally even a bergschrund at the base of the route.

Climb

Belay opportunities abound throughout, and pitch lengths can be varied to suit. The route is described here in five long pitches.

Pitch 1, 50m
Roughly five metres up from the very lowest toe of rock is a clean, right-slanting diagonal V-groove. Ascend this to a vegetated area at about 20m. Follow the continuation of the same diagonal groove line up this mucky bit to reach a steep, awkward chimney crack. This leads to a ledge and spike belay.

Pitch 2, 40m
Follow a left-leaning open corner, then a short section of level arete. Savour the drop to the left, slabs curving off into Douglas Gibson Gully.

Pitch 3, 50m
This pitch tackles the obvious craggy tower directly overhead. Climb a deep right-angled corner on the right side of the ridge, leading up to a blocky ledge (possible belay). Now tackle the impending rock above, with big rounded holds and amazing exposure. As the ground steepens step up and work slightly right into a vague recess (peg runners), before moving briefly left to surmount a very awkward step. This is the first crux. Belay in a deep slot above, often referred to as the Sentry Box – perhaps misleadingly, since it has no roof.

Pitch 4, 50m
Make a high step out of the slot, then cross a second level arete and a short delicate slab, which

133

Airy slabs at the top of the ridge

leads up to a grassy ledge just right of the crest. This runs into the base of another clean-cut corner with a slabby left wall. Bridge up this to top out onto a knife-edge with an exhilarating gulf on either side. Teeter upright, organise a bomb-proof runner, and then tackle the short steep wall above. The gear is reassuring but the holds are hard to use, particularly if wet or verglassed. Reach for a small fin just over the lip of the wall, then heave up onto safer ground to belay. This is traditionally considered the crux of the route, and said to be the only spot in which first ascensionist JHB Bell ever resorted to aid.

Pitch 5, 50m
Take a short level arete, with big air below, to reach a last impending wall. Here either move onto a little concave slab on the left, or climb tentatively up and right across the wall to gain an easy scoop (hollow-sounding blocks). Whichever option is taken, continue steeply up blocks. Above here it's tempting to work diagonally up and right on grotty ground, but a better choice is to go straight up into a small groove, via an unlikely high step that actually constitutes the technical crux of the whole route, a meaty 4b. Airy-but-easy slabs then lead up right to the top of the ridge.

Descent
To bag the summit turn right along the corrie rim over a minor top, passing the deep incut of Black Spout before striking briefly across open plateau to the granite blocks and panorama display on Cac Carn Beag (literally 'Little Shit Cairn', a name not to be sniffed at). Now follow the well-used walker's path back towards Glen Muick. This steers clear of the cliff edge, descending from the summit plateau and leading over a minor top (great view of the North East Corrie) before winding delightfully down a steep boulder slope to the Meikle Pap col. In naughty conditions an alternative descent from the top of the Ridge is due S, then SE along the Glas Allt to reach Loch Muick – quicker to lose height, but longer overall.

Route 25 – Mitre Ridge, Beinn a'Bhuird

Grade	165m Hard Severe (as described)
Distance	32km minimum
Ascent	960m minimum
Time	12 hours
Start/finish	Car park off the A93 just E of Bridge of Dee (NO188912)
Map	OS Landranger (1:50,000) 36 for large part of route; Landranger 43 for first few km
Accommodation	See Route 24
Sleeping out	Garbh Choire translates as 'Rough Corrie', and it's not named so for nothing. There are, however, enough grassy plots between the boulders. It's also possible to camp in a fold by a little burn on the summit plateau – for easy identification, this watercourse forms the winter climb The Flume.
Public transport	Bus from Aberdeen to Braemar
Seasonal notes	Given the long and often snowed-up approach, Garbh Choire is a very serious place to climb during winter's short days. Mitre Ridge normal route is V,6, while Cumming-Crofton merits VI,6. Both are said to be superb objectives for strong parties.

Lurking in the depths of the eastern Cairngorms, Beinn a'Bhuird's Mitre Ridge is the archetypal Scottish mountaineering challenge, a line of class, considerable difficulty and almost unrivalled remoteness. Thanks to this last quality, it lends itself to an extended stay in the wilds. The 16km approach march alone exceeds the total distance of many other routes in this book, but it's a small

Mitre Ridge (middle distance) and Garbh Choire from the Sneck

135

THE CAIRNGORMS

price to pay. Garbh Choire is among Scotland's most isolated climbing venues, with impressive summer and winter lines on monolithic chunks of perfect granite. Mitre Ridge is a truly compelling feature, a huge saw-toothed wedge projecting from the mountainside. There are two classic ways up the ridge, both completed on the same day in 1933, marking a high point of pre-war Cairngorms climbing. Mitre Ridge original route is great, but the Cumming–Crofton line described here is perhaps greater still.

Approach

Long but non-strenuous, either from the N along Glen Avon or from the S. The latter option is described here. From the car park take a forest track past the estate building, following signs for Alltdourie and Gleann an t-Slugain at the occasional track junction. Eventually reach the Allt an t-Slugain, soon afterwards leaving the trees to enter the upper glen, where a little grass-bottomed gorge offers idyllic wild camping. It's possible to cycle this far, then stash the bikes. Climb the well-made path past a ruin into the wide reaches of Glen Quoich (scene of path improvements at the time of writing). Keep heading broadly N, with enticing views of Beinn a'Bhuird's eastern corries, to a path junction. Branch right beside the Glas Allt Mor, climbing to the Sneck in a further 2km. This is the col between Ben Avon and Beinn a'Bhuird. Drop diagonally left down scree and broken rock onto the upper floor of Garbh Choire. Contour under the crags to the slabby base of Mitre Ridge.

Climb

Mitre Ridge Direct (220m HS) climbs obvious slabby grooves from near the bottom toe of the ridge, then continues via chimneys and walls close to the crest, joining Cumming–Crofton between the First and Second Towers.

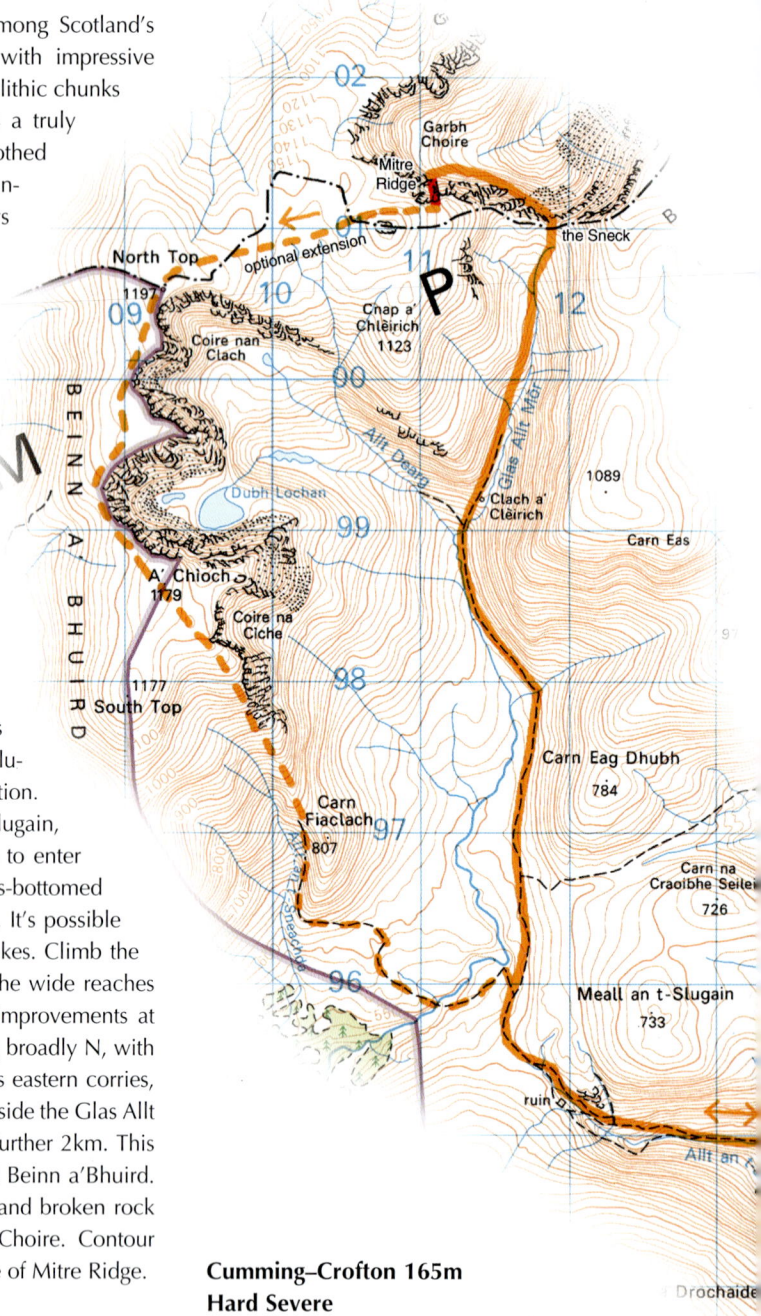

Cumming–Crofton 165m
Hard Severe

This climb has a sense of scale out of all proportion to its actual length. Rucksacks are likely to feel like a hindrance, so consider leaving them at the Sneck. Start up and right of the slab apron, below a corner system that runs almost the full height of the prow.

25 – Mitre Ridge, Beinn a'Bhuird

Pitch 1, 40m
Ascend broken ground to a grassy terrace. Take a deep corner crack to a second platform, then climb a short deep chimney directly above by bridging and back-and-foot. The chimney is steep, with hard moves to reach and surmount a jammed block at the top. Belay on the next ledge.

Pitch 2, 15m
Step down and right onto the W Face, traversing a little ledge to reach a smooth diagonal V-groove. This is delicate and balancey – perhaps the technical crux of the route. It's worth placing a high runner in a vertical crack on the left before committing. The groove then widens; climb it until a series of diagonal moves leads leftwards across a short exposed wall (peg runner) onto a sloping ledge below a big right-angled corner.

Pitch 3, 20m
Climb the corner; it is steep, but offers generous holds and plentiful protection. Belay on the first wide ledge.

Pitch 4, 40m
Go a few metres up a wide crack in the left wall of the corner before taking an obvious rightwards traverse line onto a sloping ledge. Continue in the corner up a further steepening to an area of broken rock and gravel. Climb this mucky open gully to gain the pinnacled crest between the First and Second Tower.

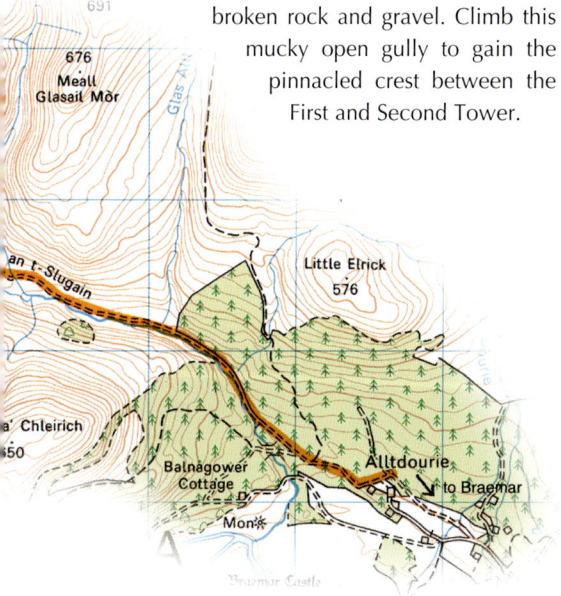

Mitre Ridge

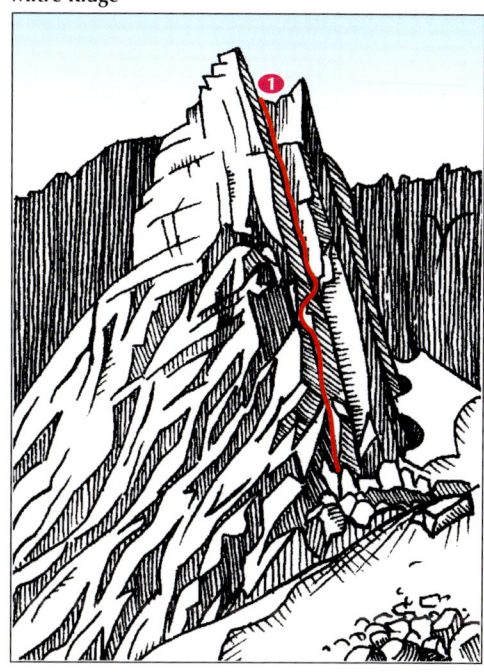

❶ Cumming–Crofton Route

Pitch 5, 20m
Of several onward choices 'Bell's Variation' on the Second Tower is the most spectacular, and constitutes the psychological crux of the route. Gain a right-slanting ramp leading around the corner onto the tremendously airy W Face. Climb a right-leaning crack in a shallow groove to stand heart-in-mouth on top of a big spike below a final short wall; a crack overhead swallows a good medium wire. Climb up and rightwards across the wall via some rather tenuous sidepulls, gaining the top of the tower with elation.

Pitch 6, 30m
Follow the level arete in a fantastic position, at one point stepping down into a mini 'Tower Gap' (see Route 17) before climbing a last easy-angled wall to the top.

Descent

For those not camping out, the quickest way home is the approach route.

The Cairngorms

The corner on pitch 3 – steep, but plentiful holds and gear

25 – Mitre Ridge, Beinn a'Bhuird

The jagged crest of Mitre Ridge, seen from the top

Continuation

Given time it's nice to explore the rest of Beinn a'Bhuird. Head W over featureless tableland to reach the North Top (the highest point), then turn S along the rim of the mountain's scalloped eastern corries to regain the approach path in Glen Quoich.

Enthusiastic climbers should consider staying in Garbh Choire for a couple of days – after all, how often are you likely to make it this far? The corrie's other gems include Slochd Wall (HVS) and the perfect Squareface (VDiff).

Route 26 – Pygmy Ridge and Afterthought Arete, Stob Coire an t-Sneachda

Grade	Pygmy Ridge 95m Moderate; Afterthought Arete 150m Moderate
Distance	9km
Ascent	800m
Time	6 hours
Start/finish	Coire Cas car park, Cairngorm ski centre (NH989061)
Maps	OS Landranger (1:50,000) 36
Accommodation	Cairngorm Lodge Youth Hostel (0870 004 1137)
Sleeping out	There are few better settings for a wild camp than the crag-rimmed Loch Avon basin. Pitch a tent by the loch or bed down under the famous Shelter Stone, where a natural chamber beneath the largest of a group of boulders has been converted into a relatively weathertight howff, with room in comfort for around six plus kit. The stone is marked by a cairn. A smaller version nearby provides overspill accommodation in busy periods.
Public transport	One of those rare Scottish routes for which public transport is practically as convenient as driving. Bus or train to Aviemore, from where a regular bus service runs to the Coire Cas car park.
Seasonal notes	Pygmy Ridge is IV,5 in winter, frequently in nick thanks to its high N-facing position. Afterthought Arete is III; S-facing and quite a bit lower, it can be a clean, dry rock climb while adjacent crags are still wintry. Both are a sure bet for mixed climbing fans.

What's in a name? Tagging 'Pygmy' onto a mountain feature makes it sound too diminutive to bother with, while demoting a route to the status of an 'Afterthought' seems hardly more promising. But don't be fooled.

The names are misleading; downright unkind. Although relative tiddlers, these are climbs with spirit. Quality of line, exciting positions and reliable rough rock give them both a memorable edge. Combining the two creates a logical day out, with

Stag Rocks (left) and Loch Avon from the approach to Afterthought Arete

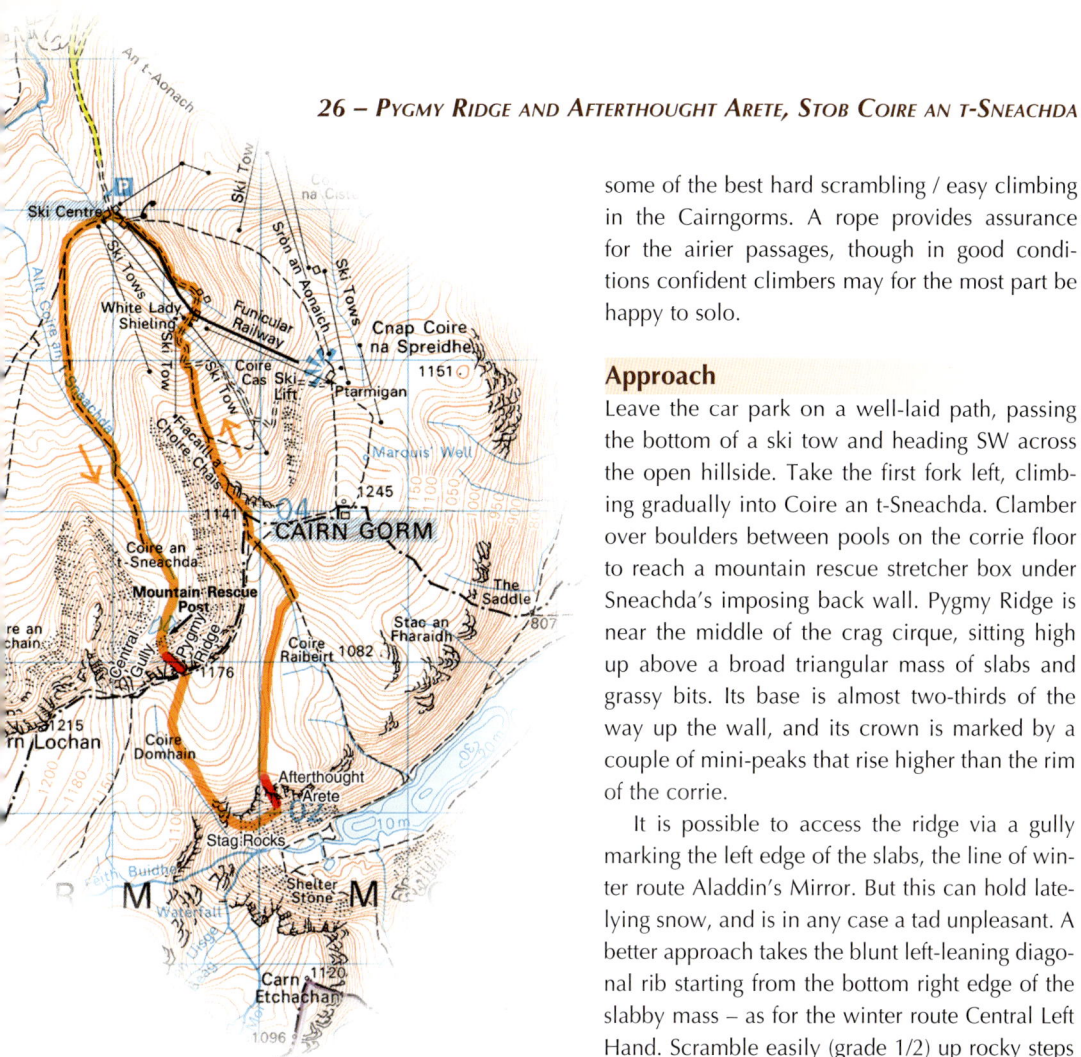

26 – Pygmy Ridge and Afterthought Arete, Stob Coire an t-Sneachda

some of the best hard scrambling / easy climbing in the Cairngorms. A rope provides assurance for the airier passages, though in good conditions confident climbers may for the most part be happy to solo.

Approach

Leave the car park on a well-laid path, passing the bottom of a ski tow and heading SW across the open hillside. Take the first fork left, climbing gradually into Coire an t-Sneachda. Clamber over boulders between pools on the corrie floor to reach a mountain rescue stretcher box under Sneachda's imposing back wall. Pygmy Ridge is near the middle of the crag cirque, sitting high up above a broad triangular mass of slabs and grassy bits. Its base is almost two-thirds of the way up the wall, and its crown is marked by a couple of mini-peaks that rise higher than the rim of the corrie.

It is possible to access the ridge via a gully marking the left edge of the slabs, the line of winter route Aladdin's Mirror. But this can hold late-lying snow, and is in any case a tad unpleasant. A better approach takes the blunt left-leaning diagonal rib starting from the bottom right edge of the slabby mass – as for the winter route Central Left Hand. Scramble easily (grade 1/2) up rocky steps and patches of greenery, with the occasional wobbly rock, moving left after nearly 100m to the clean-cut base of the ridge.

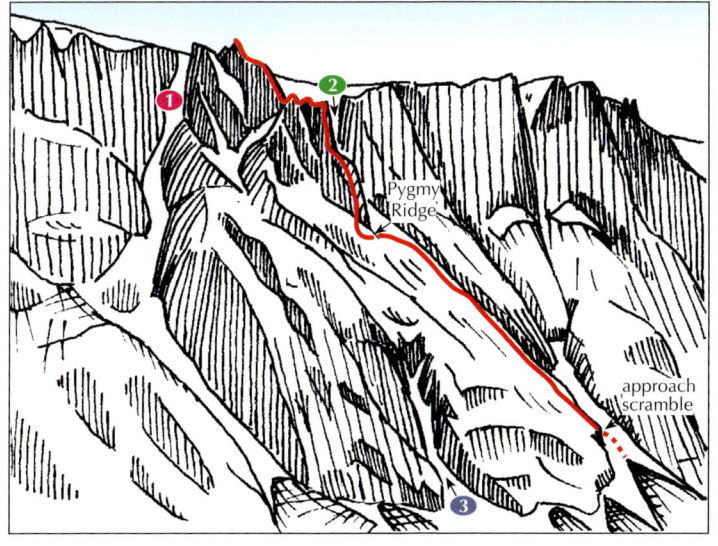

Climb

**Pygmy Ridge, 95m
Moderate**

The best line is marked by crampon scratches and scuff marks. It is worth roping up, at least for the

Pygmy Ridge

❶ Aladdin's Couloir
❷ Central Gully
❸ Aladdin's Mirror

141

The Cairngorms

On the level crest, Pygmy Ridge. Behind is the Fiacaill Buttress (Route 27)

abrupt first pitch. Start at the lowest toe of rock, climbing the steep face overlooking the corrie. Begin by moving from left to right to gain a little chimney feature, despatched by a stiff pull (nice layback). Above this stay left briefly, but soon move slightly right onto the square-cut arete, following it direct to belay in a big rubble-floored niche at about 35m.

Exit the niche up its left side before moving right to regain the frontal arete, following it to reach a little level crest after another 35m. The level toothed section leads to grassy ground at the head of the funnel-shaped gully bounding the right of the ridge. It is possible, though an anticlimax, to clamber onto the plateau up the final scrappy slope right of the clean rock (can carry a remnant cornice into summer). However the ridge offers one final blocky tower; climb right to left over piled boulders to gain a final short crest leading to the plateau.

Approach

Head S over the plateau into the shallow scoop of Coire Domhain, following a rough eroded path on the left bank of the stream as it plunges into the Loch Avon basin. Afterthought Arete is near the W end of Stag Rocks, one of several major crags ringing the valley. The crag starts just E of the Allt Coire Domhain. At about the 870m contour pick up a faint path traversing the heathery hillside under Stag Rocks. Pass below a small seeping wall, then cross a snow/scree-filled gully that descends from the plateau. Afterthought Arete rises out of the messy mass of rock just right of this gully. It's far better than it looks from below.

26 – Pygmy Ridge and Afterthought Arete, Stob Coire an t-Sneachda

Moving together on the level crest of Pygmy ridge

Afterthought Arete

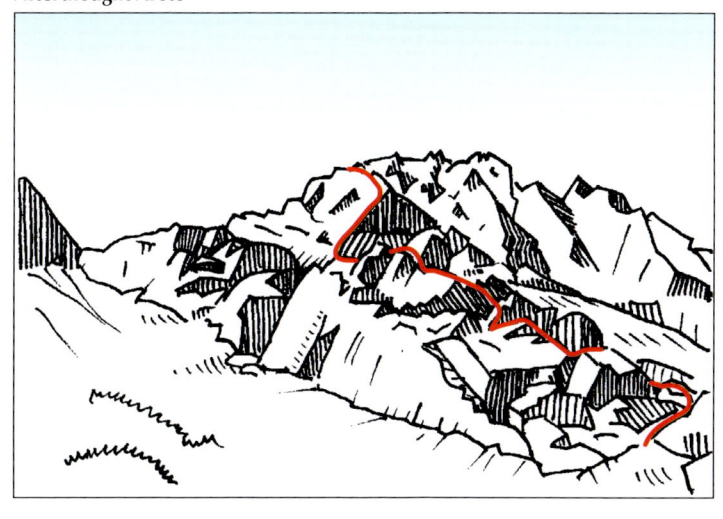

Climb
Afterthought Arete, 150m Moderate

A slabby triangular rock patch marks the foot of the ridge. This can be climbed via an obvious groove. It is rather harder than Moderate, but easily avoided by a well-worn line on the right. Once above the slab, clamber straight up some big blocks to reach a clean vertical step. The brave will sidle left here onto the left flank of the ridge overlooking a little vegetated gully before climbing a steep 10m wall back up to

THE CAIRNGORMS

Rope-free exposure high on the spine of Afterthought Arete

a ledge on the crest; good holds, but exposed. A gentler alternative slinks round right of the vertical step to reach the same ledge.

Now the ridge pinches into a long sharp spine of perfect clean rock. It remains well defined for at least the next 100m, the best passage of sustained Moderate climbing in the Cairngorms. Follow this fabulous granite staircase, with many short interesting steps and intervening stances on which to take stock or to belay. On either side steep heathery gullies rise with you, creating a sense of reduced fall potential without diminishing the excitement of the situation. It is sometimes possible to step into the right-hand gully in order to avoid particularly daunting moves on the crest, though none of these turn out to be really that difficult. The crest eventually peters into grassy slopes. Afterthought or no, you'll be thinking about this climb long after you've done it.

Descent

Stroll over the Cairngorm plateau, rimming Coire Raibeirt on about the 1060m contour, before climbing briefly to gain and then descend the Fiacaill a'Choire Chais ridge back to the Coire Cas car park.

Route 27 – Fiacaill Ridge, Cairn Lochan

Grade	150m I/II / 1/2 scramble
Distance	7km
Ascent	620m
Time	3½ hours
Start/finish	Coire Cas car park, Cairngorm ski centre (NH989061)
Maps	OS Landranger (1:50,000) 36
Accommodation	See Route 26
Sleeping out	Considering its accessibility, sleeping out under this route in winter would seem a bit barmy; but if you must, spots might be found between the boulders around the pools on the floor of Coire an t-Sneachda.
Public transport	See Route 26
Seasonal notes	A straightforward scramble in summer conditions – grade 1 if the difficulties are skirted to the right; grade 2 if taken direct. It can prove an awkward customer under fresh snow.

Easy scrambling aretes are not a major feature of the bulbous Cairngorm landscape. Most ridge climbs here follow steep buttresses on corrie headwalls, and are fairly challenging affairs. From the point of view of low-grade winter climbers and summer scramblers the range is not exactly brimming with eastern promise. Fiacaill Ridge is one of two notable exceptions (the other being Route 28). Dividing the spectacular headwalls of Coire an t-Sneachda and Coire an Lochain, this blocky crest is an excellent route onto the Cairngorm plateau. Brevity and ease of access make it an ideal half-day option. Since many difficulties are avoidable, and its setting is the least serious in the Cairngorms, Fiacaill Ridge is also well suited to novices. If only it weren't so short! Few good things last as long as they ought, so enjoy it while you can.

Approach

The ski road whisks you to 600m, an hour's walk at most from Coire an t-Sneachda and Coire an Lochain, the twin Northern Corries. Winter climbing is rarely packaged so conveniently; easy access to quality routes inevitably attracts the climbing hordes. Solitude is unusual here.

The approach is as for Route 26, just into the mouth of Coire an t-Sneachda. The back wall of the corrie grows steadily more imposing, but Fiacaill Buttress is still hidden in a fold of hillside. Fiacaill Coire an t-Sneachda bounds the glen on the right,

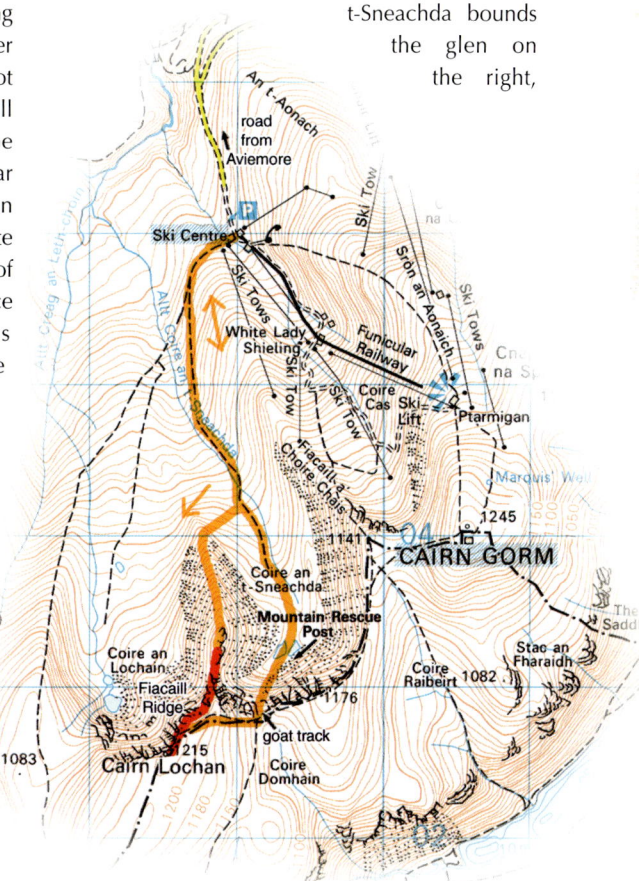

145

Coire an t-Sneachda (middle) and Coire an Lochain (right), divided by the Fiacaill Ridge, seen mirrored in Loch Morlich

saddle follow a more or less level section until the ridge rears up in a steep pile of blocks. This is the crux (II if taken direct). Sticking close to the left edge, a short chimney/groove provides an abrupt line onto the upper crest. With plenty of cracks and rounded blocks there is a wide choice of handholds, axe placements and even protection, should you want it. An easier alternative traverses briefly right before clambering back left up bouldery steps to the little level crest above. Continue along this, and then up a final steepening to reach easy ground at a broad headland, soon merging with the rolling plateau. Howling over this open vastness, the wind here can be alarming – sometimes downright dangerous. Head right along the rim of Coire an Lochain to the summit cairn of Cairn Lochan, if so inclined.

Descent
Go down to the broad saddle at the lip of Coire an t-Sneachda, between Cairn Lochan and Stob Coire an t-Sneachda (the col is marked as spot height 1111m on the 1:25,000 map). It can be nice to continue ENE around the edge of the corrie, perhaps bagging Cairn Gorm before returning to the car park on a neatly laid flagstone path (or snow) that descends the blunt spur of Fiacaill a Choire Chais. Soupy visibility or belligerent wind may render this option unattractive.

The quickest way to lose height and regain relative shelter in Coire an t-Sneachda is via the Goat Track. This zigzags down steeply between the Fiacaill Buttress (on your left if facing down) and Fluted Buttress on the main corrie headwall, eventually curving right below the latter to reach the pools on the corrie floor. Substantial snow masses often sit on the lip of this slope; when icy or unstable these can be hazardous. Under snow the entire descent requires care. Once back on ground that can't be fallen off, clamber over a boulder field, threading through the pools (often buried) and continuing back to the ski centre along the approach path.

appearing as a conical headland from this angle; it leads to your ridge. At around the 850m contour cross the burn, heading due W over rocks and heather onto the broad crest. The going is rough, but there's a trace of path leading through granite blocks onto the minor summit, a graceful perch by Cairngorm standards.

Scramble down easily from here, skirting right of a little blocky tower to reach a saddle before the steep buttress of the Fiacaill Ridge. Coire an Lochain is below on the right, and Coire an t-Sneachda to the left; either can be gained from here.

Climb
Fiacaill Ridge, 150m I/II or 1/2 scramble
The following route description applies in both summer and winter, but to maximise the challenge (and therefore the fun) it is best left for snowy conditions.

Throughout the climb broken slopes are accessible on the Coire an Lochain side, but the crest is more entertaining, the vertical Fiacaill Buttress providing a dose of exposure on the left. From the

27 – Fiacaill Ridge, Cairn Lochan

Entering the crux chimney/groove

Looking back along the ridge from near the top

THE CAIRNGORMS

Descending the Goat Track in a gale, Fiacaill Ridge forming the skyline above

Easy ground at the start of the Fiacaill Ridge

Route 28 – North East Ridge, Angel's Peak

Grade	300m 1/2 scramble
Distance	29km
Ascent	1500m
Time	9–11 hours
Start/finish	Sugarbowl car park at a hairpin on the ski road (NH985074)
Maps	OS Landranger (1:50,000) 36
Accommodation	See Route 26
Sleeping out	The Garbh Choire bothy (NN959986) is perfectly positioned to split the route over two days. Walk in on the afternoon of day one, then do the route and continue over Braeriach back to the car park on day two. The bothy is rustic to put it mildly, scarcely more than a heap of stones and some plastic sheeting – but it keeps the weather out. It comfortably holds only three with their kit; tall people may not be able to stretch full length. Consider bringing a tent in case the bothy is occupied.
Public transport	See Route 26
Seasonal notes	Though the ridge is only winter grade I, the length, remoteness and great altitude of this circuit makes it a relatively serious proposition. Bear in mind that the Garbh Choire bothy may be buried under snow, and remember that wild weather on the Braeriach plateau can be life threatening. Given a firm freeze the Lochan Uaine waterfall can be climbed as a fitting prelude to the ridge, 100m II.

This is a journey into the heart of darkness, a landscape so isolated and immense that the mere fact of its existence here in Scotland seems barely credible. The route treks long miles through the country's grandest hill pass to enter the vast bowl of An Garbh Choire, perhaps the snowiest, wildest and most magnificent corrie system in the land. The North East Ridge of Angel's

Braeriach (right) and Angel's Peak (left) with the North East Ridge in profile, viewed from Ben Macdui

THE CAIRNGORMS

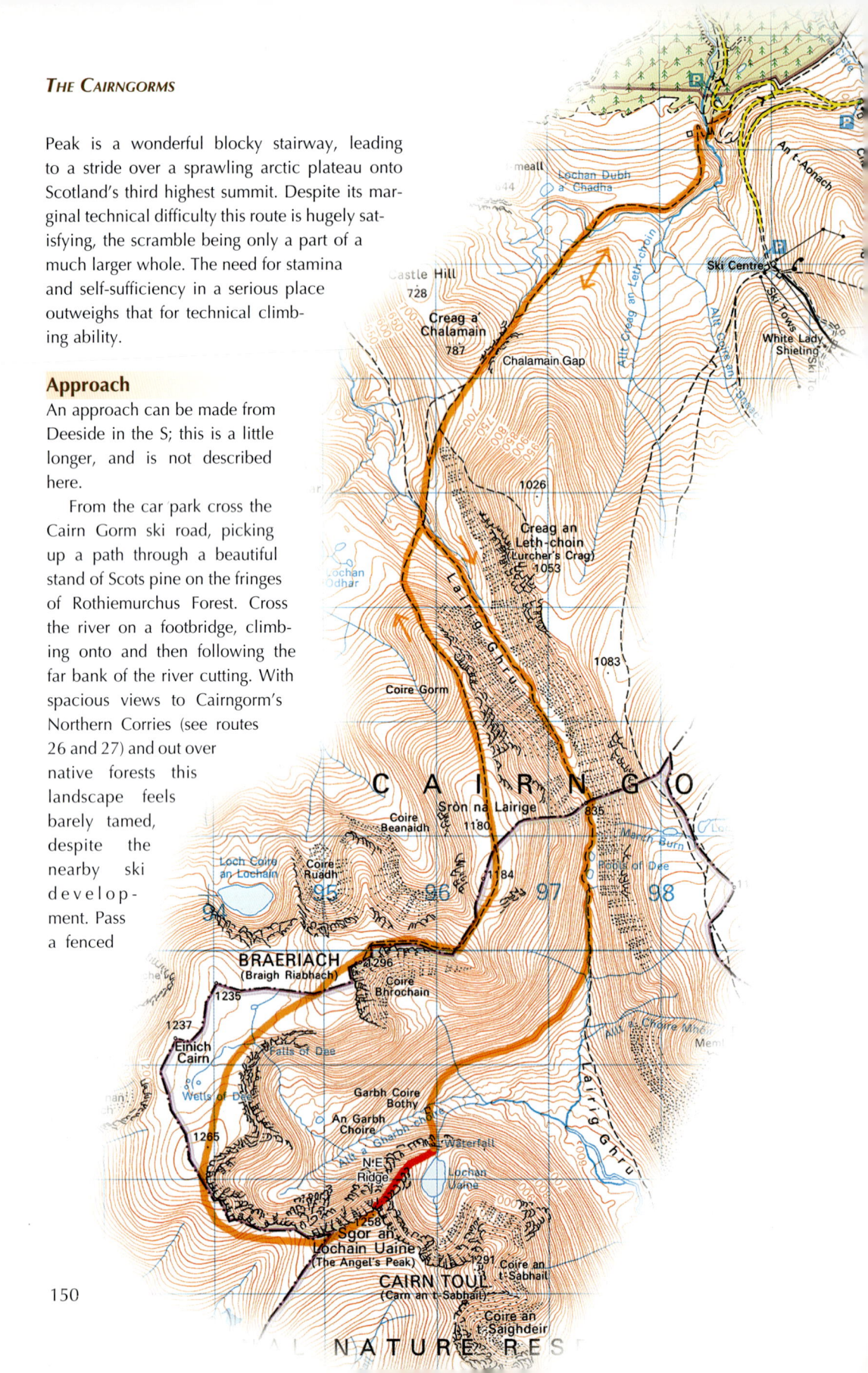

Peak is a wonderful blocky stairway, leading to a stride over a sprawling arctic plateau onto Scotland's third highest summit. Despite its marginal technical difficulty this route is hugely satisfying, the scramble being only a part of a much larger whole. The need for stamina and self-sufficiency in a serious place outweighs that for technical climbing ability.

Approach

An approach can be made from Deeside in the S; this is a little longer, and is not described here.

From the car park cross the Cairn Gorm ski road, picking up a path through a beautiful stand of Scots pine on the fringes of Rothiemurchus Forest. Cross the river on a footbridge, climbing onto and then following the far bank of the river cutting. With spacious views to Cairngorm's Northern Corries (see routes 26 and 27) and out over native forests this landscape feels barely tamed, despite the nearby ski development. Pass a fenced

28 – North East Ridge, Angel's Peak

The long, long walk-in: Angel's Peak (left) and Garbh Choire from the Lairig Ghru

enclosure where reindeer are often kept, sticking with the well-engineered path up to the Chalamain Gap. Clamber over heaped boulders in the floor of this curious dry gulch, emerging to see Braeriach looming ahead.

Drop to the floor of the Lairig Ghru, an enormous trench that divides the major Cairngorm massif in two, and follow the well-used path beneath its rotting craggy walls. Even on still days this section can act as a wind tunnel. The rocky high point is reached after about 3km gradual climb. Descend past the Pools of Dee; the driest path stays just E of the burn. At a height of 750m ford the stream to pick up a faint path contouring into An Garbh Choire, a great central bowl split into four semicircular hanging corries. This is a sight so enormous it makes you feel Lilliputian.

The ridge is now unmistakeable dead ahead, but the path disappears into heathery hummocks some way short of the mountain. One kilometre of tough going brings a brief respite at the tiny Garbh Choire bothy, dwarfed beneath the Angel's Peak. The North East Ridge is guarded by a slabby band, the lower lip of the hanging corrie sheltering Lochan Uaine. Climb steep broken slopes a little way W of the waterfall into the upper corrie. The loch shore would make a novel camp site, though who in their right mind would lug a tent up here? The North East Ridge is the right-hand skyline.

Garbh Choire bothy. Spartan lodgings, but what a location!

Climb
From a broad bouldery base the ridge steepens and narrows all the way to the distant summit. Plod up the easy lower section. Occasional pockets of scrambling begin to merge into something more significant, a succession of blocky steps and slabby ribs on perfect rough granite. There is a choice of line throughout, and the harder sections are all optional – including at one point a teeter along the rounded top of a garden-wall-type feature. A final steep blocky buttress leads all too suddenly to the summit. With the vast corrie complex arrayed below, this is a place to pause and marvel.

Continuation
From here the circuit around the An Garbh Choire to Braeriach isn't so much a continuation to the day as the quickest way home. It also happens to be the best walk of its kind in Britain, a grand stride over a huge empty plateau at 4000ft. This featureless country is a stiff test of navigation in the mist. Loop round W onto Carn na Criche, following the rim of the crags. Monster cornices can be left plastered around the lip of the corries long after snow elsewhere has melted, slowly sagging through the spring to leave weird crevasse features and tracks of avalanche debris. Not for nothing are these hills classed as sub-arctic. The gravelly

28 – NORTH EAST RIDGE, ANGEL'S PEAK

On the 'garden wall', a snowy Braeriach behind

wastes are gentle on the feet, and you'll soon be crossing the baby River Dee where it plunges over the cliffs. The summit of Braeriach comes a while later, poised above the pinnacled Coire Bhrochain crags, some of the largest in the Cairngorms.

Descent
Continue along the well-defined east ridge. Before the final top on the ridge the most-trodden path peels off left, descending to a saddle below Sron na Lairige. The trail now climbs briefly, passing just right of this minor summit and then staying fairly close to the edge overlooking the Lairig Ghru as it descends a rough rocky ridge heading towards your route of approach. Where it makes a steep descent at the end of the ridge, the path (formerly eroded but much improved in 2013) leads quickly into the floor of the Lairig Ghru. Cross the burn here and hike, footsore, back up through the Chalamain Gap.

THE NORTH AND WEST HIGHLANDS

Including everything north and west of the Great Glen fault line, this section covers by far the largest single area in the book. Here as nowhere else you can revel in a sense of the ancient, and a feeling of elemental rawness quite alien to the tameness of the rest of Britain. It is our frontier country, our Wild West, a place where climbers can still be genuine pioneers. With row upon row of mountains, frayed at the edges and fragmenting into water, this is perhaps the most special part of Scotland. Each hill has a startling oddball form, no two alike. The unique novelty of the landscape makes ridge climbing in the north-west particularly rewarding.

Loch Toll an Lochain and the incomparable Corrag Bhuidhe pinnacles from Sgurr Fiona, An Teallach (Route 40)

Route 29 – Great Ridge, Garbh Bheinn

Grade	Severe as described
Distance	12km
Ascent	880m
Time	9 hours
Start/finish	Layby off a section of old paved road in Glen Tarbert (NM928597)
Map	OS Landranger (1:50,000) 40
Accommodation	Most visitors will base themselves in Lochaber, as there are limited options on the other side of the loch. The Inchree Centre at Onich is the most affordable accommodation close to the Corran ferry (01855 821287). In Strontian, try Glenview Caravan and Camping Park (01967 402 123).
Sleeping out	Where it's not boggy the ground is either steep or boulder-strewn. In terms of camping spots, the best of a bad bunch are beside the burn high in Garbh Choire Mor.
Public transport	Ardgour is best accessed from the A82 via the Corran ferry, which takes both cars (expensive) and pedestrians/bikes (free). There is a regular bus service from Fort William.
Seasonal notes	Despite its relatively low altitude, Great Ridge is in winter condition more often than might be supposed, though less reliably and enduringly than elsewhere. The original line is grade III, while the Direct Start is IV, and may prove hard if the slabs aren't well iced; enter from the right to avoid the first pitch.

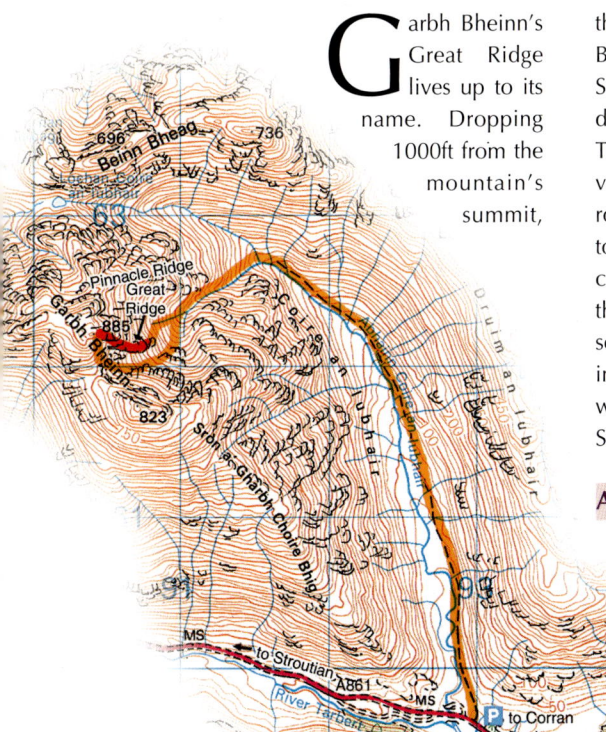

Garbh Bheinn's Great Ridge lives up to its name. Dropping 1000ft from the mountain's summit, this huge feature is well seen from Ballachulish Bridge on the opposite shore of Loch Linnhe. Standing across the water in the little-visited depths of Ardgour, it makes an intriguing sight. Though of sub-Munro status, Garbh Bheinn is very craggy indeed, with a wealth of fantastic rock climbing. Why do so few people bother to make the five-minute ferry crossing? While crowds throng nearby Glencoe you can enjoy this mountain's perfect rough gneiss in virtual solitude, pestered only by midges. With absorbing airy climbing, a rugged setting and fantastic west coast views, Great Ridge Direct is one of Scotland's mountain classics.

Approach

Head up Coire an Iubhair, following a path on the right side of the burn. What looks from a distance like lush grass becomes on closer acquaintance a soaking morass, in fact one of the mushiest approaches

The North and West Highlands

in this book. Enticing plunge pools and an unfolding view of Garbh Bheinn's jagged skyline keep your spirits – if not your legs – out of the mud. After about 4km of bog hopping, cross the stream and turn left, climbing rough ground below rocky hummocks and the shark's fins of Pinnacle Ridge (worthy scramble; see 'Descent', below), into the mountain's dramatic upper cirque, Garbh Choire Mor (not named on the Landranger map). Great Ridge is up on the right, looking vaguely reminiscent of the Ben's NE Buttress. The lower section is a mound of slabs split by grass terraces; the upper section a clean rock prow. Steep scree and boulders lead past the mouth of Great Gully, then left of a lone slabby tier to the hem of the main slab apron. The inferior original line (Diff) gains the clean upper ridge via mixed rock and grass to the right of these slabs, and just left of the gully. The Direct route is far superior.

Climb

Great Ridge Direct, 325m Severe

The exact location of the Direct route has been known to cause confusion, particularly perhaps for those who incline to the left. Start near the rightmost toe of the slabs, a few metres right of a steep corner, directly below a right-facing ramp which leans diagonally rightwards. Alright? Pitch lengths can be varied at will, particularly on the upper ridge.

Pitch 1

Climb a short bulging slab – short, that is, on both protection and holds – to gain the right-slanting diagonal ramp. Follow this, with unexpected exposure, to belay about halfway along. Seepage can be extensive on this and the following pitch.

Pitch 2

Continue easily to the end of the ramp. Step airily onto a blunt spike leading to an upper tier. Head slightly left, then straight up over layered slabby ledges. There's a big step-up between each layer, enlivened by small handholds and minimal gear. Enter a short steep corner – often wet. Climb this with interest to a well-worn grass ledge. Belay at the foot of a second steep corner.

Pitch 3

From the outside end of the ledge step up left onto the face, then climb easily to a second grass ledge. There's an obvious chimney flake in the wall above; climb the front face of this on good holds. Belay from a perched boulder on the lip of the third and largest grass terrace.

Pitch 4

The end of the Direct start. Walk diagonally right up grass to a dank little gully. Tackle this on slime and vegetation or – better – clean rock steps to the left. At the top cross yet more grass to the base of the continuation ridge. This pitch may prove too long to tackle in one go, forcing an intermediate belay at the top of the gully.

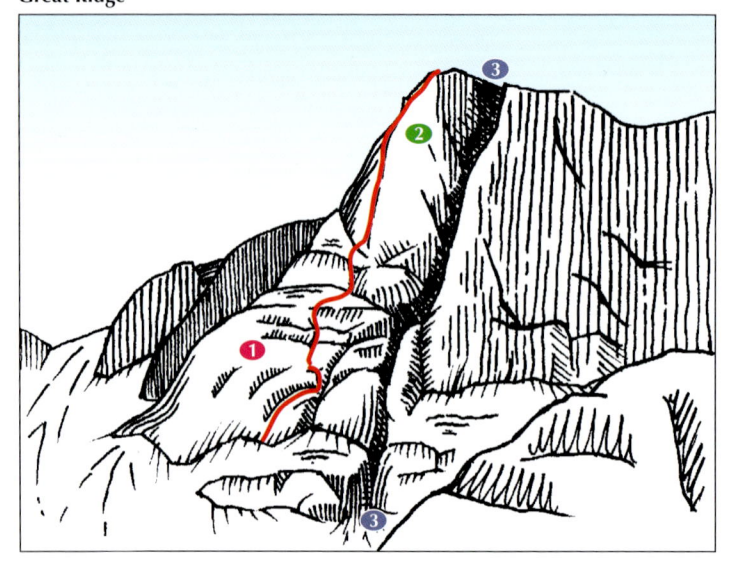

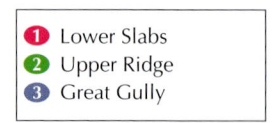

Great Ridge

❶ Lower Slabs
❷ Upper Ridge
❸ Great Gully

29 – GREAT RIDGE, GARBH BHEINN

Wild camp below Garbh Bheinn's Pinnacle Ridge (right). The upper section of Great Ridge follows the distant left-hand skyline.

Since this whole section is relatively easy, a sensible alternative might be to move together with running belays.

Upper Ridge
Competent parties might move together for the remainder of the route. On paper this is fine, since the upper ridge is officially graded only Diff. In practice, though, many people will prefer to pitch it until the angle eventually relents; pitch lengths can be varied at will. The grade seems in places to be an underestimate, especially compared to a benchmark Diff such as Tower Ridge; Great Ridge is both more sustained and, arguably, more exhilarating. The line offers a variety of tougher and easier options, but even the gentlest variants have their moments. The holds are generous, the moves interesting and the situations awesome – what more could you ask for? Nearing Garbh Bheinn's summit the difficulties ease, and moving

Hundreds of metres of air on the upper ridge

together becomes an option for all. The end, when it finally comes, is abrupt, depositing you right at Garbh Bheinn's summit cairn.

Descent
The quickest descent is to head briefly W towards a satellite top, soon picking up a path that curves round S, skirting the upper crags of Garbh Choire Mor (fantastic climbing) to reach a col at the corrie's head. Drop down steep scree and boulders under Great Ridge to regain the approach route.

Detours
For a good hillwalking circuit scramble N from Garbh Bheinn's summit down to the tiny lochan at the head of Coire an Iubhair. Climb onto Beinn Bheag and follow the rocky ridge back to the car park.

Alternatively, the energetic might enjoy climbing Pinnacle Ridge for good measure. From the top of Great Ridge descend back into Garbh Choire Mor, then head N to reach a slabby shoulder. The route climbs the first prominent pinnacle (actually no more than a step in the ridge, but sustained at Moderate), then continues more easily up the lovely crest above to land on the second tower. For details see *Scrambles in Lochaber* by Noel Williams (Cicerone).

Ant-like climbers, dwarfed by the upper ridge

THE NORTH AND WEST HIGHLANDS

Route 30 – North-North-East Ridge, Sgurr Ghiubhsachain

Grade	3 scramble as described (harder and easier variations exist)
Distance	16km
Ascent	1170m
Time	6½ hours
Start/finish	Riverside Forestry Commission car park at Callop (NM924793)
Maps	OS Landranger (1:50,000) 40
Accommodation	Glenfinnan Station Self Catering (01397 722 295). For options in nearby Lochaber see Route 14
Sleeping out	Convenient low level camping can be found both up the Allt na Cruaiche and on the grassy verges of the track along Loch Shiel.
Public transport	Buses and trains from Fort William to Mallaig stop at Glenfinnan
Seasonal notes	This route lends itself much more to summer scrambling than to winter climbing. The many rock buttresses would provide a succession of interesting little technical mixed pitches, but the amount of walking in between each would make for a very disjointed day out, the rope and rack constantly going in and out of the bag. The N-facing summit crags of Sgurr Ghiubhsachain might, however, merit further investigation in their own right, either in winter or summer.

The Mallaig road passes through wonderful country, all wrinkled rock and lush west coast vegetation. Between the long glens rise rugged mountains, fairly low but very striking. The peaks surrounding fjord-like Loch Shiel have nothing to offer the Munro bagger, and neither are there many major crags to lure climbers. They are all the more attractive for their relative unpopularity.

The hills are studded with outcrops, and dozens of short climbs and scrambles must be awaiting discovery. Of the established routes the NNE Ridge of Sgurr Ghiubhsachain is a corker, stringing together a succession of little buttresses, on which difficulties can be varied at will. The line lacks continuity, but the rock is impeccable and each section of scrambling seems better than the last.

Sgurr Ghiubhsachain from the lochside approach track

30 – North-North-East Ridge, Sgurr Ghiubhsachain

Approach
Take the bike-friendly woodland track, soon passing the turn-off to a made-up trail from Glenfinnan (possible alternative start point). The track now follows the shore of Loch Shiel for several kilometres to reach a cottage and fish farm at Guesachan. Just beyond the burn by the cottage, turn S onto a rudimentary boggy path that climbs onto the blunt NNE ridge.

Climb
There is plenty of hands-in-pockets walking to come, but a lot of optional scrambling too on outcrops of rough, dependable gneiss. The best line up the ridge crest seeks out each little buttress in turn, and though any of them could be completely avoided there should be no need to do so. Scrambling sections can be varied to suit, at any grade from 1 to at least VDiff; the line described is just one of many possible variables, technically at the upper limit of what can be considered a scramble.

Start scrambling low down on the ridge on a little raised rib of perfect rock. Above this a steep wall provides a few metres of vertical fun – quite butch if climbed on the right, but easier to the left. Pockets of escapable scrambling lead on, becoming more frequent. Climb the first major buttress direct, steep at first and then slabby. A second big outcrop offers a choice of lines leading to the minor summit of Meall a'Choire Chruinn. Clamber down to the shallow col (optional scrambling on the way) where a number of little pools offer a pretext for a breather.

The ridge now rises to the mountain's conical NE summit. Pass left of a steep wall (too hard for a scramble) to reach the foot of a long slab on the left side of the ridge, easily identified by the huge detached boulder underneath. Gain the slab, climbing its right edge in an exciting position for 30m or so. The summit crowns a steep set of crags; further walking and little outcrops bring you to the foot of this final and largest obstacle.

If necessary the steep face directly ahead can be outflanked entirely by looping wide right up the grassy hillside. Better climbing options include:

Magic moments on the NNE Ridge

a) follow slabby rocks just up and right of the steeper front face (grade 3); or
b) head only briefly up and right until below an obvious slanting ledge system. Gain this via some big blocks, and follow it up left. It's possible to stay with this line of minimal resistance, but better (VDiff) to quit it for the steep airy wall on the right, where good holds lead up to a niche.

All roads lead to a ledge below the last rock section. Here move slightly left to reach a rib bounding a slabby corner, and climb this with some exposure. Easy rocky ground now leads to the NE summit. The main summit is a little further on, marked by a large cairn.

Descent

To avoid a mass of slabs immediately below, backtrack to the gap between the two summits to descend a steep grassy slope almost due E onto the wide peaty saddle. If you've left bikes at Guesachan it's feasible enough to drop from here down Coire Ghiubhsachain back to the lochside track.

Continuation

Better, though, is to extend the circuit over Sgorr Craobh a'Chaorainn. A crag tier guards this fine rocky summit. In its middle the wall is steep, but there are nice grade 3 options either to the left or right.

Now descend the rugged NE ridge, bearing slightly right to avoid vegetated crags. From a level section climb over the pointy mini summit of Meall na Cuartaige and continue down rough ground to a soggy path in the Allt na Cruaiche glen. Soon meet a vehicle track at a small hydro development, and follow the W bank of the Allt na-Cruaiche back to the car park.

30 – North-North-East Ridge, Sgurr Ghiubhsachain

Is it really a scramble? The exciting wall on the summit crags.

THE NORTH AND WEST HIGHLANDS

Route 31 – Forcan Ridge, The Saddle

Grade	2 scramble
Distance	15km
Ascent	1380m (including ascent of Sgurr na Sgine)
Time	6 hours
Start/finish	Roadside car park on the A87 in Glen Shiel (NG968143)
Maps	OS Landranger (1:50,000) 33
Accommodation	Ratagan Youth Hostel (0870 004 1147), Kintail Lodge Hotel bunkhouse (01599 511 275), campsite in Shiel Bridge
Sleeping out	The Bealach Coire Mhàlagain is a potential wild camping spot, far from the madding crowd (if not the maddening clouds).
Public transport	Citylink buses to Portree run though Glen Shiel
Seasonal notes	The Forcan Ridge is one of the mainland's best winter traverse routes. The difficulties are high on the mountain and quite often snowed up. The climb is a much tougher proposition then, and fully earns grade II. People tend to abseil the steep descent from Sgurr nan Forcan.

Ridge walks are to Glen Shiel what the proverbial coals once were to Newcastle. You can barely set foot in the place without stubbing your toe on several. The glen is walled in by dozens of charismatic peaks, linked into complex strings by graceful curving crests. It is one of Scotland's finest mountain groups, enhanced still further in sunshine and snow. The landforms make for aesthetic hillwalking, though visitors of the mountaineering persuasion will be disappointed to discover that most ridge routes fall tantalisingly short of being truly engaging. Happily, there are at least two notable exceptions: the Forcan Ridge on the south side of the glen and Mullach Fraoch-choire (Route 32) on the north are described in this book. The route to the lofty summit of The Saddle is an engaging scramble on an exposed arete, with far-reaching west coast views. It is the best line in the area.

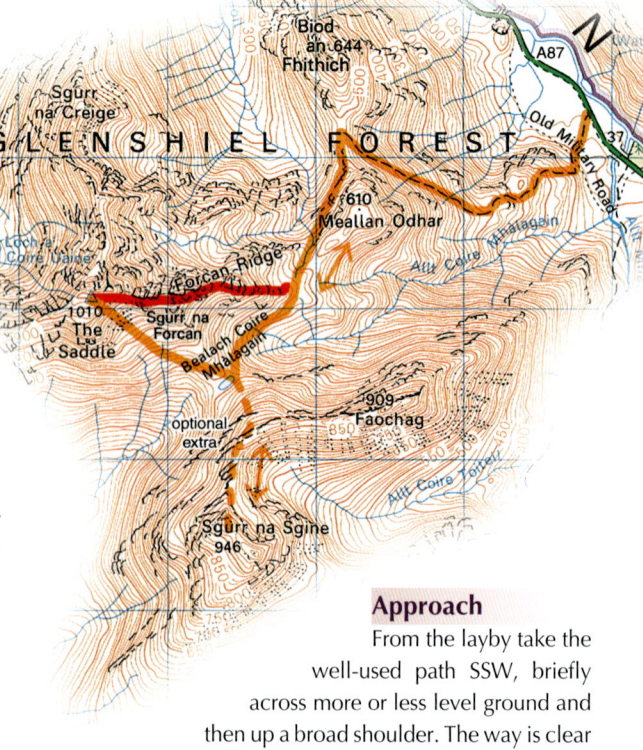

Approach

From the layby take the well-used path SSW, briefly across more or less level ground and then up a broad shoulder. The way is clear and friendly underfoot. The path effects a rising traverse of the steep Glen Shiel face of Meallan Odhar, landing you on a small col between this top and Biod an Fhithich. Stay with the path as it skirts

31 – FORCAN RIDGE, THE SADDLE

Sgurr nan Forcan (left) and the Saddle (right) from the Glen Shiel approach

Hand-traversing the clean-cut arete near the west end of the ridge, with Sgurr nan Forcan behind

THE NORTH AND WEST HIGHLANDS

Looking back at the Forcan Ridge and the Five Sisters from The Saddle

the head of Choire Chaoil, with the jagged Forcan Ridge now unmistakeable ahead.

Climb

Ascend grass and rocky bits to a small slab. Above is a corner, which might slow your progress in the damp. It's about as hard as anything further up, though short lived. Beyond this you're on the summit ridge of Sgurr nan Forcan, a sharp arete flanked by steep drops. Sticking with the crest is – as ever – the most entertaining option, with a few interesting blocky problems and plenty of exposure. The rock is very good, and the harder obstacles soon succumb with a bit of thought. An eroded path just below and to the right of the arete steers walkers past most of the trickier stuff at about grade 1, though to use it would be a wasted opportunity – both you and the route deserve better.

Airy Sgurr nan Forcan is a top spot for a brew. Just beyond is a sudden sharp descent into a gap. It's not more than 20m, but looks polished and scary. This is somewhat misleading, however, as it actually goes at a comfortable grade 2; best tackled by the most direct line. Easier but inferior earthy gullies cut down to either side; those with a sporting attitude will ignore them. On clearing the gap, a path follows a grassy crest, with occasional scrambly moments. At one stage you can hand-traverse a clean-cut arete, though sadly it's not compulsory. A brief steep ascent then gains the east top of The Saddle. Stroll past a couple of tiny lochans to the trig point.

Descent

One plan would be to continue W around the head of Coire Uaine, though this would steer you far from your start point. Easier is to descend SE into a little boulder-filled bowl, then on down grassy slopes to the Bealach Coire Mhàlagain. Assuming you've the motivation it's nice to climb Sgurr na Sgine while you're here; it's fairly steep, and longer than might be thought, but nowhere hard. The reward is a great view, including an unusual perspective on the Forcan Ridge in profile. Back at the bealach take an obvious path into Coire Mhàlagain, which wends its way down to your approach route.

Route 32 – South Ridge, Mullach Fraoch-choire

Grade	I winter
Distance	17km
Ascent	1200m
Time	8 hours
Start/finish	Roadside car park on the A87 in Glen Shiel (NH087122)
Maps	OS Landranger (1:50,000) 33 just barely covers the route. In case of an unplanned descent to the E bring Landranger 34 too.
Accommodation	For an extended stay in the wilds you can't beat rustic Glen Affric Youth Hostel (grid NH079203) (tel 0870 155 3255), only accessible on foot. This is a great base from which to tick the climb, plus many other backcountry peaks. For roadside accommodation options see Route 31
Sleeping out	An Caorann Mor is a suitable – if breezy – spot
Public transport	See Route 31
Seasonal notes	In summer the S Ridge is simply a scrambly hillwalk, and the pinnacles can be skirted or climbed at will. Firm snow can make things similarly straightforward. But deep unconsolidated snow renders things very tricky; in such conditions this could well feel like the hardest grade I ever.

North of Glen Shiel a vast emptiness stretches out towards distant Torridon, rippled waves of mountain and glen with no through roads, no villages, not much of anything at all. There's a lifetime of wild hillwalking and backpacking here, and perhaps even a few winter mountaineering gems yet to be unearthed. Rising at the southern fringe of this area A'Chralaig and Mullach Fraoch-choire afford glimpses of the interior and over the massed ranks guarding Glen

Climbing A'Chralaig, a stormy Glen Shiel menacing our backs

The North and West Highlands

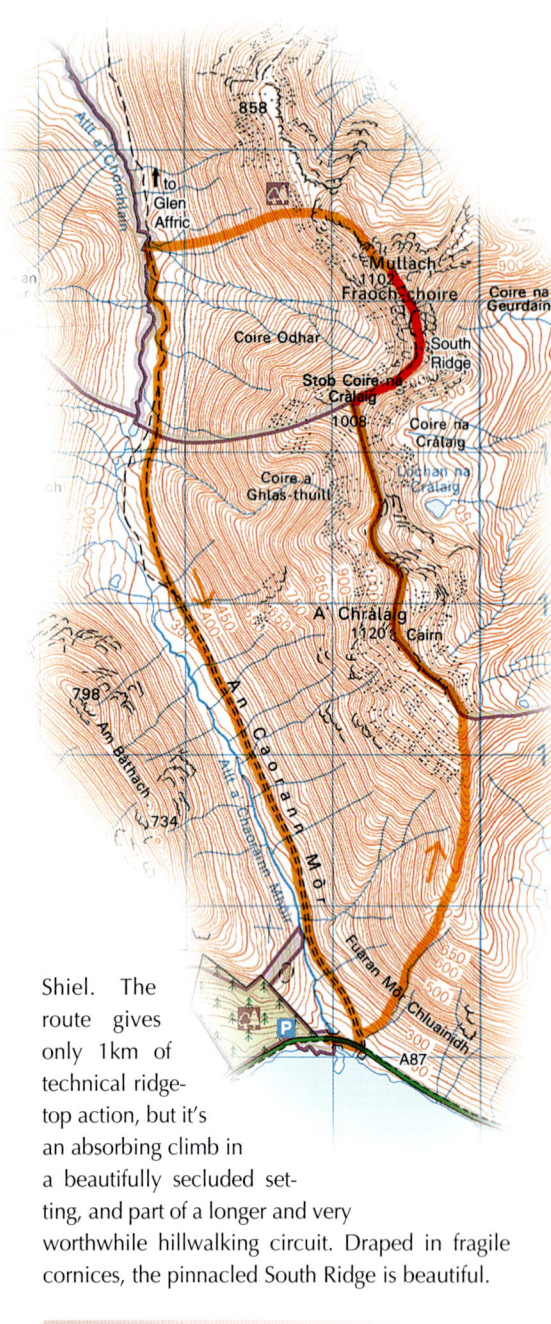

Shiel. The route gives only 1km of technical ridge-top action, but it's an absorbing climb in a beautifully secluded setting, and part of a longer and very worthwhile hillwalking circuit. Draped in fragile cornices, the pinnacled South Ridge is beautiful.

Approach

Park not far E of the Cluanie Inn at a woodside layby. Follow the track briefly into An Caorann Mor, soon branching right on a path (of sorts) that takes you direct up the breakneck grassy hillside just W of a stream bed. The 750m contour marks a welcome respite in the angle at the start of A'Chralaig's broad S Ridge. Follow the ridge, which can hold a substantial cornice. The ground grows stony underfoot as you near the summit, marked by a substantial cairn.

Descend N from A'Chralaig on a wide, gentle ridge, twisting left over a minor shoulder to avoid an outcrop before reaching a levelling at the top of A'Chralaig's blunt W spur. The spur provides an uncompromisingly direct means of ascent onto the ridge for those climbing the route from a base at Glen Affric Youth Hostel. Keep heading N, descending into a saddle before climbing easily onto Stob Coire na Cralaig. Take care in poor visibility, as this summit can carry a cornice on both its E and N sides at once. Gear up for the technical traverse here.

Climb

In friendly snow conditions you might not bother with a rope, but if ploughing through untracked mounds of the stuff, skirting the sometimes very large cornices, the potential for catastrophe will not be lost on you. Soft snow turns this section into quite some undertaking. A handful of nuts and slings should be sufficient equipment, while one walking axe apiece will be better than a pair of short tools.

Descend the ENE ridge – already notably tapered, with scrambly hints of what's in store. A col at 949m is the last point of potential escape for a while, N into Coire Odhar. Climbing again, the ridge begins to swing N, the ground increasingly tricky. Now the mountain bares its teeth, the crest riven into a rank of little pinnacles crowning the apex of sweeping snow slopes. Initially, any flanking manoeuvres can be more effort than they're worth, so clamber direct over each successive airy obstacle, weaving the rope around the many sound blocks and spikes as you go.

Soon reach a distinctive knife-edged pinnacle, an insecure roost on a windy day. This can be descended at its far end down awkward blocks leading into a tight notch. If fresh snow

32 – SOUTH RIDGE, MULLACH FRAOCH-CHOIRE

Skirting the knife-edged pinnacle in foul conditions

masks all the holds it may be quicker to descend steep snow on the right (E) flank instead, then traverse underneath the pinnacle (good spike runners) to gain the notch. Either variant will be performed more safely using fixed belays, rather than moving together.

Climb the next rock steps direct, passing a wide gully mouth on your right. Not far beyond, a big rock mass straddles the ridge. A steep blocky groove at its S end gives access to the pinnacle's summit – this is the other section that might be advisable climbed as a pitch. An easier alternative flanks left of the pinnacle, via a rock ledge along its base. Without further pause for thought the ridge now climbs direct to the summit cairn, perched on one of the airiest peaks in the region.

The North and West Highlands

Descent from Mullach Fraoch-choire, and things are looking up

Descent

The NW Ridge offers the safest way home, rough at first though not in the same league as the S ridge. Those based at Glen Affric Youth Hostel can continue straight off the end of the ridge, but if returning to Glen Shiel stay with the crest for only about 800m, just far enough to cross a minor bump and descend to the 900m contour. Now bear almost due W. Steep uniform slopes plunge into the glen, perhaps inviting a controlled glissade. Lower down, follow a bank between stream beds to gain the valley floor. Swing S on a boggy path, hiking over the watershed and on down the track to Glen Shiel.

Route 33 – Cioch Nose, Sgurr a'Chaorachain

Grade	135m VDiff
Distance	9km
Ascent	660m
Time	7 hours
Start/finish	Layby beside the roadbridge over Russel Burn (NG814413)
Map	OS Landranger (1:50,000) 24
Accommodation	Applecross campsite (01520 744268), Gerry's Achnashellach Hostel (01520 766 232), Torridon Youth Hostel (0870 004 1154). Other alternatives in Lochcarron.
Sleeping out	Below A'Chioch the ground is rough and boggy; best bet for a wild camp is beside the lochan in Coire a'Chaorachain.
Public transport	This area is not known for ease of access, but buses do run from Loch Carron to both Applecross and Shieldaig. Strathcarron is the nearest train station.
Seasonal notes	Due to its low altitude and coastal setting this crag rarely develops ideal winter climbing conditions. When in nick Cioch Nose is a hard grade IV mixed route, and the continuation onto the mountain's summit makes a long and committing day.

Taking a bold and challenging line up a superbly steep sandstone buttress, Cioch Nose must be the most impressive route of its grade in the country. Out pioneering in 1960, Bonington and Patey were no doubt surprised when the fierce frontal face of A'Chioch yielded so 'easily'. To modern visitors the idea that this formidable nose is breached by a mere VDiff seems just as unlikely – an impression not entirely dispelled when they get on the route. To paraphrase a notable wag, in Scotland the grade Very Difficult actually means very difficult; a particularly apposite comment in this case. Cioch Nose leads to a more rambling buttress above, leading in turn to the crest of Sgurr a'Chaorachain's scrambly East Ridge. Its succession of squat towers provides a satisfying conclusion to this mountaineering adventure.

Cioch Nose

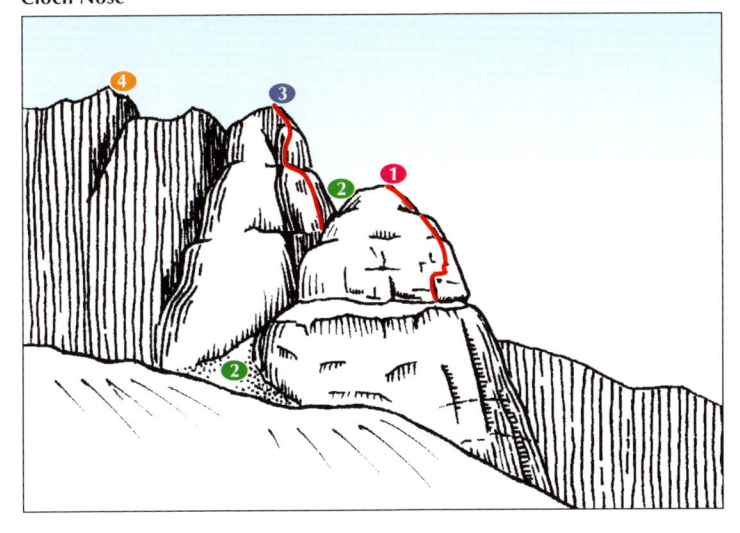

Approach

Even from the car park A'Chioch looks stunning. Cross the roadbridge and stroll up the road to the first sharp bend, where you take a gated track that splits off right to Loch Coire nan Arr. Quit the track at the dam to follow, lose and

❶ A'Chioch
❷ South Gully
❸ Upper Buttress
❹ Ridge scramble

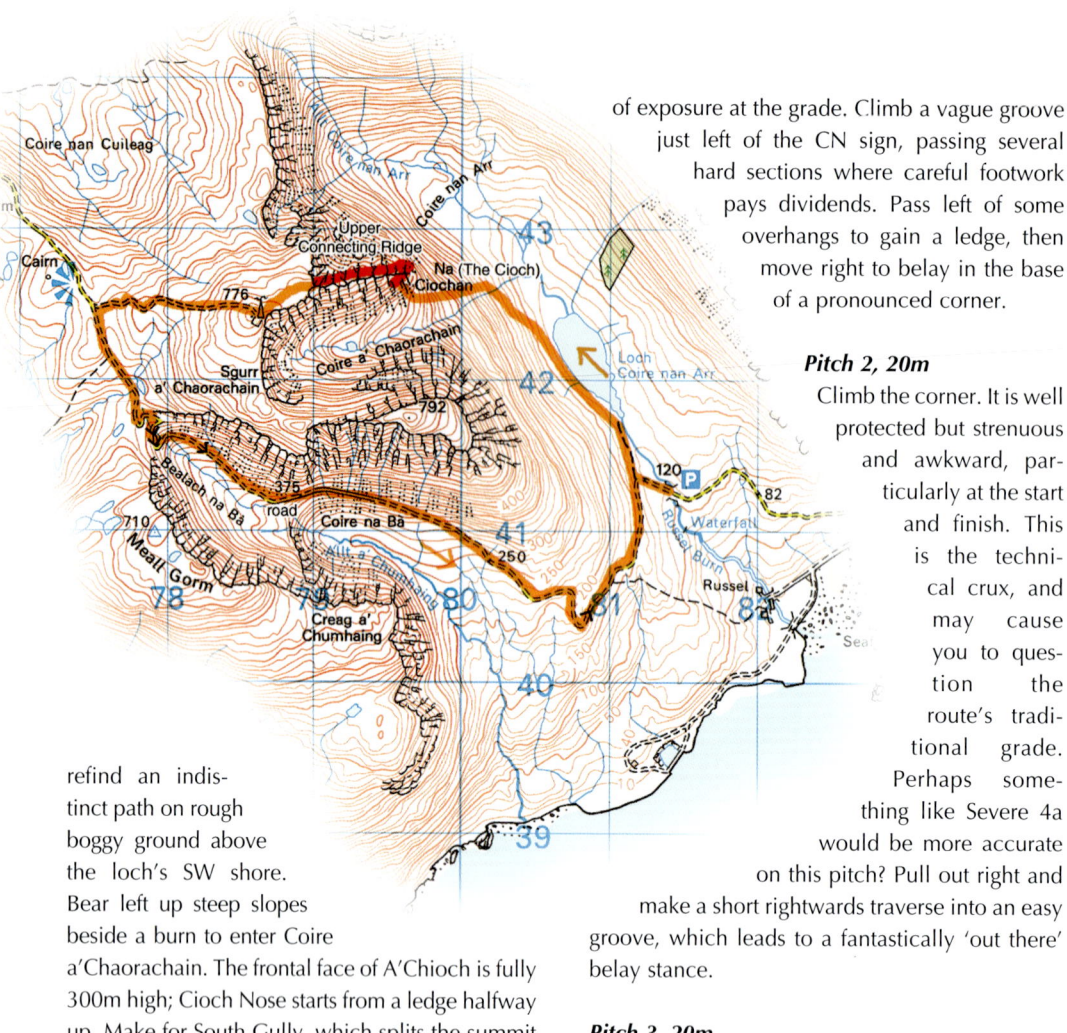

refind an indistinct path on rough boggy ground above the loch's SW shore. Bear left up steep slopes beside a burn to enter Coire a'Chaorachain. The frontal face of A'Chioch is fully 300m high; Cioch Nose starts from a ledge halfway up. Make for South Gully, which splits the summit of A'Chioch from the ridge behind. Head up a scree fan directly below the gully, tackling a short rock step to reach the grassy terrace of Middle Ledge. Head out right along the increasingly exposed ledge, climbing a short groove to belay some way beyond a line of low square-cut overhangs, where CN is scratched on a rock. It is possible to reach this point by climbing a route up the lower tier first – Cioch Corner Superdirect (160m HVS) is said to be the best choice (details in *Northern Highlands Rock & Ice Climbs*, vol 1, SMC).

Climb
Cioch Nose, 135m VDiff
Pitch 1, 25m
With over 150m of air beneath your heels from the off, this route has an almost unrivalled sense of exposure at the grade. Climb a vague groove just left of the CN sign, passing several hard sections where careful footwork pays dividends. Pass left of some overhangs to gain a ledge, then move right to belay in the base of a pronounced corner.

Pitch 2, 20m
Climb the corner. It is well protected but strenuous and awkward, particularly at the start and finish. This is the technical crux, and may cause you to question the route's traditional grade. Perhaps something like Severe 4a would be more accurate on this pitch? Pull out right and make a short rightwards traverse into an easy groove, which leads to a fantastically 'out there' belay stance.

Pitch 3, 20m
Psychologically speaking, this is the crux. Step right onto a wall in an improbable position, with the full height of the crag sweeping away below. Swing straight up on generous holds – steep but straightforward – past a rusty wire runner and an ancient peg. Bear slightly left to reach a reassuring stance directly above the previous one.

Pitch 4, 25m
Make a hard step-up to start, then follow easy ground, passing left of an overhung mass, then back right up a deep little groove onto a spacious grassy ledge and a block belay.

Pitch 5, 45m
Walk to the right end of the ledge, where another CN is scratched on the rock. Climb easier-angled

33 – Cioch Nose, Sgurr a'Chaorachain

From the approach, Cioch Nose promises great things. From near the right end of the horizontal grass ledge the route goes direct up the superb upper buttress.

ground. The holds are large and plentiful, though beware the odd loose chunk. The exact line can be varied at will, and the rounded pate of A'Chioch is soon won.

Possible descent
Walk to the neck connecting A'Chioch to the ridge behind. If time or weather threaten, it's possible to bail out here by descending left down South Gully. This is vegetated and unpleasant, making a very inferior end to the day. It's far better to continue up, thus turning a cragging route into a mountaineering expedition.

Continuation
The continuation route tackles the vegetated buttress immediately above A'Chioch. It starts as more of a scramble than a climb, with several short rock steps separated by much greenery. The drops, however, are still formidable, and moving together isn't out of the question. The last and biggest rock band leads to a grass terrace below

Pulling out of the crux corner on pitch 2

33 – Cioch Nose, Sgurr a'Chaorachain

A tricky descent on the East Ridge high over Coire a' Chaorachain

a prominent steep wall, a good 60m high. Going straight up the middle of this is said to be about Severe in standard, though the correct line doesn't exactly stand out. If in doubt head left. Just before a deep, dank gully, a clean groove cuts up and slightly right. Climb this at around VDiff, passing a couple of hollow-sounding blocks, two rubbly ledges and then a final wall.

On reaching the ridge crest stash climbing kit in the sacks and swap rock shoes for boots. Follow the ridge over a succession of squat rounded towers, forming the summits of the big North Buttresses (much scope for winter climbing). This is for the most part a rough, scrambly walk, though there are a number of interesting little grade 3 scrambling descents at the gaps between the towers. Thanks to the difficulty of access this fantastic stretch of ridge feels almost untouched. A cairn marks the summit plateau of Sgurr a'Chaorachain. Wander over to the surreal weather station for evocative views towards Skye's Cuillin.

Descent

Given the inclination it's worth returning to the car by a rugged hillwalking circuit around the head of Coire nan Arr – go N from the weather station, then curve E onto the summit of Beinn Bhan, the other great sandstone mountain of Applecross (see Route 34). A ridge then leads SE back to the road.

Much quicker, though, is to descend W down the weather station's access track onto the road at the Bealach na Bà. As this is one of Scotland's most dramatic road passes, the tarmac tramp or hitchhike back to the car can hardly be considered a chore.

175

THE NORTH AND WEST HIGHLANDS

Route 34 – A'Chioch Ridge, Beinn Bhan

Grade	150m II,3
Distance	9km
Ascent	940m
Time	8 hours
Start/finish	Verge-side parking on the causeway over the River Kishorn (NG835423)
Map	OS Landranger (1:50,000) 24
Accommodation	See Route 33
Sleeping out	The floors of corries Feola and Poite would make ideal campsites, though the walk-in from the road is quick enough to render winter camps redundant.
Public transport	See Route 33
Seasonal notes	Beinn Bhan's seaside position and low elevation conspire to make winter conditions less enduring than on bigger peaks inland. If caught in a cold snap, however, its major ice lines are among the best anywhere. As a mixed route, A'Chioch Ridge doesn't need such a prolonged freeze, and may prove to be a goer when higher hills are shrouded in new snow. A summer Moderate with more than its fair share of loose rock and greenery, this is a scenic and exciting trip at any time of year.

Of several Scottish rock features dubbed the Cioch, two crop up in Applecross barely three crow-flying kilometres apart. Thankfully confusion can be avoided. All they share is a name, being very different sorts of animal in the flesh. Sgurr a'Chaorachain's Cioch Nose (Route 33) is a justly celebrated rock climb, while Beinn Bhan's A'Chioch is best saved for winter. Given some white stuff, it too becomes one of the finest trips of its grade in the country. Route 33 starts

Approaching Coire na Feola – A'Chioch is the bulbous peak centre frame, the Upper Connecting Ridge obvious to its left

34 – A'Chioch Ridge, Beinn Bhan

the eye follows the ridgeline back into Coire na Poite, a vast tiered scoop down which tumble world-class icefalls. A'Chioch comes next, a bulbous limb set at right angles to the mountain's body. Left again is Coire na Feola, home to yet more great climbing. And so, to action.

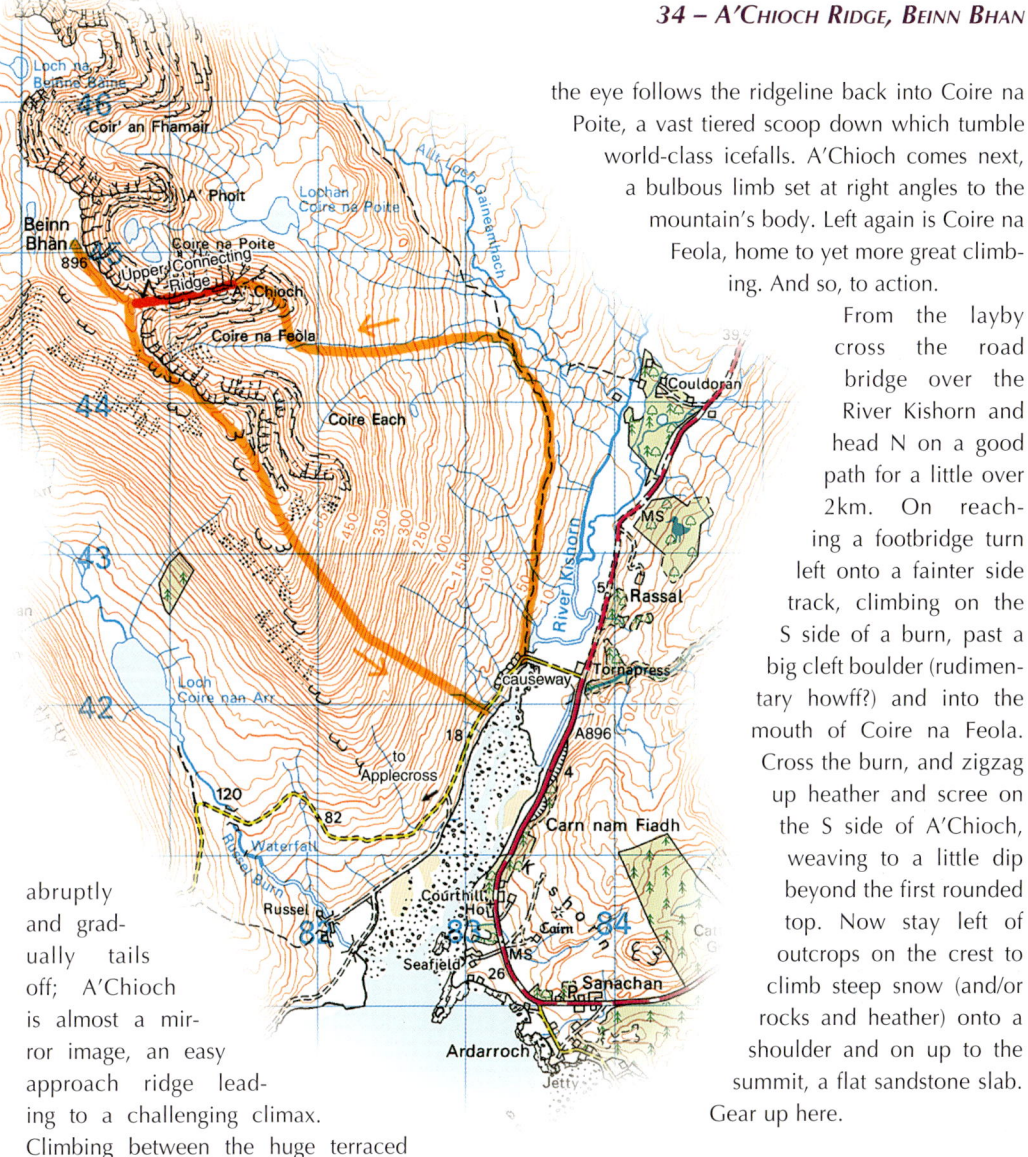

From the layby cross the road bridge over the River Kishorn and head N on a good path for a little over 2km. On reaching a footbridge turn left onto a fainter side track, climbing on the S side of a burn, past a big cleft boulder (rudimentary howff?) and into the mouth of Coire na Feola. Cross the burn, and zigzag up heather and scree on the S side of A'Chioch, weaving to a little dip beyond the first rounded top. Now stay left of outcrops on the crest to climb steep snow (and/or rocks and heather) onto a shoulder and on up to the summit, a flat sandstone slab. Gear up here.

abruptly and gradually tails off; A'Chioch is almost a mirror image, an easy approach ridge leading to a challenging climax. Climbing between the huge terraced headwalls of Beinn Bhan's ice-streaked corries, it is impossible not to feel humbled.

Approach

Before starting, drive up the A896 beyond Couldoran for a panorama of Beinn Bhan's E side, a truly unique display of rock architecture. On the right is the striking 'big wall' of Coir'an Fhamair, one of the steepest crags around. Jutting in front is A'Phoit, sister ridge to A'Chioch, with a giant breast-shaped terminal buttress. Leading to the mountain's summit plateau, its Upper Connecting Ridge is a rubbly Severe (winter IV). Scanning left,

Climb

The initial grade I ridge traverse is best tackled moving together – there are many blocks to weave the rope around. Now alive to the possibility of a fatal fall, descend broken boulders to reach the top of a short steep rock groove. Downclimb this with care (optional runners) into a little notch. Go up a turfy depression just left of the crest for 50m or so, emerging onto a dramatic narrow arete; follow this until overlooking the next saddle, at the foot of the Upper Connecting Ridge. Less experienced climbers might appreciate a fixed belay for this next section, which will

177

The North and West Highlands

The airy ridge crest – the Upper Connecting Ridge climbs the big rocky buttress ahead

require a full ropelength. Do not descend direct to the saddle. Instead, just before the abrupt end of the ridge cut rightwards down moderately steep snow for 20–30m, then cross back left on a ledge below the terminal nose, passing possible spike runners on the col to belay at its far end, just beneath the Upper Connecting Ridge.

Upper Connecting Ridge, 150m II,3

The climb now ups a gear or two. Customarily it is given II, though there are several mixed moves that would not disgrace a harder route, and I've graded it accordingly.

Pitch 1, 40m

Zigzag up straightforward turfy ground, with the odd interesting step, to belay almost at will.

Pitch 2, 25m

This pitch breaches a steep rock band. Go up and right into a clean-cut groove, providing good wire protection. Bridge up it, with several hard moves (hooks and torques for those that like that sort of thing) until quitting the groove at the first opportunity to sidle right along a turf ledge, and then back left above the top of the groove, traversing across some little rock spikes to belay on a generous ledge.

Pitch 3, 40m

Move up, then step right to gain a shallow turfy groove system. Continue in this with no notable difficulties to belay at the base of a vertical tier. Ensure that the second is positioned clear of any falling rock that might be sent down the following pitch.

34 – A'Chioch Ridge, Beinn Bhan

Looking back along the impressive A'Chioch crest from the Upper Connecting Ridge

Pitch 4, 45m
Go straight up a little chimney/gully above the belay, the only breach in the rock tier. Surmount a chockstone (tough in poorly consolidated conditions) and continue more easily to reach a short steep corner/groove, perhaps the technical crux of the route. Both protection and reliable axe placements can be hard to find here, so don't rush things. Pull out onto safer ground, the end of difficulties coming shortly after at a wide belay ledge.

Do not be tempted to try to outflank this crux groove up a tottering rib of stacked blocks to the left – unless, that is, bombarding your partner in a kamikaze shower of falling boulders and flailing axes appeals. Take the author's word for it, this diversion will only lead to a memorable wobble.

From the ledge at the top of the graded climb continue roped together up the final exposed snow and rock arete, soon emerging onto Beinn Bhan's plateau. The true summit is a few minutes' stroll to the NW.

Descent
Turn S along the rim of Coire na Feola and over a minor top above Coire Each. There's a photogenic perspective on A'Chioch in profile and, SW, to the Cioch of Sgurr a Chaorachain. Descend the ridge a while longer to outflank crags, before dropping ESE at about the 650m contour, making a direct descent down boggy heather slopes to the road.

THE NORTH AND WEST HIGHLANDS

Route 35 – Beinn Alligin Traverse

Grade	I
Distance	10km
Ascent	1200m
Time	6 hours
Start/finish	Car park near Torridon House (NG869577)
Maps	OS Explorer (1:25,000) 433, OS Landranger (1:50,000) 24
Accommodation	Torridon Youth Hostel (0870 004 1154), adjacent campsite for hardy souls, Kinlochewe Hotel Bunkhouse (01445 760 253)
Sleeping out	Ample wild camping options beside the Abhainn Coire Mhic Nobuil, so long as you don't mind the odd tussock.
Public transport	No laughing matter. Infrequent buses connect Diabaig and Torridon with Kinlochewe and Achnasheen
Seasonal notes	Grade 1 scramble in summer, and very worthwhile. At its best, however, under snow, when it makes a perfect intro to winter mountaineering ridges.

There are few more evocative sights than a snow-dusted Beinn Alligin at dawn, especially so if you're lucky enough to be setting out on this route. The rounded Horns and the remarkable cleft of Eag Dhubh are compelling features, inviting closer inspection. Romantics will be keen to learn that Beinn Alligin means 'Jewelled Mountain', a tag that is fully deserved. It's a wee gem. The traverse of the mountain in summer is a popular hillwalker's route with airy situations and a reasonable amount of scrambling interest (barely grade 1). However it's not on a par with the exciting Fasarinen pinnacles of neighbouring Liathach (Route 36). To maximise mountaineering enjoyment you're best off waiting for a snowfall, at which point the Horns show their teeth – if you'll pardon the mixed metaphor.

Approach

Follow the E bank of the Abhainn Coire Mhic Nobuil on a good path, at first through a patch of Scots pine and then onto open ground. After nearly 2km cross the Abhainn Coire Mhic Nobuil on a footbridge, then turn left at a trail junction to ascend towards the

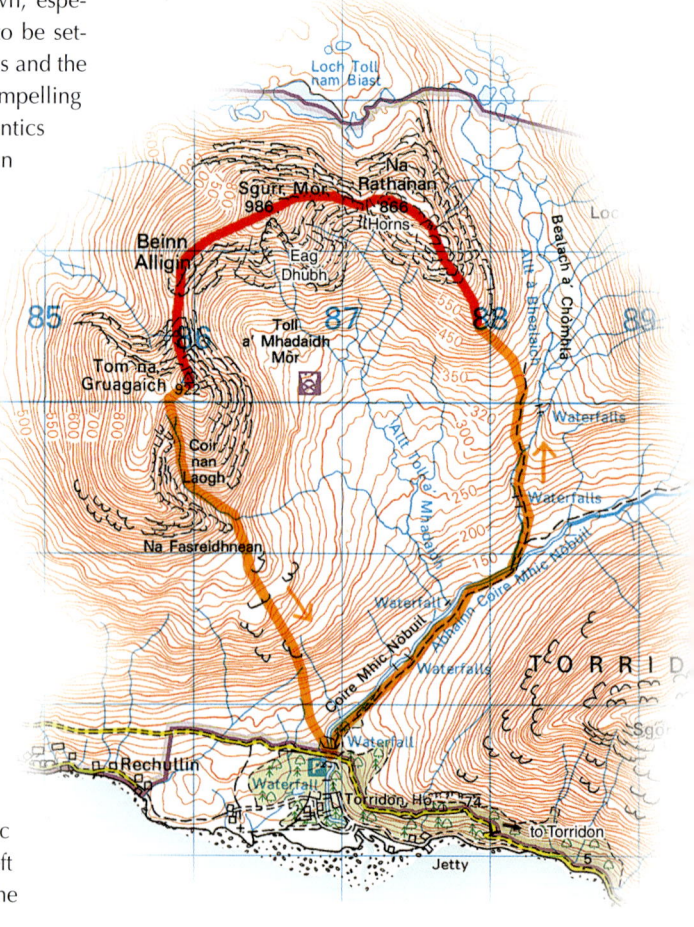

Beinn Alligin from across loch Torridon. The Horns are prominent on the right, while Eag Dhubh cleaves the centre summit.

Bealach a' Chomhla. Cross the Allt a' Bhealaich on a second footbridge, then soon after branch left where a cairn marks a path junction.

Climb
The terminal buttress of Na Rathanan looms above. A well-made path winds steeply up the heathery crags, and some simple scrambling is required on coarse weathered sandstone. Pass over a pronounced shoulder to make the final climb towards the lowest and most dramatic of the three Horns.

Note
Not far below this rocky peak a path can be met to traverse the broken slopes just left of and below the Horns; though this misses out the scrambling of the ridge crest it's worthwhile in its own right. In snow it may prove no safer than the Horns.

Once up on the summit of the first Horn typical Torridonian terraces plunge away on all sides beneath you, and in winter conditions beginners might appreciate a rope. Descend a series of sloping ledges and short steep rock steps (crux of the route) to reach a narrow col below the second Horn. This gives a rough ascent with some hands-on fun. There's a little more light scrambling in the descent to the gap on the far side of the second Horn. From here another climb up broken rocky tiers gains the third Horn, the summit of which forms a short level rock crest. Now descend to a low col before plodding up the long convex slope leading onto Sgurr Mhor, Beinn Alligin's principal peak.

The summit view is among the best anywhere. Near at hand, the Horns, Beinn Dearg and the two big Torridon monsters look awesome; at your feet the glittering expanse of Loch Torridon stretches out to sea and the isles. Just beyond the

The eastern-most Horn and distant Liathach (Route 36)

top, the ridge broadens above the enormous rift of Eag Dhubh – staying close to the left edge is the most entertaining course. Easy ground leads over a minor top to a dip before Tom na Gruagaich. With a little easy scrambling along the way, skirt the rim of the huge (and often ice-smeared) corrie face to gain this final summit.

Descent

Head briefly SW to a shallow col, then drop into the steep-floored trough of Coire nan Laogh. A well-used path descends the corrie beside a burn to reach the moors below. It then passes over a rough knobbly shoulder before making the final descent to the roadside by the car park.

The Horns and Beinn Dearg from Sgurr Mor

THE NORTH AND WEST HIGHLANDS

Route 36 – Liathach Traverse

Grade	II
Distance	12km
Ascent	1300m
Time	9 hours
Start/finish	Coire Dubh Mor car park (NG957568). Starting here adds some distance to the day, but gives the most interesting route onto the ridge.
Map	OS Landranger (1:50,000) 25 and Explorer (1:25,000) 433 (recommended)
Accommodation	See Route 35
Sleeping out	People have been known to camp wild in secluded bits of Glen Torridon, though in winter there's little to be gained from this.
Public transport	See Route 35
Seasonal notes	A hillwalker's favourite, Liathach is among the mainland's best summer ridge traverses, up there with Aonach Eagach and An Teallach. Minus snow the Fasarinen Pinnacles are a beautiful grade 2 scramble; in these conditions most difficulties can be avoided via a rough airy path on the S side of the crest (unpleasant if banked out with late-lying soft snow).

Tier upon crumbling tier of sandstone, layered up looming ice-streaked faces to a skyline of shrouded pinnacles and white-caked summit cones; wintry Liathach is a monstrous mass, uniquely brutish, a shameless hogger of the limelight. Is there a finer mountain anywhere? Sweeping straight out of Glen Torridon in a vertical elevation not far short of El Capitan, few Highland scenes make a climber's palms sweatier. Except, of course, the view of the other – even more impressive – side of the same hill. The Liathach traverse is a winter mountaineering classic, a route of great atmosphere, challenge and exposure, but often without undue technicality. Surrounded on all sides by steep, complex ground that permits few chances of escape, the dominant feeling is of being cut adrift from the world below, thrown upon your

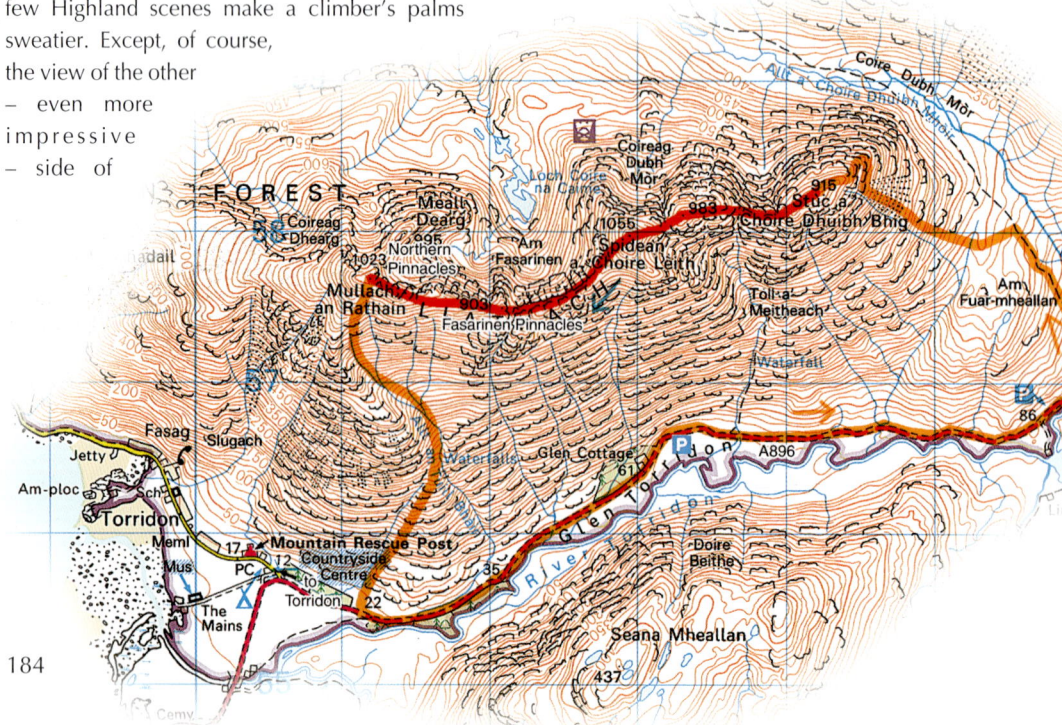

Liathach hogs the limelight above Glen Torridon

own resources. No wonder Liathach is generally considered to be mainland Britain's most serious winter mountain traverse. As with the chapter on Aonach Eagach (Route 13), the route description is for snowy conditions, though it also holds good for a summer visit.

Approach

Some guidebooks advocate an approach from the layby in Glen Torridon just E of Glen Cottage: climb a well-laid path N beside the cascading Allt an Doire Ghairbh into the high cirque of Coire Liath Mhor; keep E of the burn to scramble over rough blocks onto a more or less level saddle on the main ridge between Stob a Choire Liath Mhor and Bidean Toll a'Mhuic. This is the quickest and easiest way to gain the ridge E of the main summit, and should also be borne in mind as the best descent route at the end of the day for those who have done the traverse W–E (say, after an ascent of the Northern Pinnacles, Route 37). However, there is a more exciting option, described below.

From the car park follow the major path up Coire Dubh Mor. At about 300m altitude look for a cairn that marks a junction with a less-clear path. Turn left onto this, aiming for the E slopes of Stuc a'Choire Dhuibh-Bhig at a point a healthy distance left of the dank terminal crags. Rough going gains steep scree and vegetation; zigzag up, not far right of a burn issuing from a prominent gully in the big crag band above. Some way short of the crag band, bear right, crossing easy snow slopes (or vegetated sloping terraces) above the terminal nose to gain the blunt NE Ridge of Stuc a'Choire Dhuibh-Bhig. Follow this ridge to the summit, scrambling up entertaining blocks – a great introduction to the amusements in store. Above the scrambly sandstone band you move onto a cap of quartzite scree, the weird feature that gives Liathach its distinctive conical summits.

Climb

Over the first few summits the ground underfoot is all stony scree, making for rough going. Although neither technical nor particularly exposed, the route as far as the Fasarinen Pinnacles requires care in the winter, uniform

The North and West Highlands

Is there a finer mountain anywhere? Sunset stains the Fasarinen Pinnacles, as seen from the Northern Pinnacles (Route 37)

snow slopes meeting in roof-top crests, dropping on all sides to the great vertical sandstone layers lower down the mountain. An accidental slide would be unthinkable.

Descend around the head of Coireag Dubh Beag, crossing the saddle as reached by the Coire Liath Mhor path (see above). Continuing W, the ridge narrows briefly above a deep gully dropping S into Coire Liath Mhor. Climb easily over the twin heaps of Stob a Choire Liath Mhor to reach a tight little col beyond. *Gullies on either side of the crest give a possible means of escape here, though the N side is a grade I downclimb, and the S involves tricky route finding through crag bands.* Carry on up to the mountain's main peak, Spidean a'Choire Leith. With luck the stony summit ridge will have been transformed into a gently corniced crest, the cleanest of curving lines.

The summit affords the first pulse-quickening view of the Fasarinen Pinnacles, a rank of teeth with giddying gulfs to N and S. Meall Dearg and the Northern Pinnacles (Route 37) are also well seen from here, and the impression is of austere majesty, more Alpine than Scottish. Descend with mounting trepidation, skirting the lip of Coire na Caime along a gently inclined crest to a notch before the Pinnacles. Gear up here. The rope can be woven around blocks and spikes as you go, so a few extra nuts and slings should do.

As with the crenellated sections of other great ridge traverses, a variety of lines is available at any given point; the ground is so complex in close up that a blow-by-blow route description would prove more a hindrance than a help. Sticking as close as possible to the crest provides the soundest rock and the purest climbing experience,

Approaching the Fasarinen Pinnacles

grade II throughout. There are innumerable short mixed passages up and down the tight-packed towers of blocky sandstone, and even a balance along a tightrope spine, the kind of airy situation normally associated with space walking. Should the adrenaline prove too heady, it is possible at many points to move down onto an eroded flanking path that traverses breakneck slopes to the S of the crest. In summer this inferior option tends to be preferred by the less audacious, but when banked by fresh or slushy snow it is insecure and a dubious choice.

Between here and Am Fasarinen there are several teeth, the first flat-topped, and the third in particular very spiky. It's all so thrilling, so absorbing; the only regret is that it doesn't continue for longer. After about 700m things begin to ease off, a level platform signalling the end of the main event. The rim of Coire na Caime now rears up towards its apex at Mullach an Rathain. Plod W over a minor peak to the trig point on Liathach's most elegant summit.

Descent

Descend about 200m SW into the steep scree shoot of Toll Ban, which is descended for several hundred metres. Hard snow here demands caution, though in benign conditions the course of the burn offers a tremendous glissade. Reach a broad, gently sloping bay. At around 530m cross to the W side of the burn on a clear path that soon quits the course of the stream and heads S onto a rocky shoulder, winding down through sandstone bands and bogs to regain the road beside a small plantation. Slog back E along the tarmac for nearly 5km, waving a hopeful thumb at any passing traffic – if there is any.

THE NORTH AND WEST HIGHLANDS

Route 37 – Northern Pinnacles of Mullach an Rathain, Liathach

Grade	150m II/III
Distance	15km
Ascent	1000m
Time	9½ hours
Start/finish	Coire Dubh Mor car park (NG957568). Starting here permits the possibility of making a full traverse of Liathach, the reverse of Route 36.
Map	OS Landranger (1:50,000) 25 and Explorer (1:25,000) 433 (recommended)
Accommodation	See Route 35
Sleeping out	The lochans cupped between Liathach, Beinn Eighe and Beinn Dearg, at the junction of Coire Dubh and An Drochaid, provide fine wild camping. However, after this climb it may not prove easy to descend back to a tent sited here.
Public transport	See Route 35
Seasonal notes	A summer Moderate. Derided by some for loose rock, the Northern Pinnacles are actively recommended by others, and the issue of looseness said to be overstated. Given the generous vegetation, random scree piles and general wobbliness, a sensible compromise is to suggest that it's probably a worthwhile climb in summer, if treated with respect.

Mountaineers can be a misanthropic bunch. But then stirring isolation is an essential part of the game, and an aspect it's hard to appreciate with other idiots milling about all over your chosen hill. So here's one for all you Victor Meldrews out there – you'd better believe it. Hard to reach and serious for the grade, the Northern Pinnacles are rarely crowded. But why? Passing through some of the most awesome positions on a mountain known for nothing else, this is a challenging Torridonian adventure, up there with the best. Thanks to its unjustified neglect, the line is often free from the trough of footprints guiding parties along the adjacent Am Fasarinen crest (Route 36). Coupled with the full Liathach traverse, the Pinnacles make one of Scotland's most sought after winter outings, an ambitious goal that only fast-moving teams are likely to achieve.

Approach

Parking at Coire Mhic Nobuil as for Beinn Alligin (Route 35) makes for a moderately shorter day, with a descent of Mullach an Rathain's broad W ridge instead of a final tarmac tramp. An approach from the E is recommended, though, if only for the view of Liathach's stupendous wild side, home to some of the UK's most celebrated ice climbs.

Take the well-laid Coire Dubh Mor path, under the nose of Stuc a'Choire Dhuibh-Bhig (see Route 36). Some while later pass the turn-off for Beinn Eighe's Coire Mhic Fhearchair, weaving through hummocks along the N shore of a group of lochans. Beyond the outflow from Loch Grobaig, ford the main burn and continue towards Meall Dearg on rough, pathless ground, crossing several smaller streams to reach the NW foot of the mountain (arduous if breaking trail in deep snow). Skirt right under Meall Dearg's big terraced wall until below a scree bowl on the W side of the mountain, rising into Glas-toll Bothain. Climb steep turf and scree left of a little burn (occasionally copious ice), continuing into the upper spike-rimmed corrie. The Northern Pinnacles form the left-hand skyline.

Climb

Though originally graded II, the Northern Pinnacles are more of a proposition than other IIs in the book, and I've felt obliged to give them a modest upgrade. From Coire na Caime, a full traverse of Meall Dearg en route to the Pinnacles

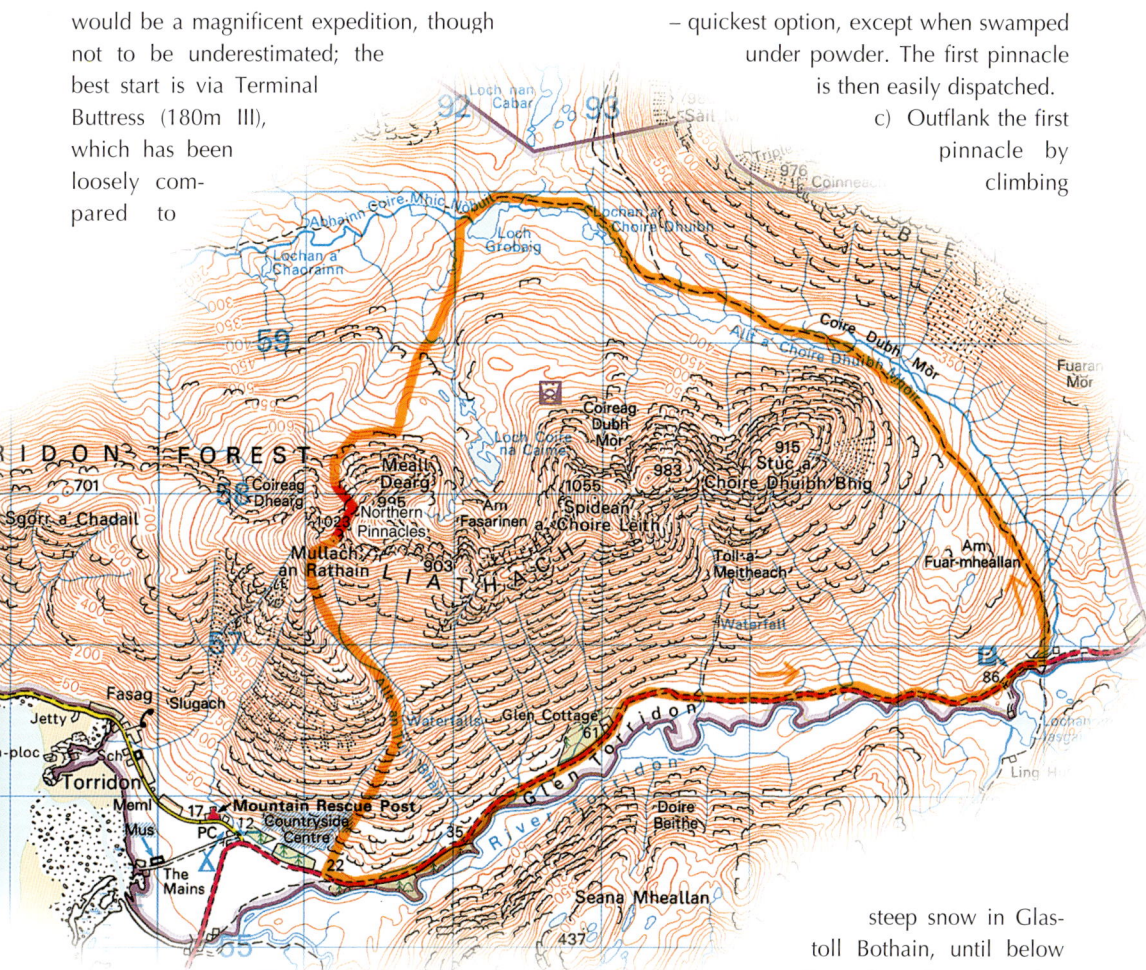

37 – Northern Pinnacles of Mullach an Rathain, Liathach

would be a magnificent expedition, though not to be underestimated; the best start is via Terminal Buttress (180m III), which has been loosely compared to Tower Ridge. The catch is its low altitude, and thus the rarity of good nick. Most will be content with the Pinnacles themselves.

Numbered from one to five, the Pinnacles look like separate towers from some angles, though on close acquaintance they turn out to be an ascending series of rock steps in a ridge, with minimal descent between each. From Glas-toll Bothain there are several ways to the ridge crest.

a) Climb due E up steep turf (a solid freeze desirable) to Meall Dearg's pointed summit, then descend the thin arete to the foot of the Pinnacles.
b) Climb an obvious narrow gully (grade I) between Meall Dearg and the Pinnacles – quickest option, except when swamped under powder. The first pinnacle is then easily dispatched.
c) Outflank the first pinnacle by climbing steep snow in Glas-toll Bothain, until below a line of weakness running right–left up the side of the ridge. Two pitches of I/II up snow, frozen turf and icy rock steps gain the level crest between the first and second pinnacles, at the start of the major difficulties. There's a good rock belay at the foot of the second pinnacle.

Pitch 1

Forming a keen blade, the second pinnacle is too hard to attempt direct. Traverse right of the blade on a rocky terrace to reach a short, tricky wall. Place gear in the corner on the left before committing; a few tough moves gain easy ground beyond the diving-board tip of the second pinnacle. Continue a little way up the third pinnacle to belay below a steepening.

189

The North and West Highlands

Meall Dearg (right) and the Northern Pinnacles from Am Fasarinen (Route 36)

Pitch 2
There are hard mixed moves straight off the belay, with blocks to hook and wire placements for protection. Gain a shallow icy groove above. Move up this past a couple of little steps to reach a steep rock mass, which must be outflanked. Move left tentatively, seeking out cracks for wire protection and axe torques, into another groove line. Continue to a block belay.

Pitch 3
Step left, then up a slabby groove to reach the base of a vertical tower. There is now a choice:
a) climb the tower via a cracked wall on its left side, overlooking Coire na Caime – tricky but well protected
b) otherwise, sidle right a few metres to enter a short icy chimney leading to the top of the third pinnacle.

Pitch 4
Descend until between the third and fourth pinnacles, at a neck where gullies on either side of the ridge meet up. Go up easily until directly beneath the rotten-looking tower of the fourth pinnacle. Now move right on a terrace system for around 15m. If gear placements are buried, this can feel a tad necky. Continue into a little vertical groove; climb it (tip: hook blocks with your axes) to a chock and sling belay at the top of the fourth pinnacle.

The fifth pinnacle is just a scree heap en route to Mullach an Rathain, though with steep snow slopes plunging below it's worth staying roped up to the summit cairn. After all this, only fast parties are likely to have time for the continuation traverse over Am Fasarinen (the reverse of Route 36).

Descent
Those who have parked as for Beinn Alligin (Route 35) simply have to descend Mullach an Rathain's broad W Ridge. If returning to the E end of Liathach, however, see the descent for Route 36.

Pitch 1: skirting the second pinnacle, on a day of questionable weather

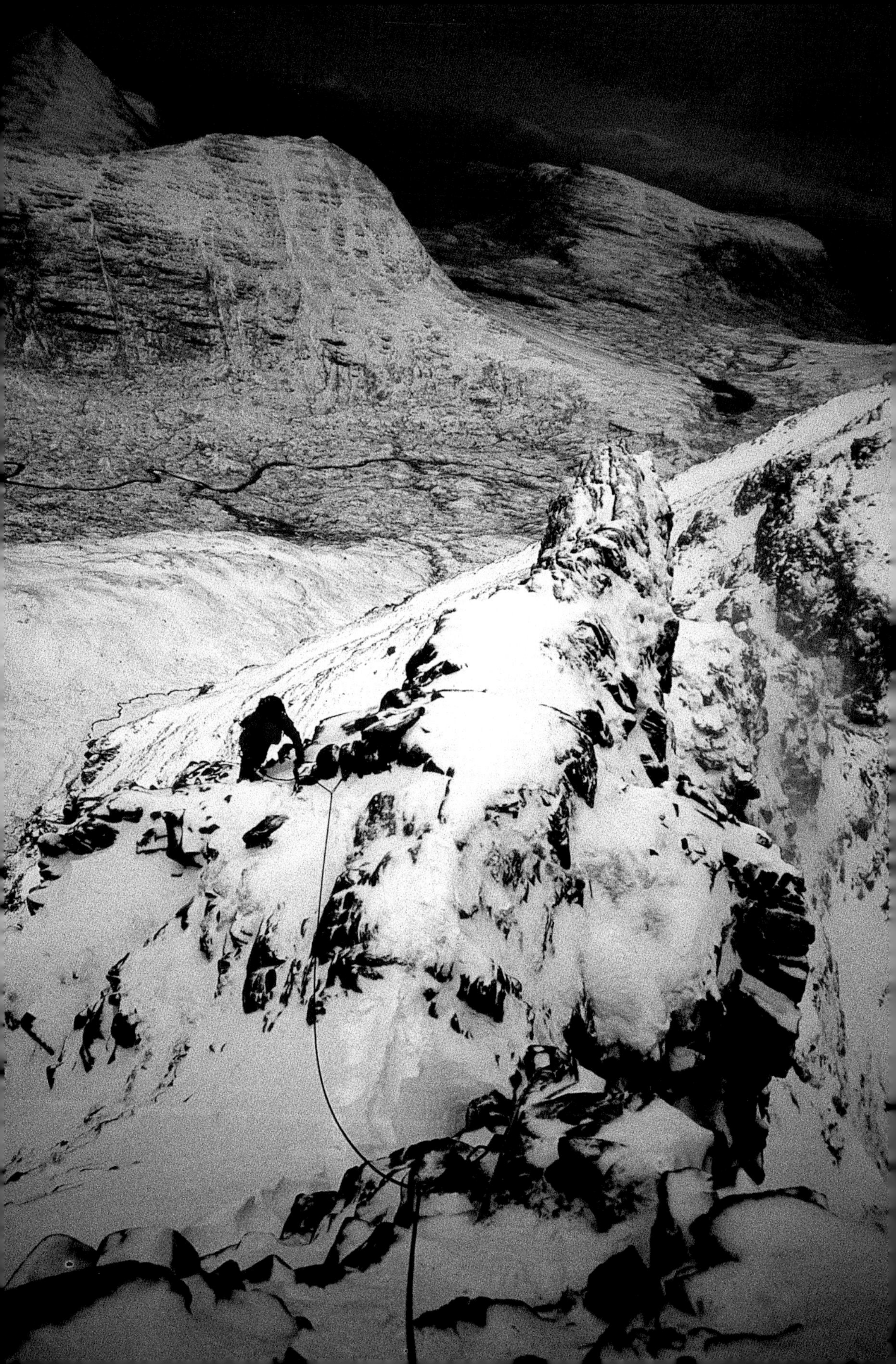

THE NORTH AND WEST HIGHLANDS

Route 38 – Marathon Ridge, Beinn Lair

Grade	390m Difficult (treat with caution)
Distance	36km
Ascent	980m
Time	16 hours
Start/finish	Riverside car park in Poolewe (NG858808)
Map	OS Landranger (1:50,000) 19
Accommodation	Carn Dearg Youth Hostel near Gairloch (0870 004 1110), Kinlochewe Hotel bunkhouse (01445 760 253)
Sleeping out	Because of the distances involved, and because it's an amazing place that deserves a stay of several days, it's best to base yourself at the run-down Carnmore bothy (NG977769) for an assault on Marathon Ridge. The adjacent Carnmore crag provides some of the best mid-grade multi-pitch rock climbs in Britain, and this is just one of many local attractions.
Public transport	Buses connect Gairloch with Inverness and Ullapool; some of these go via Poolewe.
Seasonal notes	A rarely climbed winter grade III notable for its length and remoteness; a good freeze should firm up the loose sections. In midsummer the midges can prove unendurable.

In this overcrowded age the pioneering spirit of yesteryear is an elusive commodity. But exploratory adventures still await, deep in the remote north west. The Letterewe/Fisherfield Forest is widely touted as our 'Great Wilderness'; a hike into its interior is a pleasure in itself, and climbing a route or two while here is the proverbial cake icing. Marathon Ridge languishes in obscurity on the stupendous but largely ignored N Face of Beinn Lair. Even by local standards it receives scant attention. The climbing is a mixed bag, the mix being equal parts nice rock, choss and verdant greenery. Yet the setting is magnificent, and the ridge is both more challenging and more rewarding than might be expected. This is an almost virgin mountaineering route, in much the same state as the old-timers would have enjoyed it. The primary appeal of Marathon Ridge is its unsullied feel, and yet paradoxically the climbing quality would benefit from an increase in traffic. However, it is likely to remain one for connoisseurs of the esoteric. Polish those hobnails, dust off the tweeds… and watch out for falling rocks old bean.

Approach

The distance, ascent and time stats given above are for a single-day, there-and-back trip. Very few will be willing or able to complete the undertaking in a one-er, however. There are various possible approaches. Prettiest is from Kinlochewe via the north shore of Loch Maree and the Bealach Mheinnidh (22km). The nautically minded have been known to canoe directly across the loch to Letterewe, cutting nearly 3/4 of the distance off the former walk. For those lacking boats the 'shortest' hike is from Poolewe (14km), as described here.

Take the riverside minor road past the school, staying left at a turn-off after about 2km. Keep on the now unsurfaced track through the farmstead at Kernsary (petting the piglets and puppies is optional), soon entering a forestry plantation near a rickety stile. Follow the track to a cairned path branching off slightly right. This climbs gradually over open moorland, with the huge northern flanks of Beinn Airigh Charr, Meall Mheinnidh and Beinn Lair prominent ahead. These are the most extensive exposures of hornblende schist in Britain, offering Alpine-scale climbs. Pass beneath the extravagant overhangs of Beinn Airigh Charr,

38 – MARATHON RIDGE, BEINN LAIR

The final arete of Marathon Ridge, seen from Beinn Lair's summit plateau. Behind is the North West Ridge of A'Mhaighdean (Route 39), with the 'molar' visible on the skyline. In the far distance are the clustered peaks of An Teallach (Route 40).

The North and West Highlands

where there's certainly scope for hard new routes. Continue under Meall Mheinnidh to reach a junction with the path descending from Bealach Mheinnidh (overlooked by another set of beefy overhangs). You're now in the rugged heart of the wilderness, with Carnmore bothy just 2.5km along the shore of Fionn Loch and over a short causeway.

For Marathon Ridge, climb the Bealach Mheinnidh path until just below the col. Turn left on an obvious path traversing beneath the crags of Beinn Lair. This peters into nothing at a stony saddle. Hold roughly the same contour for nearly 2km along a boggy terrace scattered with boulders. The complex face above is very imposing, offering a number of fabulous low grade climbs. Descend gradually into Gleann Tulacha, with Beinn Lair's conical Summit Buttress high on the right. Marathon Ridge lies some way beyond. The base is clean and tapered, while up near the top is a chunky detached tower. The mountain opposite has a vaguely saddle-shaped summit marked on the 1:50,000 map as spot height 652m. The left end of this saddle is on a rough bearing of 23° grid from the base of Marathon Ridge – one way to confirm your position.

Climb

Marathon Ridge, 390m Difficult

Move-for-move Diff is a fair technical grade. However (and this is a big proviso), the grade belies its seriousness, both in terms of the ground encountered and the remote setting. Marathon Ridge is best suited to those with experience of route finding and rockfall on big mountains – in the Alps, for instance. The hornblende schist bedrock is basically sound, but surface debris and vegetation abound. This mess would be cleared with traffic, if there ever were any. There are many incuts and slots, for which a selection of small and medium cams is invaluable. The rock is treacherous when wet.

Climb the lowest nose, which provides 60m of interest. Moving together is a sensible approach from the off. It is steeper than it looks, and there is a stack of delicately poised blocks at half height. Above is a grassy section, and then a steep wall of about 30m.

Marathon Ridge

① Tower

38 – Marathon Ridge, Beinn Lair

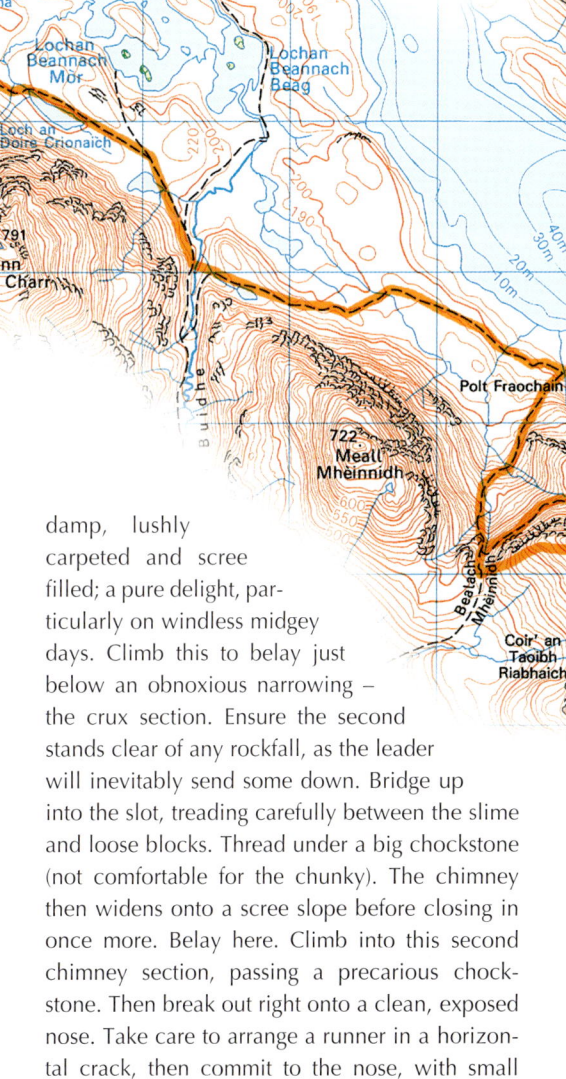

Climb straight up the middle. Another easy grassy stretch follows, leading to a second wall. Turn the difficult top section of this to the left. A mixture of vegetation and cleaner tiers then leads to the base of a big rock mass.

Make for a deep chimney at the point where a subsidiary ridge comes in from the left. This is damp, lushly carpeted and scree filled; a pure delight, particularly on windless midgey days. Climb this to belay just below an obnoxious narrowing – the crux section. Ensure the second stands clear of any rockfall, as the leader will inevitably send some down. Bridge up into the slot, treading carefully between the slime and loose blocks. Thread under a big chockstone (not comfortable for the chunky). The chimney then widens onto a scree slope before closing in once more. Belay here. Climb into this second chimney section, passing a precarious chockstone. Then break out right onto a clean, exposed nose. Take care to arrange a runner in a horizontal crack, then commit to the nose, with small holds on sound rock. Tricky.

Continue right of the crest on broken vegetated ground, reaching a grassy neck below the steep rock of the tower. Turn the initial prow on the left, climbing a crack to a sloping ledge. Don't continue along this ledge. Instead step airily right onto the crest, which is followed to cracked blocks. Above is a final level arete – walk along this, downclimbing from a small spike to reach the summit plateau. Enjoy a deep sigh of relief, then turn right to stroll nonchalantly to the summit cairn.

Descent
Descend WNW along the cliff top, curving gently left to avoid crags guarding the Bealach Mheinnidh. Regain the path down to Fionn Loch.

Above the chimney, with the Mullach Coire Mhic Fhearchair massif behind. Note the fashionable headnet, all the rage last midge season.

38 – Marathon Ridge, Beinn Lair

The north walls of Beinn Lair, Meall Mheinnidh and Beinn Airigh Charr are among the biggest in Britain

Climbing the tower

THE NORTH AND WEST HIGHLANDS

Route 39 – North West Ridge, A'Mhaighdean

Grade	1/2 scramble (not sustained)
Distance	41km
Ascent	1200m
Time	13 hours
Start/finish	Riverside car park in Poolewe (NG858808)
Map	OS Landranger (1:50,000) 19
Accommodation	See Route 38
Sleeping out	As with Marathon Ridge on nearby Beinn Lair, the distances involved and the special wilderness quality of this area make an overnight stay in Carnmore bothy the best option.
Public transport	See Route 38
Seasonal notes	Though no way sustained at the grade, the NW Ridge in full winter garb merits I/II, with brief difficulties and excitement. The overwhelming emptiness of this area should be taken into account by any visitors planning a winter foray.

A'Mhaighdean is often cited as the furthest 3000-er from any public road. Heavyweight challengers like Ben Avon and Ben Alder might leave the title open to dispute, but what does it matter? A'Mhaighdean is a beautiful peak in a truly special location in the centre of the fabulous Letterewe/Fisherfield Forest. It is surrounded by a vast expanse of water and rock, where huge bare crags sprout from carpets of peat bog and lochs lap every hollow. This route shares the thrilling wilderness feel of Marathon Ridge on adjacent Beinn Lair (Route 38), but here all similarity ends. While its neighbour is an adventurous rock climb, A'Mhaighdean's NW Ridge is a simple scramble. It may be technically among the easiest routes in this book, but it's no less a clamber for that, and more than justifies the long haul into the Great Wilderness.

Approach

As for Marathon Ridge (Route 38) the route stats are given for a single there-and-back push, something very few parties will attempt in just one day.

Crossing the Fionn Loch – Dubh Loch causeway, with the north face of Beinn Lair (Route 38) behind

Follow the Marathon Ridge approach to Carnmore bothy. Leave excess kit here to bag a place on the earth floor. This can be very grotty, and a spare tarpaulin is worth packing. From the bothy walk back past the ugly white lodge, which looks like a 1930s semi dumped incongruously in the country's most stirring middle of nowhere. Ascend diagonally E on a well-made path above the N shore of Dubh Loch, an eerily silent stretch of water fringed by towering crags. On joining a foaming burn the path curves NE up a little side valley. Follow this to a wide pass, turning off for A'Mhaighdean at the first lochan. A faint path threads bogs and rocks to reach the shore of Fuar Loch Mor, nestled below the mountain's broken N face.

Climb

From the loch's far side plod up steep pathless slopes onto the blunt NW ridge. This starts off wide and easy underfoot, rising in a series of little steps to a sudden unexpected climax. Above a small crag tier the ridge abruptly narrows to form an exposed tooth, a steep drop barring onward progress. A second fierce-looking detached molar straddles the gap beyond. Bear slightly left to descend a short steep chimney on beautifully rough sandstone – the hardest section of the route. Once in the gap, contour right beneath the second pinnacle, weaving up broken scrambly ground beyond onto the broad summit plateau. In winter conditions a delicate snow arete can form between the second pinnacle and the final slopes. It's not technical, but steep slopes on either hand ensure a pleasant thrill. Once on the plateau a brief stride gains the summit, a tremendous perch above the vast W face. From Slioch, Beinn Lair and Torridon to the jagged skyline of An Teallach, via Skye's Trotternish peninsula floating in silvery seas, the panorama ranges far and wide. On a crisp snowy day this has to be one of the finest views in the world.

Slioch (left) and Beinn Lair (Route 38) from the NW Ridge

Descent

Descend easily NE to the col below Ruadh Stac Mor, which can quickly be bagged if the urge arises. Then regain the stalker's path above the NE shore of Fuar Loch Mor, which returns you to the main Carnmore path at the Lochan Feith Mhic'- illean.

Route 40 – An Teallach Traverse

Grade	3 scramble
Distance	16km
Ascent	1400m
Time	8½ hours
Start/finish	Layby on the A832 at Corrie Hallie (NH113852)
Map	OS Landranger (1:50,000) 19
Accommodation	Sail Mhor Croft bunkhouse, Camusnagaul (01854 633 224), Badrallach bothy and campsite (01854 633 281)
Sleeping out	Wild camping options beside Loch Toll an Lochain and near Lochan na Bradhan on the shoulder E of Sail Liath. Shenavall (NH066810) is a lovely bothy, though it's not well placed for a circuit of Coire Toll an Lochain.
Public transport	As with most parts of Wester Ross, talk of buses can seem more like legend than reality. There are a few, however, if you don't mind growing old and grey while you wait. Occasional services pass through Dundonnell en route to Gairloch, Ullapool or Inverness.
Seasonal notes	The winter traverse is of a similar quality and style to that of Liathach (Route 36) and Aonach Eagach (Route 13), with a lot of absorbing grade II ground; an absolute classic.

The traverse of An Teallach is the mother of all mainland ridge scrambles, full of drama and stunningly aesthetic. Around the huge headwall of Toll an Lochain the mountain's skyline is rent into jagged teeth, framing one of Scotland's most impressive cirques. Perhaps we all carry in our heads some personal notion of the form that a perfect mountain day should take. If so, few routes can more closely match the ideal of so many. An Teallach embodies the inclusive

The Toll an Lochain skyline as seen from the Corrie Hallie approach path. Left to right: Sail Liath, the Corrag Bhuidhe Pinnacles, Sgurr Fiona and Bidein a'Ghlas Thuil

The North and West Highlands

premise of this book, offering just the right measure of difficulty to appeal to the broadest possible range of people. For the modest scrambler it might prove the trip of a lifetime; and yet, met with such daunting spaciousness and so much wonderful clambering, even the most accomplished climber will be elated.

Approach
Take the Gleann Chaorachain track, starting on the opposite side of the road from the layby. This passes through woods, then climbs steeply not far from a waterfall to reach open ground above Loch Chaorachain. Roughly 3km from Corrie Hallie a cairned path splits off right, heading for Shenavall bothy. Stay with this for about 1.5km, passing a row of outcrops on the left before branching right again on a second path (also cairned, but less well used). This soon begins to climb in earnest, zigzagging relentlessly up the rough E flank of Sail Liath. Its description as a 'path' can at times seem academic, though the general line is painfully obvious. The angle begins to relent at the 800m contour; stroll easily onto the

summit, to be met with your first close up view of the excitement to come. Walk over Cadha Gobhlach (or skirt right just below the summit), descending to the col beyond. Now follow a rough eroded path up scree, some way beneath a serrated sandstone crest, to reach a little nick below the abrupt buttress of Corrag Bhuidhe. This marks the start of technical difficulties.

Climb
With your sense of exposure suddenly heightened tenfold, climb the first slabby sandstone tier on good solid holds. From here there are now two choices, the direct route or the soft option. The former is the crux of the entire traverse, a serious grade 3 scramble nudging Moderate. To take the direct route, bear right of a little rock mass to reach a steep wall, which feels like it hangs directly over Coire Toll an Lochain. Climb right to left up a short, rounded diagonal crack. On the ledge above,

Plenty of fun in store. Corrag Bhuidhe (left), Sgurr Fiona and Bidein a'Ghlas Thuill (right) from Sail Liath

traverse briefly right before climbing a chimney-crack set in a little corner. Bear right at the top of this to summit the first of a series of pinnacles.

Alternatively, from the top of the first tier traverse left below Corrag Bhuidhe's terminal buttress, following an eroded path that snakes along the precipitous SW flank immediately below the clean rock of the upper tier. It is possible to bypass all the fabulous scrambling to come by moving down onto a lower traverse path, though it's unpleasantly loose in places and a definite anti-climax. You didn't come so far merely to slink off in defeat. When banked out by soft snow this traverse path is anything but a soft option, and not recommended. In any case, mountaineers worth their salt will feel irresistibly drawn to the crest. To get there keep traversing high, ignoring the occasional grotty groove above, until barred by a little slabby wall. Move up this delicately onto a blunt rib bounding a shallow grass gully. Climb the rib to reach the gully, and thus the crest not far beyond the first pinnacle.

Once there turn left to clamber over a succession of beautifully rounded little towers. There's generally a choice of routes, with the easiest line of ascent and descent being the most obviously well used. Even the popular variations have their moments. A short, level crest about halfway along the pinnacles provides one of the day's most nervy passages; it may be no harder than balancing along a garden wall, but were you to stumble off to the right you'd probably land straight in the lochan 500m below. Not a place for daydreaming. The final spire, Lord Berkeley's Seat, overhangs the corrie floor strikingly. Descend from its tip down blocky ground to reach a little col.

Now bear N up the summit ridge of Sgurr Fiona. There's fun scrambling on the crest, though this can be avoided by staying slightly left. From the summit a long stony descent and reascent NNE then gains the trig point at Bidean a'Ghlas

Treading carefully on the Corrag Bhuidhe pinnacles – Bidein a'Ghlas Thuill on the right

Thuill, where a large and rather menacing ewe may try to mug you for snacks (this was circa summer 2004, and so sadly she may no longer be with us).

Descent

Many people opt for the normal descent from here, which heads N from the summit to the col at the head of Glas Tholl before dropping E into the corrie to gain a path returning to Dundonnell. This is the most painless possibility, though an anti-climax.

Better, if far rougher, is to bear ESE from the trig point, heading for the offshoot of Glas Mheall Liath. At first the ridge crest is riven by a succession of towers, Corrag Bhuidhe's aspiring little brothers. These provide many fine scrambly moments (max grade 2) above a rather abrupt N face, though all the interest can be bypassed on the right. Soon there's a notable change of rock from rounded sandstone to broken quartzite blocks leading to the isolated summit, with its magnificent and under-appreciated perspective on the Toll an Lochain skyline.

Keep heading E from here down toilsome rubble, real ankle-snapping terrain. The bottom of the boulder field marks another abrupt geological switch back to sandstone. It's hard to find the safest line, particularly in poor visibility. Beyond occasional sheep tracks that appear and disappear without reason, and perhaps the odd random bootprint, there is almost no pretence at a path. Zigzag down a succession of vegetated slopes split by slimy little crag tiers. With easy ground now tantalisingly close the direct route E is suddenly blocked by a more substantial cliff; zig

40 – An Teallach Traverse

On the Corrag Bhuidhe pinnacles – using the knees for maximum adhesion, so as not to end up in Loch Toll an Lochain

right, then zag back left to thread safely through this on heather terraces. In poor conditions it may be wise to skirt ESE, outflanking this line of crags altogether. Down on terra firma follow a prominent moraine ridge that heads roughly E, then strike across open boggy ground to reach the lochan at (NH101852). Skirt left of the lochan to pick up the well-used path (you'll have been wanting one of these for some time) that descends from the Glas Tholl corrie. Follow this beside a burn, into a rhododendron-choked wood, across a stinking mire and thus to the road. Turn right to regain the car.

THE NORTH AND WEST HIGHLANDS

Route 41 – Stac Pollaidh

Grade	2 scramble minimum, with scope for harder variations
Distance	4km
Ascent	570m
Time	3 hours max
Start/finish	Roadside car park (NC107095)
Map	OS Landranger (1:50,000) 15
Accommodation	Achininver Youth Hostel (0870 004 1101)
Sleeping out	This area offers a limitless supply of prime wild camp sites.
Public transport	Local buses connect Lochinver and Achiltibuie with Ullapool, which is on the Citylink network.
Seasonal notes	Since it's so low and close to the sea Stac Pollaidh isn't often in decent winter nick, but when so the traverse is likely to prove testing, grade II via even the easiest line.

Stac Pollaidh is often cited as the best reason for not being an obsessive Munroist, and the anti-baggers have a point. This wonderful little hill falls short of the hallowed tables by a cool 300m, yet for sheer spirit it overshadows many a Munro. Poised in a blissfully accessible position overlooking Inverpolly's wild watery heartland, Stac Pollaidh's weathered crest bristles with a surreal array of curvy sandstone pinnacles. Scramblers can revert to childhood for a while as they explore this giant adventure playground, choosing their line at will – from easy paths around the obstacles to spectacular pitches above meaty drops. At barely 2km from car to summit, Stac Pollaidh is the shortest route in this book and perfectly suited to a half-day squeezed between downpours.

Approach
The Footpath Trust have replaced what was once an eroded mess with a decent path of freshly laid flagstones which now encircles the entire hill. First climb fairly gently around the E flank of the hill, coming at the saddle between the E and W summits from behind.

Climb
From this saddle first bag the E summit, climbing over a bump and then down a short slabby section into a narrow gap – care when wet. The top is just beyond. Retrace your route to the saddle and continue westwards, wending through and over a confusing array of slabs and towers. An earthy path passes initial difficulties on the right before gaining the crest up a scree gully, but this is the least imaginative option. The best fun is had by picking a line to suit your mood. Bear in mind, though, that the rounded rock makes some sections harder

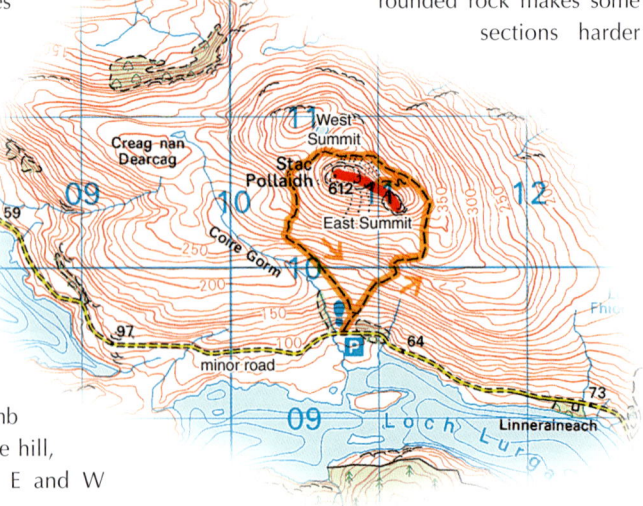

Who needs the Med? Stac Pollaidh (far left), Cul Beag and Beinn an Eoin from Achnahaird

than they look, and that despite the non-serious air a fall could be terminal. Armed with a rope and a rack (friends useful) you could spend many hours tackling the more exposed and tricky pinnacles. Passing the spine-rimmed bowl of Pinnacle Basin you soon reach a squat flat-topped tower barring the W summit. Take this direct on good holds (airy) or bypass it on the left (Loch Lurgainn) side via a little groove. This feels no easier than the face of the tower but is a little less exposed. The summit is just beyond.

Descent
Bar roped climbing the only way off is to retrace your steps to the saddle, and thence down; for variety consider following the W loop of the new path.

Stac Pollaidh and Loch Lurgainn from Cul Beag

Grim conditions nearing the west summit

Route 42 – Suilven

Grade	3 scramble
Distance	22km
Ascent	1100m
Time	10 hours
Start/finish	Layby at the end of the public section of the minor road from Lochinver to Glencanisp Lodge (NC107220)
Map	OS Landranger (1:50,000) 15
Accommodation	Achmelvich Youth Hostel (0870 004 1102), Inchnadamph Lodge backpacker's (01571 822 218)
Sleeping out	Given an early start average parties can complete this route in one long day, but for maximum wilderness impact why not plan an idyllic overnight camp? There's fantastic wild camping at the lochan-studded table beneath Suilven's N face, though the ground is hummocky and midges have the potential to be hellish in season.
Public transport	See Route 41
Seasonal notes	Though not sustained at the grade, the traverse of Suilven in full winter garb merits II, with short sharp difficulties and exposure.

The sandstone mountains of Assynt are eccentric individuals, each with its own distinct character. Their hulking shoulders and curiously weathered heads give these peaks the look of fantasy beasts springing improbably from the surrounding moorland. Although this animistic comparison has been made so often in mountain literature that it now seems clichéd, no other metaphor quite hits the spot. Here be monsters. Suilven is the area's biggest draw, an exceptional mountain with an iconic status. From some angles it resembles a lone pillar, from others a curiously elongated spine, raised high over a rumpled landscape of outcrops and water. The

Suilven from the Lochinver path. Left, Meall Meadhonach; right, Caisteal Liath

209

The North and West Highlands

traverse of Suilven's proud tops is a testing foray into the wilds, one of Scotland's all-time classic hill days. Great popularity and relatively low technicality do nothing to diminish the adventurous quality of this route.

Approach
Throughout the approach, Suilven dominates the landscape. Take the surfaced track beside beautiful Loch Druim Suardalain, and through the grounds of Glencanisp Lodge. The estate was purchased in recent years by the Assynt Foundation, an alliance of local people hoping to secure the area's future on behalf of all residents rather than a dynasty of landowners, with a view to regenerating both the local economy and the natural landscape. This was widely hailed as a flagship example of community buy-out, supported by many in the hillwalking fraternity and funded in part by landscape preservation bodies. However in the light of such support a recent proposal to build a windfarm on a prominent hillside close to Suilven seems rather ironic. Is this really in line with the Foundation's core aim 'to safeguard natural and cultural heritage of the land for future generations and the enjoyment of the wider public'?

Keep heading roughly E through fields and thickets of gorse, where the track becomes a path. For several kilometres this undulates gently, following the N bank of the wide boggy valley of the Abhainn na Clach Airigh.

Fork right at a dry stone wall enclosure near Suileag, passing a couple of reed-choked pools before crossing a wooden footbridge over the river. A few hundred metres further on, a cairned turn-off makes a beeline for Suilven. The route is so popular that it has become a veritable six-lane motorway ploughed through the peat, more like an overused stretch of the Pennine Way than a remote Scottish hill track. Wade up a couple of short boggy slopes to reach the loch-pitted table directly beneath Suilven's imposing N face. Loop around the W shore of Loch a'Choire Dhuibh to climb steeply up a scree-filled trough leading, after a lung-busting ascent, to the Bealach Mor, an obvious nick in Suilven's humpbacked spine.

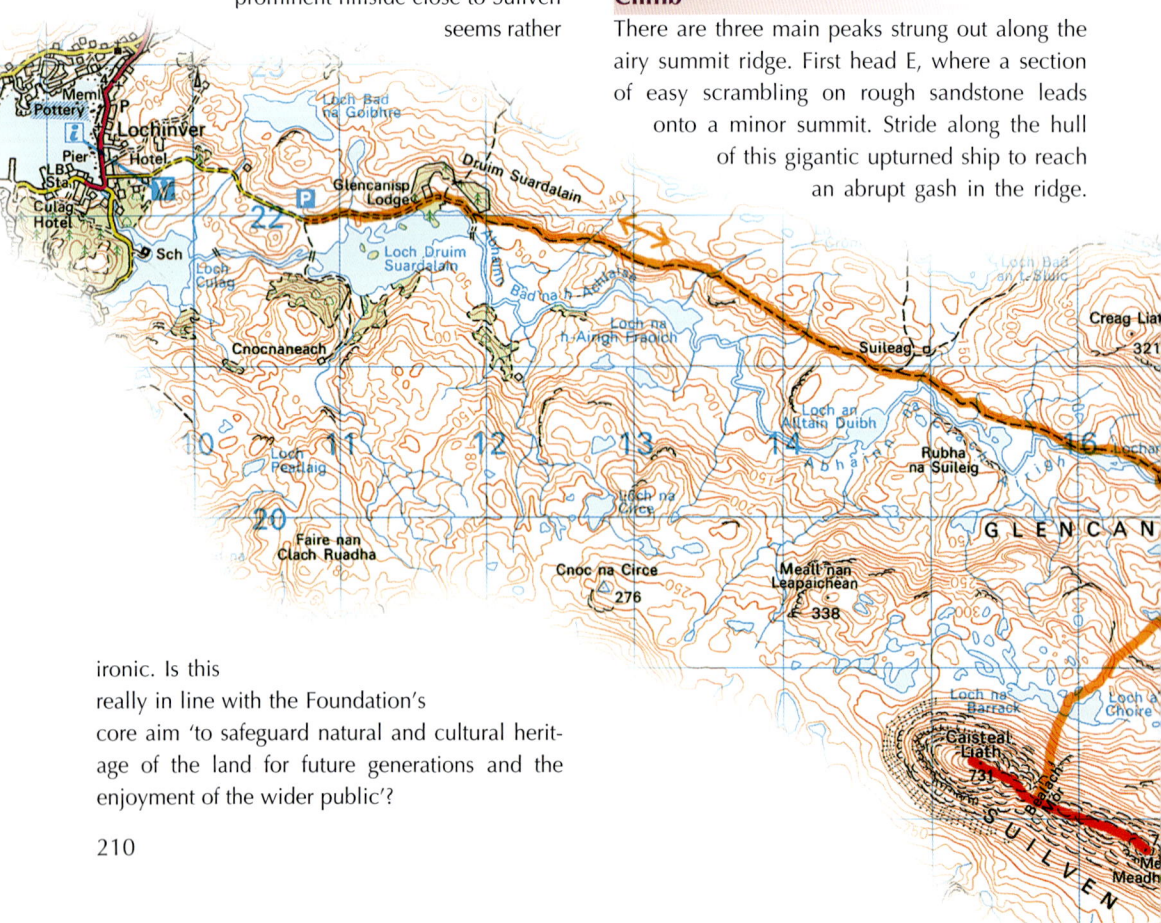

Climb
There are three main peaks strung out along the airy summit ridge. First head E, where a section of easy scrambling on rough sandstone leads onto a minor summit. Stride along the hull of this gigantic upturned ship to reach an abrupt gash in the ridge.

210

Caisteal Liath's barrel prow from Loch Druim Suardalain

Wind steeply down rock steps (simple scrambling) and loose patches before climbing out the far side on more of the same. A sandstone band bars the central summit, Meall Meadhonach; it is steep, awkward and very exposed. Bear in mind that you'll be reversing this route later.

Ascend steps to a big detached block on the right. Move left along a terrace to climb more steps onto a big ledge below the final vertical wall. Gain the top of a balanced boulder. Step airily right along a ledge to finish straight up in one quick mantel, using bedded blocks for handholds.

The flat grassy summit is then won without further difficulty, and makes a wonderful perch on which to pause and ponder.

The little E tower of Meall Bheag sprouts in a rather malformed-looking way from the side of the parent mountain, from which it is separated by a deep cleft. It is daunting, and most people give it a miss. To climb it, first descend rough zigzags into the cleft to reach a short arete. Cross this, then bear left of the tottering headwall, taking a worn path that winds up rubbly terraces on the mountain's precipitous N face. Though not technically difficult (max grade 2 scramble), the loose ground leading to this isolated summit demands care. Should the weather or your nerve fail now, it's possible to bail out by heading down the scrambly E ridge to the moorland below. Otherwise reverse the route of ascent over the two summits and back to the Bealach Mor, taking particular care with the initial descent from Meall Meadhonach.

Caisteal Liath, Suilven's highest summit, is simple compared with the previous shenanigans. Pass through a gateway in a weirdly truncated stone wall, then keep heading W on a well-used path with occasional little rock tiers, over a minor bump with a tiny pool, and on up to the airy summit dome, a cul de sac from which a reversal is the only safe descent. Overlooking a watery wilderness stretching out to the silvery sea, this is a magnificent viewpoint.

Descent

Drop yet again to the Bealach Mor, which by now feels like a home from home. A satisfying circular route descends SW from here down steep scree, eventually picking up a path back to the coast on the N bank of Fionn Loch. Most will opt instead to return the way they came.

The North and West Highlands

Cul Mor from the final steep tier of Meall Meadhonach

The shark's fin of Meall Meadhonach from Caisteal Liath, with Canisp behind (left)

SKYE AND RUM

For ridge climbing fans there is no finer destination than the Isle of Skye. The Cuillin are wonderful hills, improbably jagged and as rocky as the Moon. At times black and forbidding, at others a warm glowing red, often coyly retiring behind a veil of mist, these are mountains of dramatic mood swings. The Main Ridge Traverse is by far the toughest undertaking detailed in this book, a mountaineering challenge of the highest calibre. Compared with such riches, the nearby Cuillin of Rum are often overlooked. Yet they provide a rewarding scrambling traverse in their own right, on a wild and unusual island.

Winter perfection – Sgurr nan Gillean (left), Am Basteir and Sgurr a Bhasteir from near Sligachan

SKYE AND RUM

Route 43 – Traverse of the Rum Cuillin

Grade	Moderate as described (much easier alternatives possible)
Distance	25km including Barkeval and the return leg via the Dibidil path; 28km for a return via Ruinsival and Harris
Ascent	1900m
Time	10 hours
Start/finish	Loch Scresort campground
Map	OS Landranger (1:50,000) 39
Accommodation	Visitors should probably consider spending two nights on the island if they are to fit the Cuillin traverse into a gap in the ferry timetable. Hostel at Kinloch Castle (01687 462037) or basic camp site beside Loch Scresort.
Sleeping out	Dibidil (NM393927) is a fabulous bothy, with mod cons including a fireplace (bring coal) and a new roof. (What, no satellite TV?) Though its location is not ideal for a traverse of the ridge, it may be worth contriving a variation on the route described in order to enjoy a night or two in such a spot. To the W of the Cuillin, the shores of Loch Fiachanis and the nearby pastures of Harris offer good wild camps from which to traverse the entire ridge from Barkeval to Ruinsival.
Public transport	In an age dominated by the infernal combustion engine, the existence of a place with no surfaced roads is, literally, a breath of fresh air. Private cars cannot be brought to Rum, and this state of affairs is likely to continue indefinitely, or at least until some bright spark builds a bridge from the mainland. Despite its remoteness Rum is easily accessed by public transport, a bus or train to Mallaig followed by 1½ hours on a Calmac ferry. Sailings are not daily, so check the timetable.
Seasonal notes	These hills are low lying and subject to the warm, wet influence of the surrounding sea; a deep freeze here is relatively uncommon. Under snow the full Cuillin traverse would present a testing challenge. At a guess, the hardest passages would be III, with quite a lot of I/II ground in between. At the opposite end of the year, beware the midges of high summer; Rum's reckon themselves among the most voracious in Scotland, and this gives them a lot to live up to.

A National Nature Reserve for the last half-century, Rum is a unique and intriguing place. With its rough coastline and a hinterland of empty bog and mountain, much of the island feels untouched. The population of around 30 permanent residents, employees of Scottish Natural Heritage, is squeezed into a corner; the rest is left to wildlife. Vehicle tracks are few and even on the main summits the footpaths are rough. Skye's Cuillin are justifiably popular; Rum's are strangely neglected. If you meet another party, consider yourself unlucky. Despite their modest stature these Cuillin have far more appeal than many a range of Munros, and form a ragged mass that dominates both the island and the imagination. Their evocative Norse names roll off the tongue, exotic and ancient. When ghostly vapours smoke between the peaks, as they usually do, it is almost possible to fancy that Rum's Cuillin are not entirely of this world, that they have risen from the misty sea of Viking legend. But the cold rain soon reminds you of the here and now.

But enough wafty rambling – what about the route? It is quite simply one of the best long scrambling circuits in Scotland, a mountaineering

43 – TRAVERSE OF THE RUM CUILLIN

Askival (left) and Trollaval (right) from Barkeval

escapade par excellence. Though all notable scrambling sections can be readily avoided if necessary, distance, ascent, rough ground and route finding make this a testing day – an ideal warm-up, perhaps, for that other great Cuillin Traverse (see Route 48).

Approach

Rum's rescue services are less developed than most. The island managers are keen that hillwalkers and climbers leave a route card at the Reserve Office.

A signposted path leads through the grounds of Kinloch Castle, then follows the W bank of the Allt Slugan a'Choillich through a patch of regenerated young woodland and up into the boggy scoop of Coire Dubh. The least calf-busting onward path heads left around the corrie rim and onto the little shoulder of Cnapan Breaca, reaching the ridge some way above the Bealach Bairc-mheall. It is worth tracking W from here to visit the summit of Barkeval for a grand view over Atlantic Corrie to the main peaks. Head back to the foot of Hallival, crossing a strange gravel plain en route.

Manx shearwaters

The Rum Cuillin famously host a colony of these curious burrow-nesting seabirds, and some hilltops are riddled with their holes. The birds are a type of petrel, spending most of their life at sea on the wing and over-wintering near Brazil. The only time they land is to come to their burrows to brood their eggs and feed their chicks. Because they are prone to predation from larger birds like eagles, shearwaters only come home in the middle of the night. The chick is left alone in the burrow the rest of the time and fed once every two or three days. When landing the adults call to their mate or chick, which responds to help them locate their burrow; it is an eerie combination of moaning and cackling, quite amazing when the whole mountainside rings with it for a couple of hours in the dead of night. The colony on Rum is the largest in the UK, numbering around 60,000 pairs.

Climb

Hallival
Climb the blunt NW spur – a steep grind on rough ground where rock bands provide some easy scrambling. From the summit cairn signs of wear show the way S down more broken crag tiers (grade 1 scrambling) and patches of scree to a small col.

Askival
The North Ridge of Askival begins as a pleasingly narrow grassy arete. This soon becomes rockier and more exposed, and though a well-worn path skirts left of the hard stuff to reach the summit with only some basic scrambling, it's far better to stay with the crest. Relatively few people pass this way, as evidenced by the undisturbed moss and a general lack of polish on the rock. Blocky scrambling leads up towards the menacing square-cut Askival Pinnacle. This is more a step in the ridge than a true pinnacle, and constitutes the day's crux, a short, airy Moderate if taken direct. A little pile of stones gives a leg up onto a flake crack, and soon afterwards comes the Pinnacle. Climb its right facet, moving right under a slabby section with few apparent holds. Commit to this, happily discovering some useful little edges for fingers and boots. Climb to a narrow grassy ledge; sidle right, then go up blocks until you can see the left side of the ridge again. Continue just left of big mossy blocks on the true crest, following the occasional scuff mark up the line of least resistance over (or around) several jagged masses of rock that provide some good butch clambering, including at one point a tricky mantelshelf move. The summit trig point comes soon after.

Descend due W, the ground soon narrowing into another arete. Big blocks on the crest provide light-hearted scrambling (grade 1), though there is an easier path just to the left.

Trollaval
The continuation to Trollaval begins as a grassy slog, later developing into another short blocky ridge (grade 1/2). The twin summits are connected by an airy little ridge. In poor visibility it's easy to get confused here, overshooting the W summit and inadvertently continuing down the scrambly W ridge. **Choosing the right line of descent from this mountain is critical.** A direct line from the W summit leads to one of Rum's biggest crags. To avoid this undesirable feature backtrack to the E summit. Even from here it's possible to go wrong, ending up on an improbable Moderate descent down a series of slabby tiers – particularly hazardous in the wet. Instead keep bearing strongly left from the E summit, more SE than S, to pick up a blunt arete; descend this with some easy scrambling, skirting a few tiers of crags lower down to reach the Bealach an Fhuarain, another height-losing low point on the ridge traverse.

Ainshval
The buttress guarding Ainshval looms menacingly above, providing the last significant passage of hard scrambling on the ridge, a challenging grade 3 (slippery when wet). Though the buttress can be avoided on scree to the right, it is well worth doing. First climb an obvious right-to-left diagonal rake, and then move back diagonally right on the grassy edge of a slab to reach another slabby tier. Climb this, too, slanting back left again to reach some grass below a final steep mass of rock. Ascend a greasy, broken and slightly vegetated groove, which leads straight up to an area of sounder, rougher rock with plenty of reassuring holds, and thus to the top.

Now continue uphill, easy walking leading to a steep scree-covered slope just to the left of Ainshval's final N ridge. Although a path plods straight up this scree to reach the top, the rock arete is a much better option. Eight metres of steep grade 3 / Moderate climbing leads straight up the

43 – TRAVERSE OF THE RUM CUILLIN

vertical foot of this ridge to reach the crest. Now continue up the wonderfully sharp spine, with slabby ground to the right and a steeper drop to the left. The scrambling is reasonably amenable (grade 2/3), though some of the rock needs a light touch. The Cuillin's second summit is soon reached.

217

On the grassy arete at the start of Askival's North Ridge, cloud smoking off Hallival in the background

Sgurr nan Gillean
A broad, easy crest leads down to the next col. From here a pleasant bit of grade 1 scrambling climbs the subsequent arete onto an unnamed top at 759m. Sgurr nan Gillean is a grassy ridge-top stroll away.

Descent
There now just remains the not inconsiderable matter of returning to Kinloch, still several hours distant. There are three options.

a) Some people advocate returning to the Bealach an Fhuarain, from where a traverse can be made under Trollaval to the Bealach an Oir, and thence around Atlantic Corrie back to the Bealach Bairc-mheall. This is unattractive given poor weather or limited daylight.

b) The most popular alternative is via the Dibidil path along Rum's east coast. Avoid broken crags on the SE face of Sgurr nan Gillean by first heading down the steep S spur (600m distance should do it) before swinging E, sploshing through the sodden sponge that characterises much of Rum's low ground to reach the path not far S of Dibidil bothy. The bothy provides a welcome temporary respite from bad weather. From here it is a further 8km back to Kinloch. The path is easy to follow in the dark, if necessary, though it can be quite boggy and in wet weather some burn crossings may require real care.

43 – TRAVERSE OF THE RUM CUILLIN

Trollaval from Askival's North Ridge

c) Best for scenery and atmosphere is the longer route via Ruinsival and Harris. From the unnamed summit at 759m descend the broad Leac a'Chaisteil ridge, with a short climb at its end onto Ruinsival's rarely trodden summit, the Cuillin on one side and the sea at your feet. Backtrack from the summit to the top of the mountain's little NE ridge (NM360941), which provides a sneaky way off into Fiachanis corrie. At first this is an easy walk, though lower down several craggy tiers must be negotiated by a weaving line that requires some grade 2 downclimbing.

Once in the corrie skirt right of Loch Fiachanis, crossing moorland to the sturdy bridge over the Abhainn Rangail. Goats, deer, cattle and ponies share the lush beachside pasture of Harris, where a rippled array of old cultivation terraces shows how populous Rum must once have been. In a field on the far side of a river stands a bizarre mausoleum, a neoclassical stone edifice of substantial size, final resting place of a self-styled dynasty of island lairds. It is incongruous in this wild spot, and more than a little sinister. Time is bound to be pressing by now, and Kinloch is still at least 11km away. But fear not: a well maintained vehicle track goes all the way, leading you easily (and without bogs!) through the wild heart of the island, with views of the crazy switchback of hills over which you've been sweating all day.

Crux moves on the Askival Pinnacle

Trollaval's craggy west summit from the east summit

Route 44 – Dubhs Ridge

Grade	920m Moderate
Distance	9km
Ascent	1040m
Time	7 hours; move fast to catch an afternoon boat back to Elgol
Start/finish	Landing stage, Coruisk (NG486196)
Maps	OS Landranger (1:50,000) 32; OS Explorer (1:25,000) 411
Accommodation	Glen Brittle Youth Hostel (0870 004 1121), Glen Brittle campsite, Sligachan hotel and bunkhouse (01478 850 204), Sligachan campsite, Croft Bunkhouse Portnalong (01478 640 254), Broadford Youth Hostel (0870 004 1106)
Sleeping out	Coruisk is one of Scotland's classic wild camping sites.
Public transport	Postbus from Broadford to Elgol, then boat (*Bella Jane*) from Elgol to Coruisk. You should book the boat in advance (0800 731 3089 www.bellajane.co.uk)
Seasonal notes	As it starts from near sea level the slab section is unlikely ever to be in decent winter nick. When snowed up, the arete between the two Dubhs summits can become a tricky proposition and might merit grade II.

Dubhs is pronounced 'do', and everyone should. Doing the Dubhs is a unique climbing experience. This is widely touted as Britain's longest rock climb, and it's hard to think of a better one at such a gentle grade. In scale and quality it wouldn't disgrace the Lofoten Islands, a fabulous maritime setting on the wild side of the Cuillin adding to this Norwegian impression. Sweeping straight out of Loch Coruisk, a huge mound of overlapping slabs runs unbroken from near sea level to a subsidiary summit at 733m, perfect gabbro all the way. Thereafter the ridge narrows, with sustained interest right to the summit of Sgurr Dubh Mor. For most of its length it can be tackled as an unroped scramble, though the occasional tricky step and one airy abseil earn the route its Moderate grade. The Dubhs Ridge is an ideal choice for aspirant climbers with scrambling and abseiling experience.

Approach

For that remote island atmosphere nothing beats catching the boat from Elgol to the landing stage at Coruisk, where seals loll happily on the rocks. Pass the Coruisk Memorial Hut to the rushing outflow from Loch Coruisk, and follow the loch's boggy southwest shore into the wildly impressive horseshoe of the Cuillin. With its feet just short of the waterline your climb is unmistakable ahead. This point can also be reached by a lengthy tramp on the coastal path from Elgol, with a short scrambling section on the so-called 'Bad Step'.

Skye and Rum

On the Dubhs slabs, 'sweeping straight out of Loch Coruisk'

Dubhs Ridge

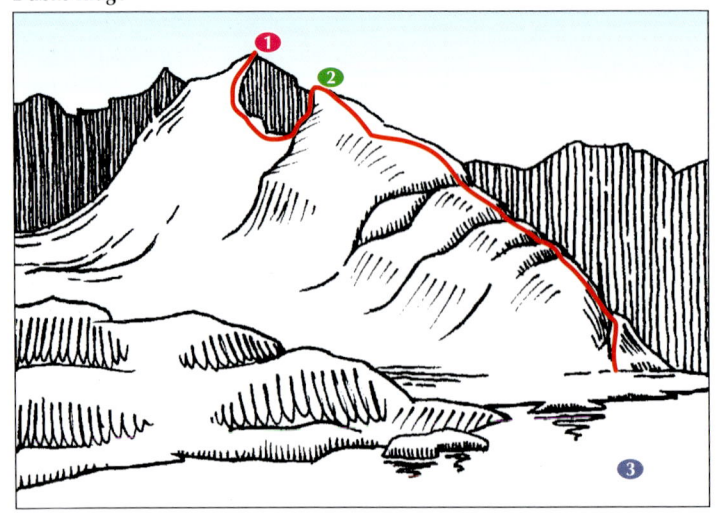

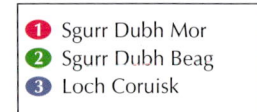

1. Sgurr Dubh Mor
2. Sgurr Dubh Beag
3. Loch Coruisk

Negotiating an overlap on the slabs

Climb

Dubhs Ridge, 920m Moderate

One beauty of the lower section of this route is that you can vary your line almost at will, seeking or avoiding the obstacles. Among the hardest bits is getting established on the slabs. The base of the ridge dips steeply towards the loch, with grassy bays cutting up higher to each side. The left-hand bay gives access to some interesting corners that feel about Diff, briefly. The right-hand cleft is easier, getting you onto rock above the tricky terminal slabs. From this point a series of steep steps leads slightly left and then gradually right again, and on these a rope might be appreciated. The broad crest beyond offers a seemingly endless succession of faultlessly rough slabs tilted at about 30°, an ideal angle for relaxed unroped padding. The odd steepening where these plates of rock overlap keeps the adrenaline flowing, but should scarcely break your rhythm. Occasional turfy escapes cut left into An Garbh-choire, if the need arises. Otherwise keep heading up, sticking more or less with the crest, to reach the sharp perch of Sgurr Dubh Beag (733m).

A new awareness of exposure suddenly arises as you descend south west a few metres to a narrow ledge above an overhang. Abseil slings are usually in place around an obvious block, and if in doubt as to their security back them up with a fresh one. Then make an exciting 20m abseil past the overhangs to level ground beneath. This isn't recommended as a first-ever abseil.

Abseil from Sgurr Dubh Beag, with Bla Bheinn (Route 47) behind

The continuation to Sgurr Dubh Mor begins as an easy scramble along a broken crest. Route finding gets gradually harder as the drop grows below. Soon you're forced left on sloping ledges some way below the crest (beware loose rock), from where you must regain the ridge. The best option is a short vertical corner, strenuous and likely to require a rope. Back on top keep following the narrow arete with some interest, eventually reaching the Munro summit of Sgurr Dubh Mor.

Descent
A brief grade 3 scramble down the W spur gains the adjacent top of Sgurr Dubh an Da Bheinn on the main Cuillin Ridge. From here the energetic could happily continue onto Sgurr Alasdair via the infamous Thearlaich Dubh Gap (see Route 48). But if you've had enough fun for now, descend the rough blocks of the South Ridge (grade 2 scramble). Down at the next bealach drop steeply left into An Garbh-choire and pick a slow tortuous route through the huge tumbled blocks that cover the upper corrie floor. In the boggy lower floor of the corrie bear left directly under the Dubh slabs to regain the Loch Coruisk path for the return sailing – or a long hike – to Elgol.

Route 45 – The Spur, Sgurr an Fheadain

Grade	400m 2 scramble
Distance	6.5km
Ascent	620m
Time	3½ – 4 hours
Start/finish	Car park on the right as the road descends into Glen Brittle (NG423258)
Map	OS Landranger (1:50,000) 32 or Harvey Superwalker (1:25,000 and 1:12500) Skye: The Cuillin
Accommodation	Glen Brittle Youth Hostel and campsite or Croft Bunkhouse at Portnalong are the most convenient options. See Route 44 for details.
Sleeping out	Few locations are more idyllic than the Fairy Pools, where wild camps come with a choice of en-suite spa.
Public transport	A bus service connects Portree with Glen Brittle, via Sligachan.
Seasonal notes	Given its prominence The Spur must have received winter ascents, though information has been hard to come by. Grade II/III seems a fair guesstimate. Sgurr an Fheadain is low, and often snow- or cloud-free when higher peaks surrounding it are anything but.

Driving out of the trees on the Glen Brittle road, the sudden sense of immensity never fails to startle. Ahead, Coire na Creiche has grown to span the windscreen, jaws gaping wide. It is a magnificent arena; skyline bitten by gammy teeth, and great gouged walls that look like they've been chewed up and spat back out. In the midst of it all is Sgurr an Fheadain, an offshoot from the main ridge that divides the corrie into two. Though enclosed by a ring of much higher peaks, this fierce little upstart commands attention, a conical mass of slabby rock heaped to a sharp summit and split down the middle by the sinister gash of Waterpipe Gully. The Spur is the obvious ridgeline to the left of the chasm. It's a good way to access adjacent sections of the main Cuillin ridge, but equally worthwhile as a half-day objective.

Approach

From the car park cross the road and head downhill on a clear path to meet the Allt Coir' a'Mhadaidh. Follow its N bank past an appealing series of cascades, aptly dubbed the Fairy Pools. Continue along the stream for just over 2km, Sgurr an Fheadain becoming ever more dominant ahead. The two upper corries are Mhadaidh, to the right of Sgurr an Fheadain, and Tairneilear to the left. Bear towards the mouth of the latter. A path cuts in from the Bealach a'Mhaim, contouring the bowl of Coire na Creiche to bisect your trail. At this point cross the burn and climb rough slopes towards The Spur. A large section of slabs sits below and left of the ridge proper.

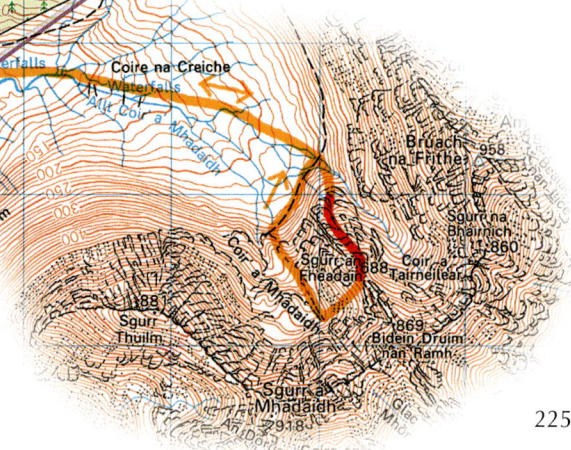

Sgurr an Fheadain (centre, front) and Bidein Druim nan Ramh (right) from the west. The Spur takes the obvious rib left of the gash of Waterpipe Gully.

Climb

Climb the centre of these slabs direct, enjoying sound rough rock set at a joyously gentle angle. Weave at will around any tricky steepenings. About 100m up, the slabs peter into an open scrappy slope. The Spur is on the right-hand skyline, guarded by crumbly crags. Traverse hard right on a faint path over a patch of scree, leading to a little niche beside a spindly tree. Climb this (the niche, not the tree) to gain the crest.

It is worth being aware of wobbly rock on the crest, though it doesn't seriously detract from the experience. Despite loose chips and the odd bigger block the bedrock is largely trustworthy, and the friction is reassuring. Follow the blunt arete direct. The ground drops away steeply towards Waterpipe Gully on the right, while the left flank is easier angled and more broken. Short steps of interesting scrambling are interspersed with grassy ledges, giving the route a non-serious feel.

Higher up the crest narrows, Waterpipe Gully now making its presence felt distinctly. From this point on, the ground requires more careful handling. Above a wide ledge, a short steep step demands a few tricky moves on questionable rock. Once this is safely dispatched a shattered arete leads without further ado to the summit crown. Pass a cairn standing near the edge overlooking Waterpipe Gully, and climb easy blocks to the true summit.

Descent

The col beyond Sgurr an Fheadain can now be seen, and the ridge leading from it up towards the

45 – THE SPUR, SGURR AN FHEADAIN

Sgurr na Bhairnich from The Spur

spiked mass of Bidean Druim nan Ramh. Direct descent from the summit to the col is not possible, ending in a lethal-looking drop-off. Instead return to the cairn. From here descend loose ground on the Coir' a'Mhadaidh side, staying just below and right of the crest. From the col there are a variety of options, described below.

Continuation
If you have time, a testing circuit around Coir' a'Tairneilear comes highly recommended. Scramble up the delightful continuation crest, and then traverse the sharp tops of Bidean Druim nan Ramh (or skirt left immediately below them), staying with the Main Ridge as far as Bruach na Frithe (all described in Route 48). Now descend the long North West Ridge of Bruach na Frithe (grade 2 scramble) to return to Glen Brittle.

If The Spur has been climbed for its own sake, rather than as an access route to an extended circuit, a quick return to the glen can be made by descending into either of the flanking corries. Both options look worse from above than they really are, though Tairneilear is a little simpler. Coir' a'Mhadaidh, however, is so spectacular that the trickier descent is worth considering. Drop direct from the col down unnervingly steep scree, weaving around minor outcrops. Just before reaching safer ground, rotten crags bar your path; bear slightly left to avoid them, and gain the sloping corrie floor. With many a pause to ogle the imposing rock walls all around, follow the right bank of the burn out of the corrie.

Route 46 – Pinnacle Ridge, Sgurr nan Gillean

Grade	Moderate/Difficult
Distance	11km
Ascent	970m
Time	7 hours
Start/finish	Sligachan Hotel (NG486298)
Map	OS Landranger (1:50,000) 32 or Harvey Superwalker (1:25,000 and 1:12,500) Skye: The Cuillin
Accommodation	The bunkhouse, campsite and hotel at Sligachan are best placed. See Route 44 for details.
Sleeping out	As this route is relatively close to a road, wild camping hardly seems appropriate; but if you must, the shoulder immediately below the ridge provides several sites.
Public transport	Citylink buses to Portree can pull over at Sligachan, as can local services.
Seasonal notes	Pinnacle Ridge is one of the finest grade III climbs on Skye. It is likely to prove time consuming, especially under fresh powder.

Sgurr nan Gillean is the archetypal pointy mountain, as drawn by children – steep flanks and serrated ridges converging from every side on the summit perch. It is a real mountaineer's peak; even the SE Ridge 'Tourist Route' involves a grade 3 scramble. This is the descent described here, but there's a much better way up. Seen in distant profile the ranked spires of Pinnacle Ridge offer an obvious and compelling challenge, with around 1000m of fall-off-able ground. This saw-toothed line is one of Scotland's best mountaineering trips, with engaging route finding and exposed

Sgurr nan Gillean (left), Knight's Peak and the Third Pinnacle (right) from the east

46 – Pinnacle Ridge, Sgurr nan Gillean

'big mountain' situations throughout. Some guidebooks bemoan the ridge's imperfect rock, though this is a small price to pay for the privilege of climbing such a grand route; indeed, patches of scree and the occasional dodgy block just add to the Alpine ambience. The route involves one abseil, which can be dispensed with at a small increase in grade.

Approach

From the A863 just W of the Sligachan Hotel take a path SW to the river. Cross the rickety old bridge and continue across moorland, making straight for the impressive Coire a'Bhasteir peaks. At about 2km branch left over a second bridge, climbing steadily to the broad saddle above Coire Riabhach. Peel off right on an indistinct path that climbs the shoulder thrown down by Pinnacle Ridge. Seen end-on the ridge now looks distinctly daunting. The shoulder becomes rockier, narrowing to give a view down into the Bhasteir Gorge on the right. Continue up scree to reach the foot of the First Pinnacle.

Climb

It is possible to ascend the First Pinnacle's NW face directly – an exposed, sustained Moderate of about 150m. The easier and more usual route slinks off left, taking the line of least resistance up grassy grooves and patches of nice rock. Keep bearing diagonally left until directly over Coire Riabhach, then slant back right up a rubbly rake to the Coire a'Bhasteir side. Traverse right briefly, then back up left to climb a short steep groove formed by an eroded basalt dyke. Head right to reach a narrow square-cut ledge on the left wall of a little gully; ascend this feature to reach easy ground and the top of the First Pinnacle.

Pass the head of a gully on your right. From here it's possible to circumvent any significant scrambling as far as the depression between the Second and Third Pinnacles simply by keeping well to the left. Better, though, is to climb right up clean slabs before heading left up a groove to the ill-defined summit of the Second Pinnacle. Scree leads to the foot of the Third Pinnacle.

The Third Pinnacle can be avoided altogether by a traverse across its E face (grade 3), but this is a wasted opportunity. For optimum enjoyment scramble right to reach a clean groove just to the right of the crest. Bridge up this, with a few stiff moves near the top. The summit is just beyond, a compact perch with air all around. The onward route into the deep gap before Knight's Peak looks menacing. Now comes the abseil. A mass of slings will usually be found in-situ around some big blocks on the summit. At the time of writing this was a confusing mess, and had to be threaded carefully. If in doubt, place a back-up anchor for the first person down. Abseil to a narrow ledge

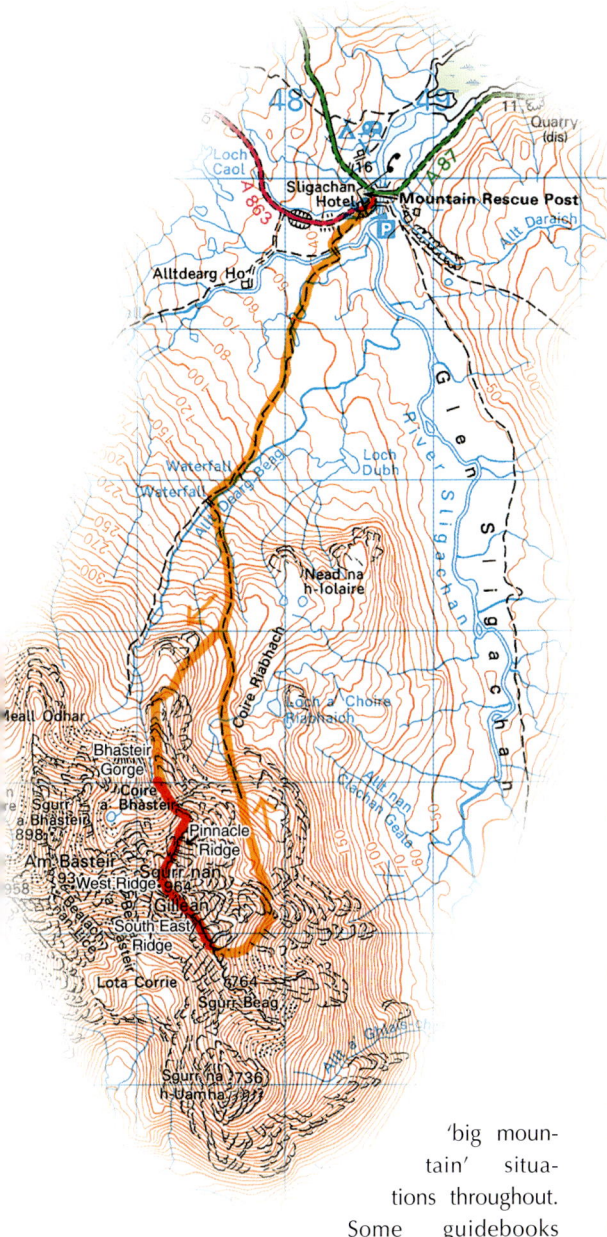

Skye and Rum

Abseil from the Third Pinnacle

Pinnacle Ridge

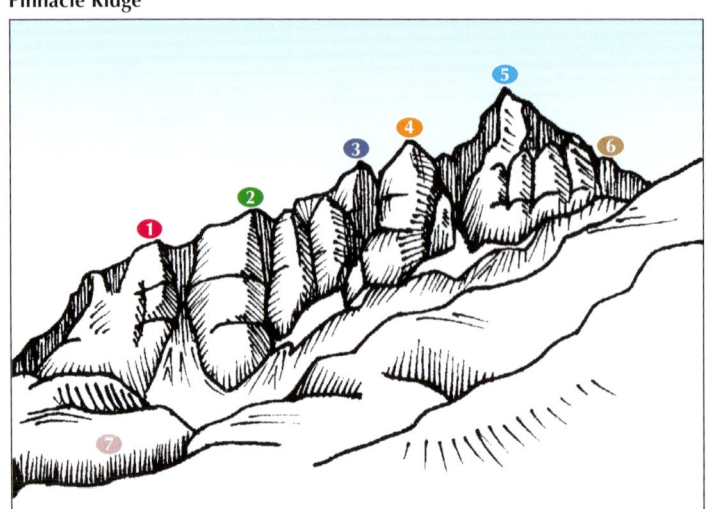

1. First Pinnacle
2. Second Pinnacle
3. Third Pinnacle
4. Knight's Peak
5. Sgurr nan Gillean
6. West Ridge
7. Bhasteir Gorge

46 – Pinnacle Ridge, Sgurr nan Gillean

The upper section of Sgurr nan Gillean's West Ridge

at about 20m. Bold climbers can also reach this point without recourse to an abseil by heading left past the thread belay to a blunt little arete, then descending W down a steep crack (good holds, but definite death-fall potential) to the ledge. This ups the overall route grade a touch. From the ledge go down an awkward little chimney to the neck between the Third Pinnacle and Knight's Peak.

Follow a clean-cut ledge leading diagonally right across the face of Knight's Peak, crossing two thin sections above a scary drop. If you stick with the ledge until directly over Coire a'Bhasteir you've gone too far. Instead, soon after the second narrowing, turn diagonally left up a sloping gritty ledge before climbing to a flat platform with a clear view W to Am Basteir. Climb a short groove formed by a dyke to reach the crenellated summit of Knight's Peak. The descent involves intricate route finding.

Return to the flat platform, then take a stony traverse path below and right of the peak. At a gap before the first of two minor towers downclimb a groove on the right, then zigzag down outcrops and scree to outflank the first tower. At the next opportunity go up and right below the right side of the second tower via some tricky moves, then up left to a ledge directly beneath the summit pyramid of Sgurr nan Gillean.

Bla Bheinn (Route 47) from the airy summit of Sgurr nan Gillean, one of the finest picnic tables in Scotland

The final slabby Moderate climb onto Sgurr nan Gillean can be bypassed via a long rightwards traverse from this point, leading eventually to the mountain's West Ridge. Better, though, is to tackle the face head on. Make a hard step up left to get established on the face, and then follow your nose up a succession of ill-defined ribs and grooves. The rock is of reassuring quality, and the situations are tremendous. Eventually you hit the West Ridge, not far short of the top; turn left and scramble up blocks to reach one of Scotland's most graceful mountain summits.

Descent

The misleadingly named Tourist Route down the SE Ridge starts as a hard exposed grade 3 scramble. Cross a thin neck to an awkward and very airy step down a steep slab, after which the blocky crest eases gradually into a broad shoulder. This marks the end of all technical ground.

Drop E into a grassy scree bowl to pick up a cairned, northward path that traverses rough ground under Pinnacle Ridge, entering Coire Riabhach down scree to the left of an area of slabs. Take care here in poor visibility. Once safely on the corrie floor keep heading north to regain the path at the shoulder mentioned in the approach route.

Route 47 – Clach Glas – Bla Bheinn Traverse

Grade	Moderate/Difficult
Distance	9km
Ascent	1200m
Time	8 hours
Start/finish	Layby near the head of Loch Slapin (NG563226)
Map	OS Landranger (1:50,000) 32 or Harvey Superwalker (1:25,000 and 1:12,500) Skye: The Cuillin
Accommodation	See Route 44
Sleeping out	The best wild camping option hereabouts is on the grassy floor of Coire Uaigneich.
Public transport	See Route 44
Seasonal notes	The traverse is a brilliant winter outing, perhaps somewhat under-graded at III. In anything but perfect snow conditions it is likely to take ages and be very awkward. Intuitive route-finding ability is important at any time, but doubly so in winter.

Springing straight out of Loch Slapin, the complex mass of Bla Bheinn and Clach Glas looks almost Dolomitic. Although detached from the Main Ridge horseshoe, these hills provide moments as gripping as anything on the Cuillin Traverse. Indeed Clach Glas – Bla Bheinn is one of Scotland's most magnificent ridge traverses in its own right, an adventure of Alpine scale and ambience. Although technical difficulties rarely seem excessive the climbing interest is sustained, with a wealth of airy situations. Perhaps the biggest challenge is steering a safe course through so much complex and daunting ground. Starting the round with an ascent of Sgurr nan Each adds a satisfying warm-up, giving more than 2.5km of scrambling interest in total.

Bla Bheinn (left), Clach Glas and Sgurr nan Each (right) mirrored in loch Slapin – almost all of the day's route is visible

Skye and Rum

Approach

Cross marshy land to gain and follow a faint path along the N bank of the Allt Aigeinn, passing an enticing series of cascades and plunge pools. Beyond a high waterfall, enter the mouth of the rugged upper corrie. Cross the stream where it splits, climbing steeply to the obvious N Buttress of Sgurr nan Each. This has been prominent on the left-hand skyline for some time.

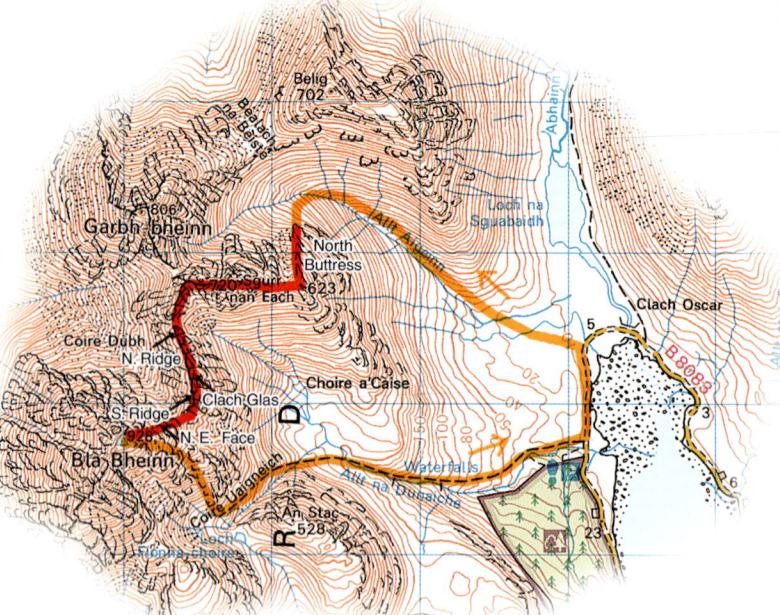

Climb

Sgurr nan Each, North Buttress, grade 2/3

Reach the first isolated toe of rock. Climb this from right to left; there's a lot of seepage, but the holds are generous. Easy broken ground and scree then lead to a short square-cut groove; follow clean rock on its immediate left. Continue to a grassy ledge, then take a short wall on brilliant rough rock. More shattered ground leads to a distinctive 'wart' or mini-tower. Climb the little vegetated groove to its left, then up the left side of a clean slab in a fine position. Above, the buttress narrows to a blunt arete; finish easily up this to reach the cairn at the minor 623m summit.

Sgurr nan Each, East–West Traverse, grade 1/2

Turn right and walk up the grassy ridge, which develops into a gentle scramble to the main 720m summit. Now traverse W along a series of rocky tops with much easy entertainment. Turn a steep exposed slab on the left, reaching a little nick in the crest just below it. The going then eases, and another minor top is soon reached. Bear SSW to the grassy col adjacent to Clach Glas. It is possible to escape E from here down steep scree into Choire a'Caise; this is the last safe descent option until the Clach Glas – Bla Bheinn col.

Clach Glas, North Ridge, Mod/Diff

Clach Glas is often referred to as the Matterhorn of Skye, and from this angle the comparison is appropriate. The awesome summit tower seems an unlikely location for a mere low-grade route, though a devious line does exist; pay close attention to route finding. Climb directly out of the bealach and take slabby ground leftwards. Cross a tight gap, then stay just right of the toothed crest, past a couple of little rock windows. Reach the top of a scree gully on the W flank. Make a tricky move right beneath an impending rock mass, and then keep traversing below and right of the crest on rubbly ledges. It is easy to be forced downhill here. Soon reach a deep scree gully bounding the summit tower.

If you've taken a low traverse line, then scramble gingerly up the boulder-filled bed to a point about 20m below the top of the gully. If you haven't yet felt the need, here might be a good place to belay. Ascend a deep v-groove on the right, bridging strenuously past a couple of smooth chockstones. Take an offwidth crack in the right wall onto a brief section of level arete leading back left to the top of the v-groove.

Turn left and climb sound, slabby rock in a magnificently tenuous position. The moves are easy, but there is one hell of a fall potential. Make directly for the crest, passing a big perched boulder at about 40m (possible belay). The crest soon broadens onto the summit platform, with its cairn poised on the edge of nothing. This must be

Low on the North Ridge of Clach Glas. Behind: Garbh-bheinn (left) and Sgurr nan Each

one of the most dramatic, least accessible places in Scotland.

Descent
Clach Glas, South Ridge, Moderate
Getting down is just as tricky as getting up – particularly in the wet. Clamber S along a blocky crest. Descend a short cracked slab on the left, with a fiendish drop from its right side and a giddying plunge of barrelling slabs ahead. This is the famous Imposter, so called for its misleading resemblance from below to the keenest knife blade. Downclimb a short steep overlap at the bottom of the slab to gain a level arete. This terminates at a vertical nose, similar in structure to the Imposter. Descend slabs to the left onto a scree-strewn ledge. Follow a worn path to an easy- angled rightwards descent down rubbly steps. Head left again below this section, taking a little nick leading to a gap in the crest with gullies dropping off to either side. Clamber out of the gap, soon entering a second gap. Climbing out of this is steep and juggy for a few moves. Head diagonally left towards a blunt pinnacle (the Bealach Tower); just before the top of this, cut diagonally left up a short groove, then abruptly descend again down a little slab on the E side. Follow a ledge back right below the tower to a gap spanned by a prominent jammed block – this looks somewhat precarious, and may not remain an identifiable feature forever. Go up easily on the right to the small grassy shoulder known as the Putting Green. At this point it's possible to bail out by dropping E, though this is steep and loose.

Descending the Imposter, Clach Glas South Ridge. It's not what it looks like.

Climb

Bla Bheinn, NE Face, Moderate

There are several possible variations from here. The route described may be the easiest, but it is also memorably weird. Head left out of the Putting Green, then right up to a gap at the top of a gully, enjoying an unusual view of the stupendous Great Prow along the way. Climb out of the gap via a short steep wall on big flat holds. Seepage can be a problem here, and as the wall tops out in scree it may be worth roping up. Then ascend this scree to the foot of a glowering face.

Make for an obvious right–left diagonal shelf, which is climbed (beware loose rubble) to an incredibly exposed ledge created by the differential erosion of a dyke. Above is a low overhang; below, a surprisingly large drop. Many parties will opt to belay here. Proceed along this gangway in a crouching crawl under the impending roof to enter a scree-filled cave at the top of a chimney. Moving out of this is the crux, and it's worth arranging trustworthy gear before committing, especially if it is slimy (hint: place a runner deep in the cave, extended on a very long sling). Beyond, the ledge system continues its diagonal line, with one more airy gap before safe ground is reached quite suddenly on Bla Bheinn's easy East Flank. Turn right, trudging up scree and outcrops to the summit trig point.

High drama on the shelf pitch, Bla Bheinn's NE face. Behind: Clach Glas and the Putting Green

Skye and Rum

Near the Putting Green, Clach Glas South Ridge. Behind: the northern Cuillin Main Ridge (Route 48)

Descent

The East Flank is the most direct way back to your starting point. Descend back past the top of the scramble, continuing behind the Great Prow and on down steep scree patches onto the lush grassy floor of Coire Uaigneich. Heavy use has made the route obvious. Follow a good descent path down the N bank of a burn, crossing the water when you reach level ground in Choire a'Caise. Stay with the path past a series of wooded waterfalls to regain the road beside Loch Slapin.

Route 48 – Cuillin Main Ridge Traverse

Grade	Very Difficult
Distance	11km climbing between Gars-bheinn and Sgurr nan Gillean; 26km total
Ascent	3000m+
Time	Varies widely depending on conditions and prior knowledge of the route. In 2013 the record stood at just under 2hrs 15mins between the southernmost and northernmost summits on the ridge. At the opposite end of the ability scale two days is common. In friendly weather average parties should reckon on something like 10–16hrs, plus a lengthy moorland tramp to start and finish.
Start	Typically, Glen Brittle campsite (NG410206)
Finish	Sligachan Hotel (NG486298)
Maps	OS Landranger (1:50,000) 32 gives a useful overview, but fails to convey the Cuillin's intricacies. OS Explorer (1:25,000) 411 is more useful, though its tangle of contours can look confusing. Harvey's 1:25,000 Superwalker Skye: the Cuillin is easiest to follow, with a useful 1:12,500 enlargement and a diagram showing non-technical descent routes.
Accommodation	See Route 44
Sleeping out	One ridge-top bivvy is *de rigeur*, though more than one would seem excessive.
Public transport	See Route 45. This is a tricky route to fit around the bus timetable; many people manage to hitchhike back to their base in Glen Brittle.
Seasonal notes	Fresh snow, heavy rain or even Skye's perennial dense fog are enough to scupper your chances. Midsummer is often wet and always midge-ridden. Spells of settled weather tend to crop up in May/June, and again in September, and these are favoured periods for an attempt. With its long daylight hours, late June seems particularly suitable. In full winter nick the Cuillin Traverse becomes a whole new game, with several days of sustained II/III and many pitches of IV. Due to its difficulty, and the ephemeral snow conditions on these maritime hills, it is completed only rarely. The Winter Traverse tends to be done from N to S so that the main difficulties can be abseiled. It's said to be one of the best routes in the universe, but only for very strong parties.
Navigation	Cuillin rock is infamously magnetic, sending compass needles into a spin (sometimes literally). While they are not distributed consistently along the ridge, these magnetic hotspots are scattered around liberally, waiting to baffle the unwary. A sensible course is to regard all bearings with a degree of healthy scepticism; when in doubt try taking a number of bearings a short distance apart, and calculating an average. If this seems like more effort than it's worth, you can always fall back on animal instinct to 'feel' your way along. Given a route of such baffling complexity, maps, compasses and GPS devices are of only limited value in any case. In poor visibility, only those with both route-finding nous and prior knowledge of the more intricate sections of the Traverse are likely to have even the foggiest notion of their location.

Rearing out of a flat expanse of bog and sea, Skye's Cuillin present an array of monstrous teeth, as strikingly jagged as any Alpine range. With fantastic rock (at its best), sweeping ocean views and climbs that stretch on forever, these soaring aretes and gnarled peaks embody all that's noble about the mountains. Linking every summit strung out along the main ridge in one audacious push, the Cuillin Traverse is the great Scottish mountaineering adventure, one of the world's top ridge climbs. The way is long and gruelling, with continuously involved route finding and all the logistical hassles of a real expedition, usually including a mountaintop bivvy. Despite

The central and northern Cuillin, as seen from Sgurr Dubh Mor (Route 44). From left to right: Sgurr a'Ghreadaidh, Sgurr a'Mhadaidh (multiple tops), Bidein Druim nan Ramh (serrated tops), An Caisteal, Bruach na Frithe, Sgurr a' Fionn Choire, the Basteir Tooth and Am Basteir

sections of rough walking it is for the most part a sustained hard scramble with continuous exposure, spiced by frequent passages of Mod and Diff soloing, several harder roped pitches and a handful of abseils. It's often reckoned that to take everything in their stride with sufficient comfort, each member of the party should be able to lead Severe. While this may be a slight overstatement, it gives a fair idea of the technical nature of the task.

As a physical undertaking the route has been compared by one well-known guide to a back-to-back ascent of Mont Blanc and the Matterhorn – but with the added frisson (and reduced friction) of Hebridean precipitation. Bearing in mind the frustrations of local weather it's clear that on top of fitness, skill and tenacity, even the most experienced climbers need a little luck. Many come year on year only to be thwarted at every attempt. But even failures here are glorious, while a successful Cuillin Traverse is one of life's richest experiences, and more than compensates for the pain and heartache.

The Greater Traverse
Unlikely as it may seem, the pleb's version isn't hard enough for some people. Including outlying Garbh-bheinn, Clach Glas and Bla Bheinn into the round adds a huge distance and an additional 1000m of ascent to an already excessive total. This one's strictly for masochistic whippets.

Logistics
Where (or if) to sleep, what to carry, whether to make a strategic mid-ridge cache of food and water before the attempt – even for old hands these questions lead to lively speculation. The great thing is, there is no single right answer. Tradition dictates a bivvy on the summit of Garsbheinn at the southern end of the ridge, followed by an Alpine start in order to tick the whole route the following day. But traditions exist to be ignored. The Traverse is such a demanding proposition that it pays to think smart. For instance, why not bag the easy southern section on the afternoon of day one, and then bivvy just short of the

48 – CUILLIN MAIN RIDGE TRAVERSE

The Coire na Creiche skyline presents some of the toughest climbing on the Traverse. Left to right: Bidein Druim nan Ramh, Sgurr a'Mhadaidh, Sgurr Thuilm.

Thearlaich Dubh (TD) Gap? That way you'll have plenty in the bag before even starting day two. If only to jump off the fence and encourage dissent, this is how the Traverse is described here.

What to carry is another question entirely. Having once lugged bivvy gear the full length of the ridge, and vowed never again, I for one recommend stashing it where you camped for retrieval later. Since the ridge crest is entirely arid (if not always dry), sufficient water has to be carried en route. Reckon on a couple of litres per person for the bivvy, plus a further couple for the climb – more in a heatwave. A short length of drinking straw allows you to suck at puddles and seeps as you go, saving the bottled stuff for later. One of the only reliable water sources close to the route is a spring just down into Fionn Choire, near the north end of the ridge. Hardware is yet another issue. Only very skilled climbers with extensive Cuillin experience should consider soloing all the way. The rest of us need a 50m rope and a stripped-down rack. And don't forget your helmet.

Approach

In summer a S to N traverse is customary, starting the approach at Glen Brittle campsite. Take the main Coire Lagan path initially, branching right after a few hundred metres and heading muddily towards Sron na Ciche. Contour into the mouth of Coire a'Ghrunnda. Traditionalists continue parallel to the ridge to ascend the horrid bouldery SW flank of Gars-bheinn. If you want to punish your climbing partner for some misdemeanour, this is the way to take them. Perhaps a 'gentler' approach is to scramble up burn-side slabs in Coir a'Ghrunnda, passing the loch to reach the Bealach a'Garbh-choire. Stash your bags here and head down to Gars-bheinn and back – round trip about 2 hours. This is a lovely ridge-top walk with a fair degree of scrambling interest, and makes a good prelude to the climbing proper. Retrieve your sacks and aim for the broken molar of Caisteal a'Garbh-choire. The direct assault up the S side and down the W is a Diff on beautifully rough rock – easily avoided by a path on the right. Climb over Sgurr Dubh an Da Bheinn and

Skye and Rum

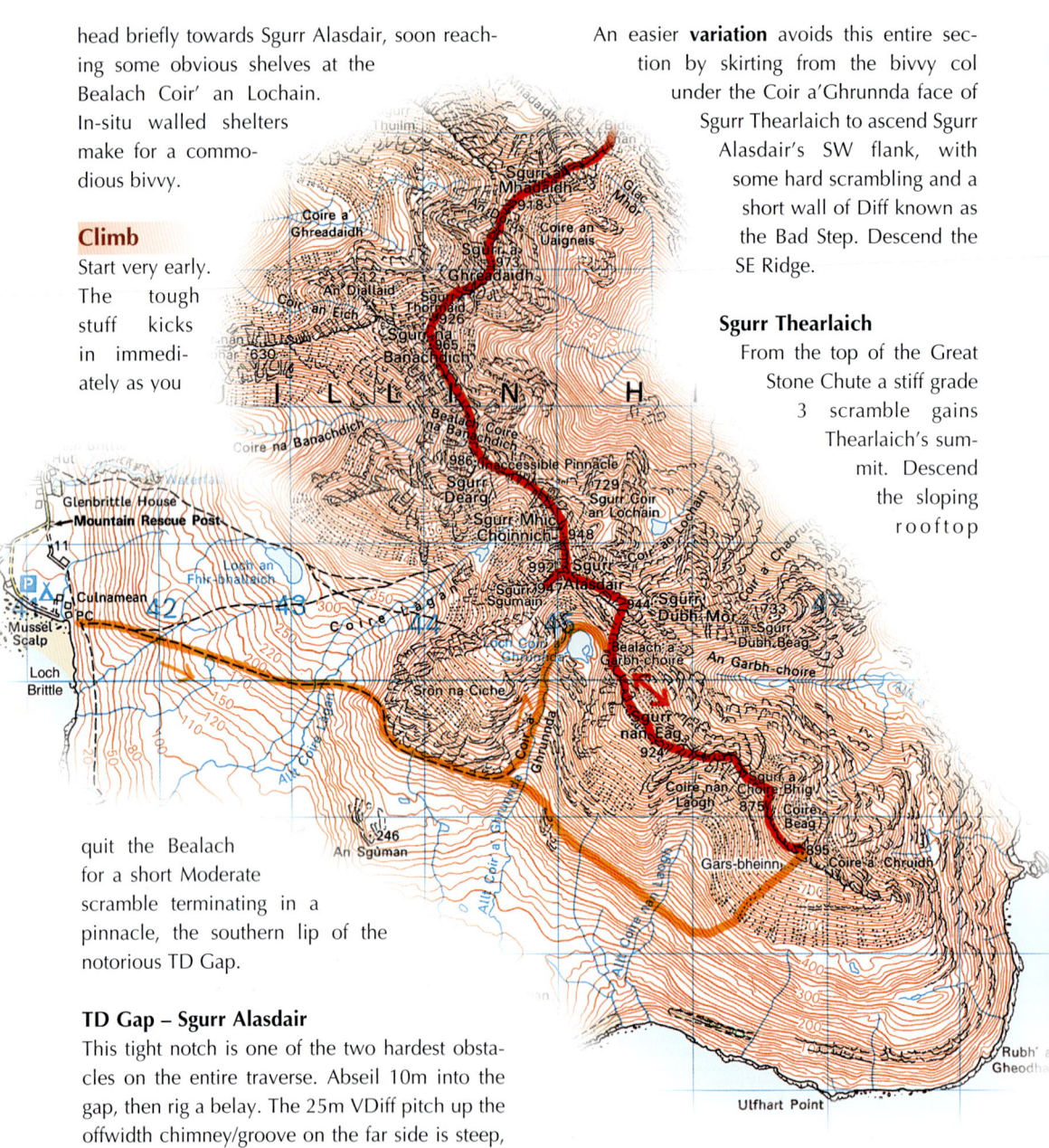

head briefly towards Sgurr Alasdair, soon reaching some obvious shelves at the Bealach Coir' an Lochain. In-situ walled shelters make for a commodious bivvy.

Climb

Start very early. The tough stuff kicks in immediately as you quit the Bealach for a short Moderate scramble terminating in a pinnacle, the southern lip of the notorious TD Gap.

TD Gap – Sgurr Alasdair

This tight notch is one of the two hardest obstacles on the entire traverse. Abseil 10m into the gap, then rig a belay. The 25m VDiff pitch up the offwidth chimney/groove on the far side is steep, awkward and polished. In the wet it can be the scene of a mini-epic. A medium cam or chock is reassuring. Scrambling leads on towards Sgurr Thearlaich. A detour bags the summit of Sgurr Alasdair, highest peak in the Cuillin; traverse leftwards across the top of the Great Stone Chute to scramble easily up the mountain's short SE Ridge. Retrace your steps.

An easier **variation** avoids this entire section by skirting from the bivvy col under the Coir a'Ghrunnda face of Sgurr Thearlaich to ascend Sgurr Alasdair's SW flank, with some hard scrambling and a short wall of Diff known as the Bad Step. Descend the SE Ridge.

Sgurr Thearlaich

From the top of the Great Stone Chute a stiff grade 3 scramble gains Thearlaich's summit. Descend the sloping rooftop roughly N towards the Bealach Mhic Choinnich. Route finding is challenging down scary Diff slabs to the col, with the easiest lines on both the Coruisk and Lagan sides being far from obvious. The natural way seems to be a direct descent instead, reaching a diving-board neck from which it is perhaps wisest to abseil into the gap.

Fighting up the TD Gap in the rain

Sgurr Mhic Choinnich – Inaccessible Pinnacle
A short steep wall gains access to the remarkable Collie's Ledge, which blazes an exposed but easy path leftwards across the mountain's W face. Either continue to its end at grade 2, then backtrack to bag the summit, or tackle the formidable King's Chimney, Diff. This pitch cuts up a corner from near the start of Collie's Ledge, and is much easier than appearance suggests – good holds lead right to pass the intimidating overhang. From the summit, scramble easily down the mountain's N ridge to the next col. The direct line up the crest of An Stac is an inescapable Moderate, which has a mixed reputation. Some consider it appallingly loose, while others maintain that the true crest is clean and even rather spiffing. Having been rained off it more than once, I'm happiest recommending the alternative route, which skirts left directly under An Stac, climbing rubble-strewn basalt slabs leading to the base of the Inaccessible Pinnacle.

Inaccessible Pinnacle
This menacing shark's fin forms the true summit of Sgurr Dearg, and is famously the only Munro that requires a rope. In truth many Cuillin Munros are similarly technical, if less exposed. The pinnacle can readily be avoided, though this would be a shame. Climb the razor-sharp E Ridge in one long roped pitch, which must rank as Britain's airiest Moderate. Abseil the shorter vertical W side, from a reassuringly substantial hawser under the summit block. A recent rockfall hasn't adversely affected the abseil, though the adjacent North West Corner (a VDiff route on the W side of the pinnacle) was damaged.

Sgurr Dearg – Sgurr na Banachdich
From the nearby slabby top of Sgurr Dearg, rough walking leads down to the Bealach Coire na Banachdich. A pleasant scramble takes the S ridge of Sgurr na Banachdich over two minor tops and on to the summit. Stay with the spine, since the flanks are loose. As this peak is both central

243

On Sgurr Mhic Choinnich, An Stac and the In Pinn soon to come (top left)

to the Traverse and fairly easily reached from the W, it's a useful place to stash food and drink prior to an attempt.

Sgurr na Banachdich – An Dorus
The ridge now juts off rightwards at 90°. Descend a loose gully to the Bealach Thormaid, below the pyramid profile of Sgurr Thormaid. This looks intimidating, but is best tackled direct by a steep grade 3 scramble up the W face. A deceptive path pretends to outflank this obstacle, though in truth it leads to harder ground. Carry on along the narrow NE ridge, passing either side of the Three Teeth. The fabulous SW Ridge of Sgurr a'Ghreadaidh comes next, a keen curved blade of rock demanding incredibly gripping grade 3 scrambling between the S and main tops. Gentler scrambling then leads down, passing left of the Wart to the gap at Eag Dubh. One brief tricky bit later you reach the pass of An Dorus, which offers a non-technical escape to the left. The following two peaks present some of the most complex climbing on the Cuillin Ridge on a confusing array of sharp tops.

Sgurr a'Mhadaidh
Sgurr a'Mhadaidh's four summits are numbered in reverse order. Climb fairly easily to the main (4th) top, then descend the narrow crest to the point where the ridge does another (approximately) 90° swing to the right. Tricky slabs lead down to a nick, which is hard to exit. Another slabby descent gains the foot of the 3rd top. Climb its right face overlooking Coruisk on slightly suspect Moderate rock. The 2nd top might be worth roping up for, and is taken direct by a short Diff pitch. The 1st top proves easier. Slabs then drop to the Bealach na Glaic Moire, where easy escapes can be made to either side.

Bidein Druim nan Ramh
Four-pronged Mhadaidh now safely negotiated, the trident of Bidein Druim nan Ramh makes your next daunting obstacle. The first peak is a

Approaching the smoking towers of Sgurr a'Mhadaidh

SKYE AND RUM

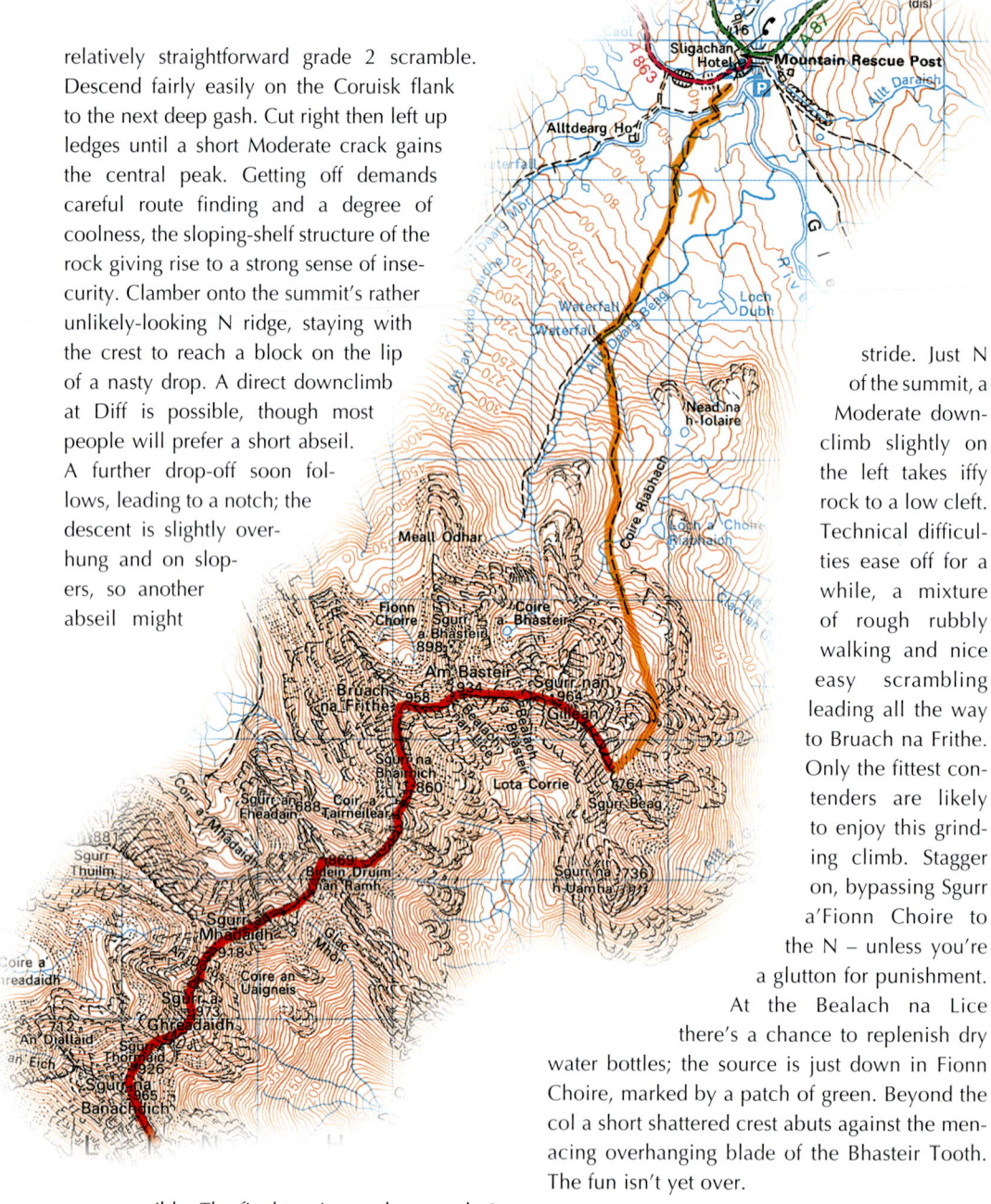

relatively straightforward grade 2 scramble. Descend fairly easily on the Coruisk flank to the next deep gash. Cut right then left up ledges until a short Moderate crack gains the central peak. Getting off demands careful route finding and a degree of coolness, the sloping-shelf structure of the rock giving rise to a strong sense of insecurity. Clamber onto the summit's rather unlikely-looking N ridge, staying with the crest to reach a block on the lip of a nasty drop. A direct downclimb at Diff is possible, though most people will prefer a short abseil. A further drop-off soon follows, leading to a notch; the descent is slightly overhung and on slopers, so another abseil might seem sensible. The final top is won by a grade 3 scramble leftwards. More grade 3 ground leads down the crest to the Bealach Harta.

Bealach Harta – Bhasteir Tooth

The crest of An Caisteal gives a relatively easy stretch of grade 2, enlivened by unexpected 'crevasses'. The widest of these calls for a scary stride. Just N of the summit, a Moderate downclimb slightly on the left takes iffy rock to a low cleft. Technical difficulties ease off for a while, a mixture of rough rubbly walking and nice easy scrambling leading all the way to Bruach na Frithe. Only the fittest contenders are likely to enjoy this grinding climb. Stagger on, bypassing Sgurr a'Fionn Choire to the N – unless you're a glutton for punishment. At the Bealach na Lice there's a chance to replenish dry water bottles; the source is just down in Fionn Choire, marked by a patch of green. Beyond the col a short shattered crest abuts against the menacing overhanging blade of the Bhasteir Tooth. The fun isn't yet over.

Bhasteir Tooth

Met with such a formidable obstacle this late in the day you could be forgiven for feeling daunted. If it all looks too much then escape down scree to the N, traversing under Am Basteir to regain the ridge at the next col. Only the mountains need witness your dirty secret – and they're not telling.

An airy stride on An Caisteal

Naismith's Route on the Basteir Tooth, a stern test of commitment at this stage in the day

The Lota Corrie route (Mod) gains the niche between Tooth and parent mountain from well down to the S via slabs, scree and grooves. It's no classic, though do-able in the wet. Being among the most challenging and sensational pitches on the entire Traverse, Naismith's Route (35m, VDiff) is best by far. This demands confidence and care in equal measure, especially from knackered traversers in big boots. Follow ledges out right over the substantial S face. A wall gains another ledge. Sidle right again, until below a deep crack. Place bombproof gear, then commit to a steep wall on small holds (may be slimy), soon leading to the crack. Climb this briefly before stepping right into another crack system and so to the top with a strenuous final mantelshelf. Pad up the Tooth's slabby top to the giddying prow.

Bhasteir Tooth – Bealach a'Bhasteir

From the nick between the Tooth and Am Basteir make an easy rising traverse to the right, gaining a loose gully. This is blocked by a short bulging nose; climb it direct with a sporty lunge or two that would rate around Severe on a roadside crag. Easy scrambling then brings you to the summit of Am Basteir. The E ridge is an undemanding scrambling descent to the Bealach a'Bhasteir, with one brief step of Moderate.

Sgurr nan Gillean

One of Scotland's finest peaks and a fitting climax to the adventure. The toothed W Ridge is an exciting Moderate. Traverse left from the col to a short chimney in the back of a recess. Climb either this chimney or the rib beside it to gain the interestingly castellated crest, which soon eases into scrambling. Thread an obvious rock window

48 – CUILLIN MAIN RIDGE TRAVERSE

Sgurr nan Gillean (left) and Bla Bheinn (right, Route 47) from Am Basteir

to reach the summit, an elevated perch with fantastic views back along the course of the Traverse. Don't relax yet – the final hurdle is best cleared before nightfall.

Descent

As for Route 46. The misleadingly named Tourist Route down the SE Ridge starts as a hard exposed grade 3 scramble. Cross a thin neck to an awkward and very airy step down a steep slab, after which the blocky crest eases gradually into a broad shoulder. This, finally, marks the end of all technical ground, and the chance to catch your breath.

Drop E into a grassy scree bowl to pick up a cairned northward path that traverses rough ground under Gillean's Pinnacle Ridge, entering Coire Riabhach down scree to the left of an area of slabs. Take care here in poor visibility. Once safely on the corrie floor keep heading north over the moors, limping into the Sligachan Hotel in time – hopefully – for a liquid celebration.

ROUTE SUMMARY TABLE

In order of route difficulty

Route	Chapter	Type	Grade	Distance	Ascent	Page
NW Ridge, A'Mhaighdean	39	Scramble	1/2	41km	1200m	198
NE Ridge, Angel's Peak	28	Scramble	1/2	29km	1500m	149
Stac Pollaidh	41	Scramble	2	4km	570m	206
Forcan Ridge, The Saddle	31	Scramble	2	15km	1380m	164
Ledge Route, Ben Nevis	16	Scramble	2	12km	1300m	96
The Spur, Sgurr an Fheadain	45	Scramble	2	6.5km	620m	225
Glen Sannox Horseshoe	4	Scramble	2/3	15km	1700m	44
Sron na Creise	7	Scramble	3	12km	1000m	57
Suilven	42	Scramble	3	22km	1100m	209
NNE Ridge, Sgurr Ghiubhsachain	30	Scramble	3	16km	1170m	160
An Teallach	40	Scramble	3	16km	1400m	201
Curved Ridge	9	Scramble	3	5km	750m	65
Rum Cuillin Traverse	43	Scr/climb	Mod	25km	1900m	224
Castle Ridge, Ben Nevis	15	Scr/climb	Mod	11km	1150m	91
A'Chir traverse	1	Climb	Mod	15km	950m	29
Pygmy Ridge/Afterthought Arete	26	Climb	Mod	9km	800m	140
Dubhs Ridge	44	Climb	Mod	9km	1040m	221
Pinnacle Ridge, Sgurr nan Gillean	46	Climb	Mod/Diff	11km	970m	228
Clach Glas – Blaven Traverse	47	Climb	Mod/Diff	9km	1200m	233
The Cobbler	5	Climb	Diff	8km	900m	48
NE Ridge, Aonach Beag	22	Climb	Diff	10.5km	1195m	120
Tower Ridge, Ben Nevis	17	Climb	Diff	13km	1300m	99
Marathon Ridge, Beinn Lair	38	Climb	Diff	36km	980m	192
Observatory Ridge, Ben Nevis	18	Climb	VDiff	14km	1300m	104
Cioch Nose	33	Climb	VDiff	9km	660m	171
Cuillin Main Ridge Traverse	48	Climb	VDiff	26km	3000m+	239
NEB via Raeburn's Arete, Ben Nevis	19	Climb	Severe	14km	1300m	107
Great Ridge, Garbh Bheinn	29	Climb	Severe	12km	880m	155
Pagoda Ridge, A'Chir	2	Climb	Severe	12km	680m	33
Crowberry Ridge via Rannoch Wall	10	Climb	Severe	5km	750m	68
Eagle Ridge, Lochnagar	24	Climb	Severe	15km	770m	130
Mitre Ridge, Beinn a'Bhuird	25	Climb	HS	32km	960m	135
South Ridge Direct, Rosa Pinnacle	3	Climb	VS	13km	779m	38
Coire Gaothach circuit, Ben Lui	6	Winter	I	18km	950m	52
Beinn Alligin	35	Winter	I	10km	1200m	180
Leachas Ridges, Ben Alder	23	Winter	I	42km	930m	125
S Ridge, Mullach Fraoch Choire	32	Winter	I	17km	1200m	167
Ring of Steall	14	Winter	I	15km	1500m	86
Fiacaill Ridge	27	Winter	I/II	7km	620m	145
CDM E Ridge and CMD Arete	20	Winter	II	18km	1000m	111
Sron na Lairig	11	Winter	II	10km	910m	72
Dorsal Arete	12	Winter	II,3	6km	990m	77
Golden Oldie	21	Winter	II	7km	740m	116
Aonach Eagach	13	Winter	II	10km	1150m	81
Liathach traverse	36	Winter	II	12km	1300m	184
A'Chioch, Beinn Bhan	34	Winter	II,3	9km	940m	176
Northern Pinnacles, Liathach	37	Winter	II/III	15km	1000m	188
Inglis Clark Ridge	8	Winter	III	8km	720m	61

APPENDIX 1
FURTHER ADVENTURES ...

Owing to the constraints of time and space, the following routes didn't make the final selection. This is no reflection of their quality, as all of them are worth a look. In addition to the following there may be other ridges out there, languishing in obscurity. Perhaps some are still unrecorded? Happy exploring.

Arran and the Southern Highlands
Pinnacle Ridge, 140m Difficult / III,4, Cir Mhor NE Face
Caliban's Creep, 150m VDiff, Cir Mhor S Face
Prospero's Prelude, 120m Moderate leading to Prospero's Peril, 125m Severe, Cir Mhor S Face

Lochaber
E Ridge, N Buttress, Stob Ban, 200m grade 3 scramble / II/III
Lancet Edge, Sgor Iutharn, grade 1 scramble / I
ENE Ridge, Sgurr Bhan, grade 1 scramble / I
Vice Chancellor Ridge, Aonach Eagach, 210m III
Traverse of Ben Cruachan via N Ridge of Stob Dearg, easy I
Hidden Ridge, Ben Starav, 200m III/IV
Traverse of Ben Starav via the N and E ridges, easy I
Western Rib, Aonach Mor, 400m II/III
Daim Buttress, Aonach Mor, 400m II/III
Solitaire, Aonach Mor, 400m II
Aonach Seang, Aonach Mor, 120m III / Difficult
The Ramp, Aonach Beag, II
E Ridge, Beinn a'Chaorainn, 300m grade 1 scramble / I/II

Cairngorms
Lairig Ridge, Sron na Lairige, Braeriach, 135m Difficult
Domed Ridge, Braeriach, 200m III / Moderate
Kookaburra, Braeriach, 130m HS
Sphinx ridge, Braeriach, 100m VDiff / III
Snake Ridge, Ben Macdui, 130m HS
Crystal Ridge, Ben Macdui, 90m Diff
Fingers Ridge, Coire an t-Sneachda, 140m Difficult / IV,4
The Glen Einich Ridges, several granite ribs up to 260m long, grades ranging from III to IV,6. Loose and dangerous in summer.

The North and West
Pinnacle Ridge, Garbh Bheinn, grade 3 scramble
Coire Dhorrcail round, Ladhar Bheinn, I
N Ridge, Aonach Air Chrith, Glenshiel, I
Lurg Mhor – Meall Mor Ridge, grade 1 scramble / I
Black Carls, Beinn Eighe, I
The adventurous won't have failed to spot the obvious potential of the impressive NW Face of Slioch: try Skyline Highway 370m HVS, or Stepped Ridge, 240m VDiff for starters.
Sgurr an Fhidhleir, Direct Nose Route, 245m HVS / VII,7
Lurgainn Edge, Cul Beag, 200m VDiff
Kveldro Ridge, Cul Beag, 200m VDiff
SE Ridge, Ben More Assynt, grade 2 scramble
Brown's Ridge, Ben Hope, grade 3 scramble / II
Bell's Ridge, Ben Hope, 240m S / III
Academy Ridge, Sgorr Ruadh, 350m III / VDiff

Skye and Rum
Midget Ridge, Sgurr na Banachdich, 120m Moderate
SE Ridge, Sgurr A'Ghreadaidh, 700m Difficult
S Ridge, Sgurr Coir an Lochain, Difficult

S Ridge, Sgurr na h-Uamha, grade 3 scramble
N Ridge, Sgurr na h-Uamha, Moderate
NW Ridge, Bruach na Frithe, grade 2 scramble
NE Ridge, Sgurr a Choire Bhig, grade 3 scramble
Druim nan Ramh direct, grade 3 scramble
Circuit of Coire na Selig, Garbh-bheinn, grade 1 scramble / I

APPENDIX 2
FURTHER READING

Of numerous books covering Scotland's mountains, and mountains in general, I have found the following both useful and inspirational over the years:

Eyes to the Hills, Gordon Stainforth (Constable 1991): A combination of evocative photographs of the British mountains and thoughtful musings.

Scotland's Winter Mountains, Martin Moran (David & Charles 1988): Essential tips and skills covering every aspect of the winter game, but also an inspiring read.

100 Best Routes on Scottish Mountains, Ralph Storer (David & Charles 1987): Is there a better hillwalking guidebook?

Scrambles in Lochaber, Noel Williams (Cicerone 1996): Details dozens of routes in this major mountain area.

The Hillwalker's Guide to Mountaineering, Terry Adby and Stuart Johnston (Cicerone 2003): Should be the first resort of every aspiring climber.

The Undiscovered Country, Phil Bartlett (The Ernest Press 1993): An erudite history of climbing, and an accomplished analysis of why we do it. An ambitious work, not yet bettered.

Mountaineering in Scotland, WH Murray (Dent 1947): A must-read; redolent of a past era, and yet still relevant today.

SMC area guides: The definitive climber's reference books to Scotland.

The material and symbolic production of landscape in the crofting counties, Ronald Macintyre (forthcoming PHD thesis), a fascinating – if weighty – analysis of land use in the Highlands, and of our perceptions and representations of the Scottish landscape.

Medicine for Mountaineering & Other Wilderness Activities, James A. Wilkerson, ed. (The Mountaineers 1992): Here's hoping you never need it; but should the worst happen then here's what to do.

And if you liked this book, you might also like...

The Ridges of England, Wales and Ireland, Dan Bailey (Cicerone 2009)

APPENDIX 3
USEFUL CONTACTS

Since the Internet is now all-pervasive, it seems unnecessary to list telephone numbers. Websites are, in general, a much better source of information.

Transport

Scotrail runs train services to Highland hubs including Aviemore, Inverness, Fort William, Mallaig, Kyle of Lochalsh and Oban (www.firstgroup.com/scotrail).

Caledonian Macbrayne operate ferries to Skye, Rum and Arran (www.calmac.co.uk).

Citylink has the most extensive bus network in the Highlands, serving every major town from Ullapool to Glasgow (www.citylink.co.uk), including a link to Skye.

National Express are also worth a look (www.nationalexpress.com)

For local buses throughout the west contact Rapsons (www.rapsons.com). Services from Aberdeen to Braemar are run by Stagecoach (www.stagecoachbus.com).

With their Postbus network the Royal Mail gets to parts other firms cannot reach (www.royalmail.com)

Comprehensive public transport journey planning is provided by Traveline (www.travelinescotland.com 0871 200 22 33), tying together the disparate timetables of a host of operators in what would otherwise be a free market chaos.

Forecasts and reports

Useful online weather forecast services are provided by various people. The Met Office is good for the big picture (www.meto.gov.uk).

Better by far, however, in terms of what the big picture actually equates to up a mountain, is the Mountain Weather Information Service (www.mwis.org.uk). During the winter season vital avalanche forecasts for the most popular climbing areas are provided by the Scottish Avalanche Information Service (www.sais.gov.uk), along with rough climbing conditions reports.

Regular winter climbing conditions reports are also posted on a variety of other websites. Perhaps the best first port of call is (www.winternet-scotland.co.uk), which has links to several sites providing conditions reports, weather forecasts and webcams trained on key peaks.

Lochcarron-based mountain guide Martin Moran provides probably the only winter climbing reports for Wester Ross (www.moran-mountain.co.uk).

Accommodation

The Scottish Youth Hostels Association runs dozens of budget hostels in prime locations (www.syha.org.uk).

This hostel network is augmented by the many independent backpacker's bunkhouses scattered throughout the Highlands and Islands, brought together on one website at (www.hostel-scotland.co.uk).

Those looking for higher-budget accommodation could do worse than visit Scotland's National Tourism Board (www.visitscotland.com) for recommendations.

Organisations

Scottish Natural Heritage work to protect and enhance wildlife habitats and landscape, running (among other things) National Nature Reserves including Rum and Beinn Eighe (www.snh.org.uk).

The Scottish Wild Land Group campaigns to protect sensitive wild land and promote the interests of local communities (www.swlg.org.uk).

The John Muir Trust has similar aims, emphasising sustainability, community ownership of land and wilderness conservation (www.jmt.org).

The Mountaineering Council of Scotland is a representative body for hillwalkers, climbers and cross-country skiers, working to protect the mountain environment and further the sport of climbing, and acting as an umbrella organisation for climbing clubs (www.mountaineering-scotland.org.uk).

The Ramblers Association fulfils a like role for the less vertically inclined (www.ramblers.org.uk). Their Scottish arm has been particularly active in recent years in campaigning to curb the damaging spread of giant windfarms in our more sensitive mountain areas, with a policy on renewable energy that is both more progressive and more conservation-minded than that of wind industry lobbyists and the Scottish Executive itself (www.ramblers.org.uk/scotland). Those in power, in both senses of the word, would do well to listen.

Most Highland bothies are privately owned, yet they are maintained on the behalf of us all by enthusiastic teams of volunteers from the Mountain Bothies Association, a charity that looks after over 100 unlocked shelters in UK mountain areas, predominantly in Scotland (www.mountainbothies.org.uk).

We all hope never to need the assistance of a mountain rescue team, but it's nice to know they're there. They are voluntary organisations, relying on donations of money, and the time and goodwill of many selfless people. Scotland's teams come together as the Mountain Rescue Committee of Scotland. Anyone interested in helping them out might like to visit (www.mrc-scotland.org.uk).

LISTING OF CICERONE GUIDES

BRITISH ISLES CHALLENGES, COLLECTIONS AND ACTIVITIES
The End to End Trail
The Mountains of England and Wales: 1&2
The National Trails
The Relative Hills of Britain
The Ridges of England, Wales and Ireland
The UK Trailwalker's Handbook
The UK's County Tops
Three Peaks, Ten Tors

UK CYCLING
Border Country Cycle Routes
Cycling in the Cotswolds
Cycling in the Hebrides
Cycling in the Peak District
Cycling in the Yorkshire Dales
Cycling the Pennine Bridleway
Mountain Biking in the Lake District
Mountain Biking in the Yorkshire Dales
Mountain Biking on the North Downs
Mountain Biking on the South Downs
The C2C Cycle Route
The End to End Cycle Route
The Lancashire Cycleway

SCOTLAND
Backpacker's Britain
    Central and Southern Scottish Highlands
    Northern Scotland
Ben Nevis and Glen Coe
Great Mountain Days in Scotland
Not the West Highland Way
Scotland's Best Small Mountains
Scotland's Far West
Scotland's Mountain Ridges
Scrambles in Lochaber
The Ayrshire and Arran Coastal Paths
The Border Country
The Cape Wrath Trail
The Great Glen Way
The Isle of Mull
The Isle of Skye
The Pentland Hills
The Scottish Glens 2 – The Atholl Glens
The Southern Upland Way
The Speyside Way
The West Highland Way
Walking Highland Perthshire
Walking in Scotland's Far North
Walking in the Angus Glens
Walking in the Cairngorms
Walking in the Ochils, Campsie Fells and Lomond Hills
Walking in Torridon
Walking Loch Lomond and the Trossachs
Walking on Harris and Lewis
Walking on Jura, Islay and Colonsay
Walking on Rum and the Small Isles
Walking on the Isle of Arran
Walking on the Orkney and Shetland Isles
Walking on Uist and Barra
Walking the Corbetts
    1 South of the Great Glen
    2 North of the Great Glen
Walking the Galloway Hills
Walking the Lowther Hills
Walking the Munros
    1 Southern, Central and Western Highlands
    2 Northern Highlands and the Cairngorms
Winter Climbs Ben Nevis and Glen Coe
Winter Climbs in the Cairngorms
World Mountain Ranges: Scotland

NORTHERN ENGLAND TRAILS
A Northern Coast to Coast Walk
Backpacker's Britain – Northern England
Hadrian's Wall Path
The Dales Way
The Pennine Way

NORTH EAST ENGLAND, YORKSHIRE DALES AND PENNINES
Great Mountain Days in the Pennines
Historic Walks in North Yorkshire
South Pennine Walks
St Oswald's Way and St Cuthbert's Way
The Cleveland Way and the Yorkshire Wolds Way
The North York Moors
The Reivers Way
The Teesdale Way
The Yorkshire Dales
    North and East
    South and West
Walking in County Durham
Walking in Northumberland
Walking in the North Pennines
Walks in Dales Country
Walks in the Yorkshire Dales
Walks on the North York Moors – Books 1 & 2

NORTH WEST ENGLAND AND THE ISLE OF MAN
Historic Walks in Cheshire
Isle of Man Coastal Path
The Isle of Man
The Lune Valley and Howgills
The Ribble Way
Walking in Cumbria's Eden Valley
Walking in Lancashire
Walking in the Forest of Bowland and Pendle
Walking on the West Pennine Moors
Walks in Lancashire Witch Country
Walks in Ribble Country
Walks in Silverdale and Arnside
Walks in the Forest of Bowland

LAKE DISTRICT
Coniston Copper Mines
Great Mountain Days in the Lake District
Lake District Winter Climbs
Lakeland Fellranger
    The Central Fells
    The Far-Eastern Fells
    The Mid-Western Fells
    The Near Eastern Fells
    The Northern Fells
    The North-Western Fells
    The Southern Fells
    The Western Fells
Roads and Tracks of the Lake District
Rocky Rambler's Wild Walks
Scrambles in the Lake District
    North & South
Short Walks in Lakeland
    1 South Lakeland
    2 North Lakeland
    3 West Lakeland
The Cumbria Coastal Way
The Cumbria Way and the Allerdale Ramble
Tour of the Lake District

DERBYSHIRE, PEAK DISTRICT AND MIDLANDS
High Peak Walks
Scrambles in the Dark Peak
The Star Family Walks
Walking in Derbyshire
White Peak Walks
    The Northern Dales
    The Southern Dales

SOUTHERN ENGLAND
Suffolk Coast & Heaths Walks
The Cotswold Way
The North Downs Way
The Peddars Way and Norfolk Coast Path
The Ridgeway National Trail
The South Downs Way
The South West Coast Path
The Thames Path
Walking in Berkshire
Walking in Essex
Walking in Kent
Walking in Norfolk
Walking in Sussex
Walking in the Cotswolds
Walking in the Isles of Scilly
Walking in the New Forest
Walking in the Thames Valley
Walking on Dartmoor
Walking on Guernsey
Walking on Jersey
Walking on the Isle of Wight
Walks in the South Downs National Park

WALES AND WELSH BORDERS
Backpacker's Britain – Wales
Glyndwr's Way
Great Mountain Days in Snowdonia
Hillwalking in Snowdonia
Hillwalking in Wales: 1&2
Offa's Dyke Path
Ridges of Snowdonia
Scrambles in Snowdonia
The Ascent of Snowdon
The Ceredigion and Snowdonia Coast Paths
Lleyn Peninsula Coastal Path
Pembrokeshire Coastal Path
The Severn Way
The Shropshire Hills
The Wye Valley Walk
Walking in Pembrokeshire
Walking in the Forest of Dean
Walking in the South Wales Valleys
Walking on Gower
Walking on the Brecon Beacons
Welsh Winter Climbs

INTERNATIONAL CHALLENGES, COLLECTIONS AND ACTIVITIES
Canyoning
Europe's High Points
The Via Francigena
    (Canterbury to Rome): 1&2

EUROPEAN CYCLING
Cycle Touring in France
Cycle Touring in Ireland
Cycle Touring in Spain
Cycle Touring in Switzerland
Cycling in the French Alps
Cycling the Canal du Midi
Cycling the River Loire
The Danube Cycleway

The Grand Traverse of the Massif Central
The Rhine Cycle Route
The Way of St James

AFRICA
Climbing in the Moroccan Anti-Atlas
Kilimanjaro
Mountaineering in the Moroccan High Atlas
The High Atlas
Trekking in the Atlas Mountains
Walking in the Drakensberg

ALPS – CROSS-BORDER ROUTES
100 Hut Walks in the Alps
Across the Eastern Alps: E5
Alpine Points of View
Alpine Ski Mountaineering
  1 Western Alps
  2 Central and Eastern Alps
Chamonix to Zermatt
Snowshoeing
Tour of Mont Blanc
Tour of Monte Rosa
Tour of the Matterhorn
Trekking in the Alps
Trekking in the Silvretta and Rätikon Alps
Walking in the Alps
Walks and Treks in the Maritime Alps

PYRENEES AND FRANCE/SPAIN CROSS-BORDER ROUTES
Rock Climbs in the Pyrenees
The GR10 Trail
The Mountains of Andorra
The Pyrenean Haute Route
The Pyrenees
The Way of St James
Through the Spanish Pyrenees: GR11
Walks and Climbs in the Pyrenees

AUSTRIA
The Adlerweg
Trekking in Austria's Hohe Tauern
Trekking in the Stubai Alps
Trekking in the Zillertal Alps
Walking in Austria

EASTERN EUROPE
The High Tatras
The Mountains of Romania
Walking in Bulgaria's National Parks
Walking in Hungary

FRANCE
Chamonix Mountain Adventures
Ecrins National Park
GR20: Corsica
Mont Blanc Walks
Mountain Adventures in the Maurienne
The Cathar Way
The GR5 Trail
The Robert Louis Stevenson Trail
Tour of the Oisans: The GR54
Tour of the Queyras
Tour of the Vanoise
Trekking in the Vosges and Jura
Vanoise Ski Touring
Via Ferratas of the French Alps
Walking in the Auvergne
Walking in the Cathar Region
Walking in the Cevennes
Walking in the Dordogne

Walking in the Haute Savoie
  North & South
Walking in the Languedoc
Walking in the Tarentaise and Beaufortain Alps
Walking on Corsica

GERMANY
Germany's Romantic Road
Hiking and Biking in the Black Forest
Walking in the Bavarian Alps
Walking the River Rhine Trail

HIMALAYA
Annapurna
Bhutan
Everest
Garhwal and Kumaon
Kangchenjunga
Langtang with Gosainkund and Helambu
Manaslu
The Mount Kailash Trek
Trekking in Ladakh
Trekking in the Himalaya

ICELAND & GREENLAND
Trekking in Greenland
Walking and Trekking in Iceland

IRELAND
Irish Coastal Walks
The Irish Coast to Coast Walk
The Mountains of Ireland

ITALY
Gran Paradiso
Sibillini National Park
Stelvio National Park
Shorter Walks in the Dolomites
Through the Italian Alps
Trekking in the Apennines
Trekking in the Dolomites
Via Ferratas of the Italian Dolomites: Vols 1 & 2
Walking in Abruzzo
Walking in Sardinia
Walking in Sicily
Walking in the Central Italian Alps
Walking in the Dolomites
Walking in Tuscany
Walking on the Amalfi Coast
Walking the Italian Lakes

MEDITERRANEAN
Jordan – Walks, Treks, Caves,
  Climbs and Canyons
The Ala Dag
The High Mountains of Crete
The Mountains of Greece
Treks and Climbs in Wadi Rum
Walking in Malta
Western Crete

NORTH AMERICA
British Columbia
The Grand Canyon
The John Muir Trail
The Pacific Crest Trail

SOUTH AMERICA
Aconcagua and the
  Southern Andes
Hiking and Biking Peru's Inca Trails
Torres del Paine

SCANDINAVIA
Walking in Norway

SLOVENIA, CROATIA AND MONTENEGRO
The Julian Alps of Slovenia
The Mountains of Montenegro
Trekking in Slovenia
Walking in Croatia
Walking in Slovenia: The Karavanke

SPAIN AND PORTUGAL
Costa Blanca: West
Mountain Walking in Southern Catalunya
The Mountains of Central Spain
The Northern Caminos
Trekking through Mallorca
Walking in Madeira
Walking in Mallorca
Walking in Menorca
Walking in the Algarve
Walking in the Cordillera Cantabrica
Walking in the Sierra Nevada
Walking on Gran Canaria
Walking on La Gomera and El Hierro
Walking on La Palma
Walking on Tenerife
Walking the GR7 in Andalucia
Walks and Climbs in the Picos de Europa

SWITZERLAND
Alpine Pass Route
Canyoning in the Alps
Central Switzerland
The Bernese Alps
The Swiss Alps
Tour of the Jungfrau Region
Walking in the Valais
Walking in Ticino
Walks in the Engadine

TECHNIQUES
Geocaching in the UK
Indoor Climbing
Lightweight Camping
Map and Compass
Mountain Weather
Moveable Feasts
Outdoor Photography
Polar Exploration
Rock Climbing
Sport Climbing
The Book of the Bivvy
The Hillwalker's Guide to Mountaineering
The Hillwalker's Manual

MINI GUIDES
Alpine Flowers
Avalanche!
Navigating with a GPS
Navigation
Pocket First Aid and Wilderness Medicine
Snow

MOUNTAIN LITERATURE
8000m
A Walk in the Clouds
Unjustifiable Risk?

For full information on all our guides, and to order books and eBooks, visit our website:
www.cicerone.co.uk.

Walking – Trekking – Mountaineering – Climbing – Cycling

Over 40 years, Cicerone have built up an outstanding collection of 300 guides, inspiring all sorts of amazing adventures.

Every guide comes from extensive exploration and research by our expert authors, all with a passion for their subjects. They are frequently praised, endorsed and used by clubs, instructors and outdoor organisations.

All our titles can now be bought as **e-books** and many as iPad and Kindle files and we will continue to make all our guides available for these and many other devices.

Our website shows any **new information** we've received since a book was published. Please do let us know if you find anything has changed, so that we can pass on the latest details. On our **website** you'll also find some great ideas and lots of information, including sample chapters, contents lists, reviews, articles and a photo gallery.

It's easy to keep in touch with what's going on at Cicerone, by getting our monthly **free e-newsletter**, which is full of offers, competitions, up-to-date information and topical articles. You can subscribe on our home page and also follow us on **Facebook** and **Twitter**, as well as our **blog**.

Cicerone – the very best guides for exploring the world.

CICERONE

2 Police Square Milnthorpe Cumbria LA7 7PY
Tel: 015395 62069 info@cicerone.co.uk
www.cicerone.co.uk